Bullying
in Schools:
and what to
do about it

For my children,
Kim, Simon, Shaun and Ella
and their mother, Jean

Bullying in Schools:
and what to do about it

Ken Rigby

Jessica Kingsley Publishers
London and Philadelphia

First published in 1996 by
The Australian Council for Educational Research Ltd

First published in the United Kingdom in 1997 by
Jessica Kingsley Publishers Ltd
116 Pentonville Road
London N1 9JB
England
and
325 Chestnut Street,
Philadelphia, PA 19106, USA

www.jkp.com

Copyright © 1996 Ken Rigby

Second impression 2000

Library of Congress Cataloging in Publication Data
A CIP catalogue record for this book is available from the Library of Congress

British Library Cataloguing in Publication Data
A CIP catalogue record for this book is available from the British Library

Printed and Bound in Great Britain by
Athenaeum Press, Gateshead, Tyne & Wear

The author wishes to thank the authors and publishers who have given permission to reproduce the following copyrighted works: p.7, *Where humans can't leave and mustn't complain*, by Les Murray, reprinted by permission of the author; p.10, photograph by Duke Dinh, Sunday Age (13/4/1995), reproduced by permission of the photographer and David Syme & Co. Ltd; p.69, from 'Original Sin on the Sussex Coast', in *Collected Works* by John Betjeman (1960), reprinted by permission of John Murray (Publishers) Ltd; p.77, 'My parents kept me from children who were rough', in *Collected Poems, 1928–85* by Stephen Spender, reprinted by permission of Faber and Faber; pp.117 & 174, from *Only playing, Miss*, by P. Casdagli, P. Gobey & C. Griffin (1990), Trentham Books, London, reprinted by permission of the author, Penny Casdagli; p.163, *Cooperation*, reproduced with permission of Quaker Peace and Service, Friends House, London, NW1 2BJ; pp.234–6, adapted from 'Cultivating the art of self-defence among victimised children', by Sonia Sharp & Ken Rigby (1993), in the *International Journal of Protective Behaviours* 1(2), pp.24–8, reprinted by permission of the Editor, International Journal of Protective Behaviours, and Sonia Sharp; p.240, 'Warning Signs', adapted from *Bullying: Another Form of Abuse* by J. Dawkins & P. Hill (1995), in *Recent Advances in Paediatrics*, 13, (T.J. David ed.), Edinburgh: Churchill Livingstone, pp.102–122, reproduced by permission of Judith Dawkins; p.260, 'Taking Steps', from *Training Students to be Peacemakers*, by D. & R. Johnson (1991), Interaction Books Co., Minnesota, reproduced by permission of the authors.

Contents

Figures and tables

Illustrations and models

Photographs

Cartoon figures and drawings

Models

Acknowledgements

This book is based partly on studies undertaken by myself and colleagues in Australia over the last six years. Many of these were undertaken with Dr Phillip Slee from the School of Education, Flinders University. I am especially indebted to him for the part he played in studies we undertook together in South Australia and upon which many of the research findings presented and discussed in this book are based.

I have also been assisted by other people who have worked with me on relevant research projects, in particular, Mr Garry Black and Ms Liz Keogh in Victoria; Ms Biruta Dietz, Ms Melanie O'Brien, Ms Alison Whish and Associate Professor Ian Cox in South Australia; and Ms Sonia Sharp from the University of Sheffield during her visit to South Australia in 1994. I have been fortunate in the help received from reasearch assistants. In the first year of the studies, both Phillip and I were greatly assisted by Ms Celia Conolly and subsequently, by Ms Kristen Oxenberry, Ms Donna Rogers and Ms Liz Pierce. I have also been assisted in the preparation of figures for this book by Ms Kelly Martin of the Visual Productions Department of the University of South Australia, and in the preparation of the indices by Ms Robyn Cunningham.

Some of the research was made possible through grants provided by the Australian Rotary Health Foundation and also through the University of South Australia. Currently I am retired from the University but am helped in continuing this work through the generous support of its Faculty of Humanities and Social Science. I am also grateful for the cooperation and assistance I have received from the Aboriginal Research Institute in Underdale where I can be contacted.

I should also emphasise that work of this nature is greatly enriched through contacts with co-workers in the field. Among these I include the many teachers and principals of schools who have given of their time and often also of their resources in discussing issues with me and in facilitating research in their schools. I should thank especially here the South Australian Department of Children's Services and Education and the South Australian Catholic Education Office. I should also like to thank the thousands of school children and many of their parents who have provided me with information about their personal experiences with bullying in schools. Without their cooperation there would have been no book at all.

In conducting these studies I have had the good fortune to meet and learn from a number of outstanding researchers or practitioners in the area of school bullying. These have included the world's leading authority in this growing area of study—Professor Dan Olweus from the University of Bergen in Norway; an entirely different figure, brilliant as a man of ideas and inspired practice, Professor Anatol Pikas from Upsalla University in Sweden; and from England, Professor Peter Smith, his wife, Professor Helen Cowie, and Ms Sonia Sharp, whose work conducted at the University of Sheffield was of very great help.

Finally, thanks be to Jean Rigby, my wife, who helped me time and time again to get on with it.

Ken Rigby
Adelaide

Foreword

Ken Rigby's book is timely. Although bullying has always been with us, it is only in recent times that people have begun to speak out about it. Victims are no longer prepared to be silent. Bullying can no longer be hidden.

There is a great deal of concern about the incidence of bullying in Australian schools. It is unacceptable that one child in six is bullied by peers on a weekly basis. Teachers, parents and children, as well as the general community, are anxious to find and implement solutions to the problem.

But before that's possible, we first have to understand bullying. Why does it happen? What are the effects of bullying on children's physical and psychological health? What are the long-term consequences? What makes a victim? How important is the parental role in all of this?

Some argue that bullying can never be eradicated but Ken Rigby gives us cause for optimism. He says there are things that can be done to stop bullying and the case he presents is convincing. But it will take a concerted effort from teachers, parents and children, particularly the latter. It will take time, too. No matter how good our intentions, bullying will not disappear overnight.

Whichever way you look at it, bullying is socially unacceptable behaviour. Worryingly, it seems to be becoming more vicious. Like other organisations in our community worried about bullying, Safety House has placed the issue high on its agenda and is playing an important community leadership role in raising awareness of the harm bullying causes. There's no doubt that a Safety House can protect children from bullies and, in the short term, offers an excellent answer to the problem but what's needed is an effective, long-term solution.

That's where Ken Rigby's expertise comes in. His academic background in economics, education and psychology, combined with his studies and intensive research on bullying in schools, means that he has enormous knowledge on the matter. What he has to say will be invaluable to educators, parents and students — and to all those trying to eliminate bullying from our schools.

For any school aiming to develop a specific, anti-bullying policy, this book is a must.

Ita Buttrose, AO, OBE
Sydney, Australia

Introduction

Bullying in schools and what to do about it

Preface

The theme of this book is a simple one. Bullying is an undesirable form of behaviour which is widely prevalent in schools, and it can be greatly reduced, if not entirely eliminated, principally by actions taken by schools and also, to a lesser degree, by parents. The purpose of this book is to provide an understanding of the phenomenon of school bullying and to suggest how it can be countered effectively.

Many teachers and parents desperately want to know what can be done. It is tempting to provide a list of things which might work: a manual, a package or tool-kit optimistically designed to remove bullying from the school environment. But, on reflection, it is clear that this will not do—it is not enough. First there must be some understanding of what bullying is, and why some children bully others, and why some children are bullied, before you can decide on a course of action.

The book is therefore divided into two parts: the first being concerned with understanding bullying, the second with what can be done about it .

Part One is about bullying in schools. I have called it *Understanding Bullying*. I see it as a necessary foundation to tackling the problem in Australian schools. It covers about one-third of the book and it consists of six chapters.

Chapter 1 asks what's new about the way we are approaching the problem of bullying today. It provides a brief account of a growing interest and awareness of the problem, both internationally and in Australia, and how some educators and schools have begun to see that there are positive, workable solutions. We examine closely what is meant by bullying in both its malign and its less vicious manifestation, how it can be distinguished from harassment, and consider the wide variety of forms it takes in schools.

Chapter 2 describes the nature and incidence of bullying experienced by boys and girls in Australian schools. It draws extensively on survey results obtained over the last five years from students in Primary and Secondary schools throughout Australia, from research conducted principally by myself and South Australian co-worker, Phillip Slee. It explores the relationship between reported victimisation by peers at school and the age and gender of students and also the type of school attended. It focuses finally on the question of how safe children are from the threat of peer victimisation in Australian schools in the 1990s.

Chapter 3 examines in some detail the consequences of bullying in schools, not only for victims of frequent peer abuse, but also for other members of the school community, including bullies who often continue to engage in the repeated victimisation of others after they leave school, and bystanders who regularly witness bullying happening around them. We look at the effects of bullying on children's physical and psychological health, and at some of the serious long-term consequences that have been reported by adults who were victimised by peers as children.

Chapter 4 poses the question of why children sometimes bully others. We ask whether bullying is an unfathomable evil or whether it is understandable in the light of what we are discovering about the biological and social determinants of anti-social behaviour. A model is proposed by which a variety of relevant, interrelated causal factors can be identified. Some are largely external to the school, such as the physical and psychological nature of the child and family and cultural influences in the home and neighbourhood; and some school-centred, such as the ethos of the school, its educational climate and the school's collective response to bullying. Research findings from Australian studies, case studies of children and observations on the behaviours of members of the school community, including teachers, are all used to illustrate the model and the influence of the suggested factors.

Chapter 5 focuses upon the school ethos, a crucial aspect of the school environment that can powerfully affect the practice of bullying in school. Again research from Australian studies is employed, this time to describe the attitudes and perceptions of school children towards victims and bullies and to relate the views and opinions of school children to their age and gender. How students feel about those who complain about being bullied is a matter of special interest, because it helps to determine whether children will tell others about it, a step which is often necessary before any action can be taken to stop bullying. Teacher attitudes as they contribute to the school ethos are also examined, including the readiness (or otherwise) of teachers to take action to help stop bullying between students.

In **Part Two** of the book we turn our attention to the practical question of *What Can Be Done About It*.

Chapter 6 provides a brief introduction to What Can Be Done, linking understanding of bullying to practical action to counter it. This chapter emphasises the need for understanding the nature of bullying and the complexity of factors that give rise to it in a school, before policies and actions are devised. Research evidence is presented to reassure the reader that there really are grounds for optimism in thinking that school bullying can be tackled effectively. We briefly revisit the earlier model of factors that affect peer relations at school (see Chapter 4) to illustrate the variety of complementary approaches that are possible and desirable in tackling bully-ing; some of these being indirect, some direct, often involving the home background of a child and/or the situation at school. Preventative approaches are emphasised. The central role of a comprehensive Anti-Bullying Policy that has broad school community support is foreshadowed.

Chapter 7 is about getting started. It is assumed that one or two or a few teachers and/or parents have got the idea that something more positive can be done about bullying in their school. From such a small beginning, we examine how things can begin to happen, first by convincing ourselves of the need for action and then by getting others 'on side'. Without the support of the school community and, most important of all, the school staff (or a substantial part of it), effective change to reduce bullying is seen as unlikely to occur. This chapter identifies some of the obstacles or impediments to progress in this area and how the process of getting others committed to act and support sensible policies and practices can be accomplished.

Chapter 8 examines the development of a school policy on bullying, the cornerstone of effective action. We look at the necessary elements in a good policy, and provide a critique of examples taken from Australian schools.

Chapter 9 This is about how students can be encouraged to support policies and practices that are directed against bullying. Research data are presented showing what boys and girls of different ages are commonly prepared to do to reduce bullying in their school. Alternative methods of gaining student support and involvement are described and appraised. We examine, too, teaching methodologies that are intended to promote cooperative behav-iour, and discuss how curriculum material that is of special relevance to understanding and countering bullying can be introduced.

Chapter 10 looks more closely at where bullying actually takes place in and around Australian schools. An account is given of where students say bullying happens. Next we address the question of what can be done about it in relation to specific locations: in the school yard at recess; in the classroom; on the way to school; and on the way home. There are tricky policy and practice issues here. Whose responsibility is it to act? What community resources can we call upon?

Chapter 11 Here I turn to the question of how a school can get reliable and adequate information about cases of bullying within its own premises. The nature and value of alternative sources of information are examined. We consider what can be learnt from the victims themselves, student bystanders, teacher observers, parents and members of the wider community. How the obtained information may be used is discussed in the light of the possible consequences of some children being labelled as 'bullies' or 'victims'. What we need to know is then seen as depending upon the actions that a school expects to take in relation to the bullying incident(s).

Chapter 12 This is about what to do *with* the bully, not (incidentally) what to do *to* the bully. Here we jump straight in and briefly entertain three different approaches, which I have called Moralistic, Legalistic and Humanistic. I delineate each and express a preference for the Humanistic.

Chapter 13 This chapter provides detailed accounts of so-called Humanistic approaches to deal with bullying. In particular, it provides descriptions of approaches devised by Maines and Robinson (The No Blame Approach) and by Anatol Pikas (The Method of Shared Concern). These and other approaches are appraised and the extent to which they are compatible with other, non-Humanistic, approaches is discussed.

Chapter 14 puts the focus on the victims of school bullying and how they can be helped by teachers and counsellors. It examines methods of working with these children, either as individuals or in groups, to develop in them greater powers of assertiveness and the capacity to protect themselves more effectively.

Chapter 15 examines further the role of parents and families in how they can help to reduce bullying in schools. It first provides advice on how parents can come to recognise signs that a child is being bullied and how the situation can best be dealt with, more especially by working constructively with the school authorities. It considers, too, how help towards more adequate parenting can be provided for families whose dysfunctionality is a cause of anti-social and bullying behaviour in their children.

Chapter 16 examines how the problem of bullying can be addressed by students themselves first learning and then employing counselling and mediational skills to help each other. Teachers are seen as having a key role in starting the process by which students are trained to take over more and more responsibility in helping peers who are experiencing problems with bullying. The thrust to empower students to tackle the problem themselves is increasingly seen as the best way to counter bullying.

Chapter 17 is really a sort of epilogue. Here more off the fence than usual, I seek to clarify what I am not saying as much as what I am.

It will soon become evident in reading this book that even though the history of the study of bullying is quite short, there are already on the market many cures and remedies, sometimes proposed with a show of remarkable and misplaced confidence. Many of these are described and critically examined. Methods that seem best in the light of current knowledge and practice are given special attention, and the critical reader will not be slow to detect some special pleading on the part of the author. But given the diversity of values and viewpoints that exist in any school community, it would be naive to expect that any proposed total solution would be enthusiastically embraced by everyone immediately on the say-so of such a book as this, or indeed any other book.

Hence this is the strategy: first to provide evidence and reasons to support a personal understanding of what bullying is — and to invite you, the reader, to discuss and question it, and work towards *your own understanding of this problem*. Then to provide descriptions of courses of action that flow from that understanding—and invite you to argue about and choose what you think might work in your own situation—as teachers with the students you teach, as parents with the sons and daughters with whom you live, and as responsible members of the community who care about the age-old problem of bullying and the devastating effects it has not only at school but in society at large.

Where humans can't leave and mustn't complain

Where humans can't leave and mustn't complain,
There some will emerge who enjoy giving pain.
A dreary intense groove leads them to each one
they pick to torment, and the rest will then shun.
Some who might have been picked, and natural police,
do routine hurt, the catcalling, the giving-no-peace,
but dull brilliance evolves the betrayals and names
that sear dignity and life like interior flames.

Whole circles get enlisted, and blood loyalties reversed
by self-avengers and failures-getting-in-first
but this is the eye of fashion. Its sniggering stare
breeds silenced accomplices. Courage proves rare.
This powers revolution; this draws flies to sad pools;
this is the true curriculum of schools.

                                        Les Murray

Understanding
bullying

Bullying
today

What's new?

Very recently—only over the last five years or so—and in many parts of the world, a remarkable change has occurred in the way educators view interpersonal relations between children in schools. For countless generations children have been teasing, harassing, bullying one another, sometimes in fun, sometimes in deadly earnest, to the amusement, horror or indifference of others, whether they be parents, teachers or other children. To many this has been simply the way things are, a natural course of events, human nature, unchangeable. But now something new is happening. We are at last beginning to see that bullying among children at school is a quite intolerable social evil; that the consequences are much greater than we had ever imagined, and, most importantly, something can and should be done about it.

Bullying is intolerable because it is cruel and repeated oppression by the powerful over the powerless, without any justification at all. It is gratuitous violence, physical or psychological. We will not tolerate it between adults. We are appalled at the domestic tyranny of husbands who abuse their wives and of parents who abuse their children. Yet for so long we have stood by and watched (or not watched) stronger children abusing weaker children.

In the 1970s the revolution in thinking about bullying in schools began in earnest in Scandinavia. The pioneer was Professor Dan Olweus from the University of Bergen. Not only was he among the first to recognise the evil of school bullying but, as a social scientist, he was able to examine its nature and incidence with care and precision as it occurred in both Swedish and Norwegian schools. He was able to persuade the educational authorities in Norway of the importance of stopping bullying in schools, and with their cooperation to mount a national campaign aimed at its systematic reduction. Two years later, evaluation studies showed that the incidence of bullying had been reduced in schools around Bergen by a remarkable 50 per cent. It was this sober, meticulous and scientifically designed intervention that encouraged educationalists in many other parts of the world to believe something could indeed be done about school bullying (see Olweus, 1993).

In the years that followed, slowly at first, and then at an accelerating rate, more and more studies of bullying were conducted in many countries across the world: in Britain, USA, Canada, Holland, Italy, Spain, Japan—and most recently in Australia.

Here in Australia interest is growing rapidly. Some of it has developed from the research of Dr Slee and myself. We began in 1989 in South Australia with a series of studies, building upon overseas research and experience. We have owed much to the generous cooperation of people in the South Australian Department of Children's Services and Education and the Catholic Education Office, and teachers and counsellors in many schools, both state and private, in many parts of Australia who enabled this research to happen, and generously shared with us their ideas and plans. Subsequently our work, sometimes conducted together, sometimes separately, was extended to include studies conducted in many other parts of Australia. In a wide range of studies more than 30 000 students and teachers in both primary and secondary schools have been questioned, sometimes using anonymous questionnaires, sometimes in face to face interviews, from over 100 schools. The bulk of this research has now been published in national and international journals (see reference section). From this work a detailed picture has emerged of bullying in Australian schools upon which our understanding of peer victimisation can be based.

In the last few years many other Australian researchers and practitioners in every state have given serious and sustained attention to the problem of bullying in schools. Those concerned have come from many professions and occupations: they have included psychologists, psychiatrists, sociologists, social workers, teachers, administrators, nurses, doctors, lawyers, the police force and parents. Bullying is no longer a curious obsession or a joke. What happens between children at school matters here and now and in the future.

Thanks to these developments, there is now a much better understanding of the kind of children who are involved as bullies or as victims (and sometimes as both) in schools. There is now first-hand knowledge available of the consequences, both physical and psychological, that bullying has for such children—and often the parents of the children as well. Through patient research, steadily an understanding has been gained of why some children become bullies—or victims; we have begun to appreciate much better the pressures that induce them to behave as they do. We can now see more clearly how the wider community and school environments each may influence bullying, and why it is rife in some schools but not in others (there are large differences between schools). Most importantly, we are learning what to do about it.

Increasingly, opportunities have been created for people to share their concerns, their understanding and their plans relating to bullying. A great deal of the learning about bullying is taking place in seminars and workshops provided for teachers and counsellors and parents at centres throughout Australia. In Melbourne this has been achieved largely through the work and support of the Australian Council for Educational Research. Many schools, health centres and hospitals have also helped in organising meetings and discussion groups. Through the continual sharing of information and the development of intervention skills, more practical advice and more effective methods are being devised and tested.

This book is an attempt to convey an understanding of bullying in schools as it has emerged largely from talking and working with children and teachers in Australian schools, attending seminars, workshops and conferences on bullying, and from numerous conversations with parents. But it would have been foolish, if not churlish, not to heed and learn from the already prolific research that has already been conducted in other countries. For instance, a great debt is owed to the team of researchers and counsellors associated with the Sheffield Project in England. Under the leadership of Professor Peter

Smith at the University of Sheffield they have carried out diligent research for several years, not only on the incidence and effects of bullying in schools but also into methods of interventions which they developed and promoted for teachers to employ in schools in the Sheffield area. This work has directly influenced what is happening in Australia.

Among the men and women of action in bullying today, two should be specially recognised. The first is the Swedish psychologist, Anatol Pikas, who has left an indelible mark on the brief history of anti-bullying practice through his bold and pioneering work, especially his work with school bullies, from whom (he has found) it is often possible to evoke feelings of concern for victims on the way to motivating them to repair hitherto destructive relationships. From him we have heard that social science and statistics are not enough: above all, that workers worth their salt in this field need to encounter the bullies, that is, those whom we often blithely demonise and treat as the enemy. Secondly: very occasionally, a research team discovers in its midst a genius for presenting and modelling methods of intervention. Such a person is Sonia Sharp, a practitioner researcher in the Sheffield team who brought her remarkable drive and flair to Australia in 1994, thereby stimulating many counsellors and teachers here to examine and try out new methods of countering bullying in our schools.

This excellent research from abroad; these wonderful people who come to Australia to tell us how; all this is grist to the mill. But millers must also learn to do their own milling from experience in their own mills. This book is an attempt to do that, blending what can be gained from overseas experience with what can be learned by us attending to what is happening in our schools and the ideas and practices that come from working here in Australia.

So what is bullying?

It has been wisely said that you may not be able to say exactly what it is, but, gosh, you know when it is happening to you. There is no mistaking it. You are in a corner and you are squirming. Your tormentor is enjoying this. You have not deserved it. Even if you get out of this (and you don't see how) it will keep going on and on. You do not know what to do.

Researchers have sought to define it. Perhaps the most persuasive definition is that of Farrington (1993), an English criminologist. He defined it as:

> *'Repeated oppression, psychological or physical, of a less powerful person by a more powerful person.'*

This, of course, refers to bullying done by individual persons, but we need to bear in mind that bullying is often done by groups. Here is the revised definition:

> *Bullying is repeated oppression, psychological or physical, of a less powerful person by a more powerful person or group of persons.*

Notice that it occurs where there is an imbalance in power between people. This imbalance is sometimes very obvious, as when a person bullies a much smaller, weaker person, or when a group of people combine to terrorise an individual. But often it is much less obvious, as when the difference in power is psychological. It is, indeed, sometimes a mystery why some people, not only children, do not stand up for themselves, but dumbly submit, even when to the outsider it seems very clear what can be done. It is as if they are transfixed, deprived of will. But the situation is grasped by the bully—and accepted by the victim.

Elements of bullying

We can distinguish between two sorts of bullying, which we call (i) malign bullying and (ii) non-malign bullying. We will begin with malign bullying.

Malign bullying

What generally concerns us about bullying is its malign intent. This is bullying that consciously seeks to do harm to someone; it is deliberate exploitation of a power differential; therein lies its malignancy. I think it is useful to think of malign bullying as typically having seven elements, as in Rigby (1994a).

1 An initial desire to hurt

This is how it begins. There is a wish on the part of the bully to inflict pain on another. We should remember that the desire to hurt others is not uncommon. Most, if not all of us, feel such an impulse from time to time, and this enables us to gain some understanding of the bully through introspection. (Isn't there a potential bully in all of us?) But a powerful and indeed obsessive desire to hurt, which characterises many bullies, is not at all common. In many cases, we will argue, it can be traced to continuous negative treatment from an uncaring family. Most of us are generally able to suppress this desire to hurt, or at least to ensure that it is not expressed against innocent and virtually defenceless people. Unfortunately this is not the case for the bully.

2 The desire is expressed in action

Whether the desire is expressed depends on a number of factors: the sheer strength and persistence of the desire to hurt; the modelling effect of others in the home or in the peer group who behave aggressively; the encouragement (or discouragement) of significant others; and the opportunity to hurt someone with relative impunity.

3 Someone is hurt

Whether an aggressive action is hurtful depends upon the vulnerability of the person(s) against whom it is directed. Therefore, bullying cannot be defined without taking into account the incapacity of a person to defend himself or herself, that is at a particular time and in a given situation.

4 It is directed by a more powerful person or group against someone less powerful

It is this imbalance of power between people that makes bullying possible. Among schoolchildren this power differential is often due to inequalities in physical or psychological strength between individuals. It may also result from the formation of groups or gangs of schoolchildren who seek to harass others.

5 It is without justification

As long as we believe that the more powerful may sometimes justifiably coerce others (as when a group of children formulate and apply sanctions against aggressors) bullying cannot be defined without recourse to criteria of justifiability. Otherwise the Law is a bully! We label coercive behaviour on the part of the more powerful as 'bullying' when we cannot see any reason for it.

6   Typically repeated

Although bullying may conceivably include 'one-off' actions, typically the bully, having found a suitable and unresisting victim, repeats the hurtful behaviour. It is this repetition and the expectation on the part of the victim that the harassment will keep going on interminably, that gives the bullying its oppressive and frightening quality.

7   With evident enjoyment

In bullying the submission of the weak is an essential element, and is enjoyed by the bully.

Non-malign bullying

Not all bullying is malign, that is, motivated by malice. From the point of view of the victim this may not matter. The hurt that is experienced may hurt just as much. The distress is quite as real.

We can distinguish two kinds of non-malign bullying: one we may call 'mindless bullying' and the other 'educational bullying'. They have in common a lack of awareness on the part of the perpetrator.

Mindless bullying

As our knowledge of children who often bully others increases, it is not uncommon to find that they simply do not fit the description we have given of the malign bully. These bullies are not full of malice. They may not appear to be hostile at all. There may be no history of being physically or psychologically abused in the home. Surprisingly, the bully may strike you as good-natured, balanced, even likeable. Is it a case of mistaken identity?

On many points the stereotype I have drawn does not apply. Yet someone is being repeatedly targeted by a more powerful person—perhaps more powerful because of membership of a gang—and without any justification, too. And the nice, likeable person before you is undeniably to blame.

We began with the view that bullies were all malign monsters. And we may still think some are. But it has become clear that many may be better described as conformists who scarcely know what they are doing. For them bullying—teasing they might call it—is a game, a seemingly harmless practice from which some sort of pleasure is gained, largely from a sense of belonging to a group that approves of that sort of thing. Typically this bully does not know the harm he or she is doing. The bullying is almost literally mindless. It is maintained less by the evil will of the bully; more by a vague desire to be part of a bit of fun.

Yet its seriousness should not be ignored. It may even be to the victim a greater disgrace and disaster to be the constant butt of 'ordinary kids' than the victim of a bully whom everyone knows is deviant and vicious.

Educational bullying

There is another kind of bullying in which there may be no hint of malice, no conscious desire to hurt, still less any exultation at another's misery. Indeed, to those who practise this kind of bullying—and even to some who observe it—the bullying may be seen as for the victim's good.

A confession—my own experience

A few years ago, I was taking a tutorial class at the University of South Australia on research methodology in which a young man read a paper he had carefully written on aspects of the scientific method; not a good paper in my opinion. Bent on straightening out the kinks in the student's 'logical thinking' and exposing the limitations of his conceptualisations, I proceeded to find fault after fault, as Socrates himself would have, only to be stopped in my tracks by a sudden desperate cry from the student: 'Stop picking on me!' Bewildered by this astonishing regression into childishness, flabbergasted in fact, I appealed to the group. Surely, I wasn't picking on him. 'Yes, you are', was the verdict. The student was 'in a corner'; he couldn't defend himself (he was trying to defend himself, not his arguments); and he was suffering dreadfully.

Bullying can be destructive, unintentionally. You can break another's spirit with the best of intentions. Being an intellectual bully is an occupational hazard for any teacher. The judgement is really a fine one between providing rigorous and justifiable (?) criticism and engaging in a ruthless and insensitive exposure of the limitations of someone who is, in some respects, not your equal. Lest it be thought that non-malign bullying is a product of intellectual arrogance only, remember that there are many other areas in which a person's 'inferiority' can be exposed (for his or her own good, naturally): in Sport, Music, Literature; in Gardening; in Good Taste; in Cookery—you name it. Wherever there is a power imbalance, whatever its source, an individual can be reduced in status, and sometimes humiliated by the insensitive bully.

In this book we shall be concerned with both malign and non-malign forms of bullying. From the victim's viewpoint, the motive (or lack of motive) on the part of the bully is hardly the point. The consequences may be much the same.

Nevertheless, I will argue that these distinctions are important ones when we come to try to understand and change the bully's behaviour which, as we shall see, is a matter of central importance.

Bullying behaviour

Bullying behaviour can be almost infinitely varied. Whatever can be done repeatedly to harm another person by a stronger person or a group of persons is potentially bullying behaviour. We need to note however that 'stronger' does not necessarily mean physically more powerful. Other forms of strength or power frequently provide the opportunity for bullying to occur, as we shall see.

Some children impose upon others because they have more powerful personalities. They are mentally tougher, more determined, sometimes less sensitive. They may have certain skills which enable them to hurt others without being hurt themselves. These may include physical fighting skills, but also well-developed verbal abilities, quickness of mind and tongue, which enable them to ridicule others to the point of humiliation. Besides such abilities, which are so easily abused, children may be more powerful than others because they have acquired status as group leaders, and can call upon others to give them support.

Forms of bullying

It is useful to distinguish between types of bullying behaviour. The most basic distinction is between physical and psychological forms. In the former we include hitting, beating, kicking; in the latter, verbal abuse, name calling, threatening gestures, stalking behaviour, malicious telephone calls to a student's home, repeatedly hiding another's belongings, leaving people out of desired activities and spreading malicious rumours about someone. Some of these methods of bullying others can be described as direct, as when a student persistently hits or ridicules another; others indirect, as in spreading stories about someone. Table 1.1 provides a way of classifying different forms of bullying.

Table 1.1   **A classification of forms of bullying**

	Forms of bullying	
	Direct	**Indirect**
Physical	Hitting	Getting another
	Kicking	person to assault
	Spitting	someone
	Throwing stones	
Non-physical		
Verbal	Verbal insults	Persuading another person to insult someone
	Name calling	Spreading malicious rumours
Non-verbal	Threatening and obscene gestures	Removing and hiding belongings
		Deliberate exclusion from a group or activity

In practice the different forms of bullying often occur together. Physical intimidation is often accompanied by verbal abuse. One is used to reinforce the other, as when a child is repeatedly struck and called names. In bullying we are concerned not only with physical injury: the constant undermining of an individual by taunts, jeers and name calling can be equally devastating.

Vulnerability

Assessing the potential damage of bullying actions is, in fact, extraordinarily difficult since it depends very much on the vulnerability of the person being victimised. So what appears to one person as playful teasing (which may sometimes be actually enjoyed by teaser and teased) can in some circumstances be extremely hurtful. Most children say that they are adversely affected by attempts to bully them. But some say that it doesn't bother them, and although there certainly can be an element of 'denial' in this response, there are students who appear to be unperturbed and unaffected and who deny that it has any real effect. One child may become deeply distressed by being constantly stared at, especially if the action is performed deliberately to annoy or upset. To another the action may have no effect whatsoever. The rule is that if the 'aggressor' knows that the action is distressing another and is aware that the victim wants it to stop—and still continues—that is 'bullying'. However much we may think that the victim is 'over-sensitive', the action cannot be condoned.

Harassment and bullying

Harassment is a term that is frequently used as a synonym for bullying and to some extent its use is culturally determined. In Britain the term 'bullying' is used more frequently than in the United States where the term 'harassment' is more popular. In Australia we appear to be half-way between these sources of linguistic influence. When teachers have been asked which term they prefer to use for what we have been talking about, whether 'bullying' or 'harassment', there is often an equal division. There are good reasons for preferring 'bullying', but I cheerfully abandon that word or alternate it with 'harassment' if the issue becomes a potential barrier to communication.

A first concern is that in using the term 'harassment' we understate or limit the scope of the problem. For many people it suggests 'sexual harassment'. This is only one aspect of the bullying problem, and a very serious problem in its own right. But it is extensively covered in Carrie Herbert's excellent book, *Sexual harassment in schools: a guide for teachers* (Herbert, 1992) which is based on first-hand knowledge of Australian schools, and I do not intend to examine it further in this book.

Although what is called harassment can be very damaging, the term is often employed to described to describe less violent and abusive behaviour.

For more physical forms of aggression, the term 'bullying' is more frequently used. Both words can, and sometimes are, used to describe abuses of power that include a wide range of abusive behaviours. However, for the not-so-serious behaviours, such as pestering someone in an annoying way, 'harassment' is the word more likely to spring to mind. Thinking exclusively in terms of harassment can sometimes result in physically abusive behaviour being excluded from consideration. In fact, this is one of the reasons for the popularity of 'harassment'. It enables principals in particular to deny that more serious forms of bullying are occurring at their school: 'only a bit of harassment', they might say.

I propose this distinction between bullying and harassment. Harassment is a *kind* of bullying, usually of a non-physical nature, wherein the victim is repeatedly treated badly by a stronger person or group *because* of his or her membership of a social group. So we have racial harassment when a person is being bullied because he or she belongs to an identifiable racial or ethnic group; sexual harassment, when bullying is directed at persons because they are female or (more rarely) male. Students may also be harassed because of their sexual preferences, especially if these are not mainstream or orthodox; for example, if they are believed to be gay. At the root of harassment are prejudiced social beliefs about certain groups of people.

Harassment is an extremely important aspect of bullying, but there is often, I would say, more to bullying than harassment. A prejudiced reaction towards people who belong to a social group, whether it be racial, ethnic, sexual, or religious, is not the only reason why children are bullied. Group membership may in fact be irrelevant. A child may be bullied because somebody wants to dominate him or her; domination is a goal in itself. The victim happens to be there and is vulnerable. The bully might say: 'asking for it'. It may be, and often is, the case that the vulnerability is greater because the victim belongs to a minority group or is seen in some sense as deserving ridicule or scorn. But this is not always so.

The distinction between bullying and harassment is important when we come to examine causes and counter-measures. We can find explanations for harassment in cultural prejudices that have developed towards particular groups. There are stereotyped judgements that people have formed towards those who belong to groups other than their own. Such prejudices are often based upon misconceptions or ignorance. They can be countered by providing accurate information about the group and experiences which simply disconfirm what may have been heard about the group being harassed. In short, the remedy may be educational.

But it is well to remember that bullying is not simply the consequence of prejudices people have about certain groups. Knowledge of the social characteristics of the person selected as a target may or may not be accurate. To the bully, especially the malign bully, it is enough that the intended victim is vulnerable. Dominating that person is attractive, no matter to what group he or she belongs.

What is
going on
in schools?

There are two equally misleading views frequently expressed nowadays about the behaviour of young people. One is that the youth of this country are getting completely out of hand; violence and delinquency are escalating at a frightening rate; we are on the verge of an uncontrollable nightmare. Bullying among youth is then viewed as a symptom of this disorder. The other equally misleading view is that youth are fine; they are wiser than the oldies; they treat each with respect and understanding; if they behave badly, as Andrew Denton puts it, with disarming guile, 'society's to blame'.

The first misleading view is easily put to rest if we stop taking what the media are usually saying at face value. It is their job to catch our attention and this can be done by sensational reports of youth violence and prophecies of doom. It has become commonplace to learn from the media that crime, especially youth crime, is on the rise, and with it the prevalence of bullying.

That view has even been attributed to me. *I emphatically disown it*. Nobody knows whether bullying in schools is increasing; what evidence there is of crime-in-general committed by young people suggests that it is not. (You can refer to material admirably marshalled by one of Australia's leading criminologists, Kenneth Polk (1995)). I suspect the same is true of school bullying.

The second error is to deny that bullying occurs in a school or, if it does, to accord it little significance. I have met principals of schools who have looked me in the eye and said: 'There is no bullying in this school'. It is sometimes conceded that it does occur; just occasionally there is an incident. Some have gone on to assure us that the 'mechanics' are in place—in case they are needed: 'time-out, suspension, exclusion, expulsion'—No worries.

By contrast, an increasing number of schools in Australia are trying to assess the situation as objectively as they can. Bullying is not easy to assess in a way that satisfies everybody. This is partly because it is often confused with aggressive behaviour between children, which often occurs when children of about equal strength fight or quarrel with one another. This may or may not be undesirable, depending on your perspective, but it is certainly not bullying. As I have said, bullying presupposes an imbalance of strength. Therefore, to provide a valid assessment you must have more than a snapshot of the act of aggression. You must also know about the situation and the circumstances in which an incident has occurred.

Assessing the incidence of bullying among children

There are basically three methods of assessment: (a) observe it happening directly; (b) ask questions of people who have observed it happening to others; and (c) ask students what is happening to them.

Direct observation

If we watch children in the playground we will soon see many examples of bullying, varying in seriousness; some seemingly playful (though not necessarily harmless) teasing; some vicious and even sadistic behaviours, though the latter are likely to take place out of the sight of most observers. Direct observation is instructive, but extremely limited. Not only is it very time-consuming, but it is likely to lead to a serious underestimation of the extent of bullying in a school. As I have suggested, bullying will often occur especially in places where observers are not present. Many incidents will be misunderstood or misconstrued, because the sequence of events preceding the 'negative action' will not be known, and bullying essentially involves repeated episodes. Finally, it does not allow us to gauge the degree of distress (except quite crudely) occasioned by the treatment. 'Only the wearer knows where the shoe pinches', has been well said.

Observations by others

If we turn to the judgements of people who have had the opportunity to observe bullying happening in their environment over a period of time, we are likely to gain some quite useful information. Both teachers and children are in a position to provide such judgements; more especially children because they see more bullying behaviour than do teachers, especially in the school playground, on the way to school and on the way home.

Where teachers provide judgements about the number of children who are continually being bullied by their peers, they not surprisingly provide an estimate which is much lower than that provided by the children themselves. This is a reflection of their limited awareness. Children are more likely than teachers to know what is happening, and to provide more valid judgements. *Therefore our best source of information is the students themselves.*

Asking students what is happening

At this point we must raise two important questions: Firstly, do students make a distinction between bullying and other forms of conflict? We have insisted that an imbalance of power is an essential element in any sensible definition of bullying. Do students normally incorporate this element in their judgements of what constitutes bullying? If they do not, then student judgements are not reliable. The second question is whether students are, on the whole, willing to disclose what is going on when they are asked to describe bullying. They may know, but feel reluctant to tell.

How students perceive bullying

The simplest way of discovering how students perceive 'bullying' is to ask them to draw a picture to illustrate bullying at their school. This Dr Slee and I did at a number of schools in the Adelaide area in 1990. The students obliged, and here are some typical drawings.

When you look at the drawings the most striking feature is, in fact, the imbalance in power, frequently caricatured. You will notice that the imbalance is in each case physical: the bully is invariably bigger as well as acting in an aggressive manner. The focus was mainly on one-to-one bullying; occasionally we see examples in the drawings of an individual being harassed by a group. Again we may note that the bullying behaviour depicted in the drawings tends to be physical: hitting, punching, pulling hair or ears, kicking, etc. But verbal abuse is also present, sometimes as an accompaniment to physical abuse, sometimes independently. Finally bullying was not seen as confined to boys; girls, too, were depicted as both bullies and victims. *This simple exercise*

convinced us that students do in fact distinguish between bullying and other forms of conflict at school. While depictions of bullying tended to be physical (and these are easier to represent in drawings than verbal harassment) there were sufficient examples of verbal or psychological bullying to demonstrate that bullying is not seen as exclusively physical. This last point is worth emphasising because it is sometimes argued that the term 'bullying' should be limited to incidents involving physical aggression. Not so, if we are to use terms as students use them.

But will students tell?

It depends on what you want them to tell. We should first make a distinction between (i) providing detailed descriptions of incidents in which bullies and victims are involved; (ii) the naming of students who frequently figure as bullies or victims; and (iii) reports about what has happened to you at school. And we must also distinguish between whether the information is provided anonymously or not. If it is anonymous, there is no way of checking the veracity of the report with the person providing it or, for that matter, helping him or her when help is needed. On the other hand, if the information being sought is not provided anonymously, then in some cases it will simply not be forthcoming at all.

The first kind of information, detailed descriptions of bullying incidents, can provide the richest and potentially the most interesting of all material for the researcher and for the practitioner who wants to understand what is going on. Anatol Pikas, the Swedish psychologist, has suggested that teachers ask their students to write essays as part of language lessons giving eye-witness accounts of conflicts they have observed at their school between peers. He has stressed that these should be as objective as possible, not works of imagination or fantasy. As a means of raising awareness of the problem of bullying in a class it can be most effective and lead to fruitful discussions on what can be done about it (see p. 149). Unfortunately it has been the experience of some teachers who have tried the method in South Australia that some students are reluctant to write such essays because they are worried about being identified by others (including the teacher) as bullies or victims, or as people who 'dob' others in. It is possible sometimes to reassure students that their essays will not be discussed openly, but suspicion and anxiety may remain. To be effective this method requires a high level of trust between student and teacher and this is not always to be found.

The second method, known as the peer nomination approach, is useful because it enables the researcher to identify children about whom there is a high degree of agreement about how they behave with their peers. It can provide a degree of objectivity that may be lacking when individuals provide information about themselves. This method has been much used overseas and also in work in Australia. But there can certainly be worries about how the information can be used. For example, a child may be subsequently labelled 'bully' as result of receiving many nominations as a bully from others in the class—and the label may stick and make it difficult for him or her to receive fair treatment from others even if the bullying behaviour stops. For this reason such information should remain highly confidential, the property (I would argue) of the researcher, to be destroyed after it has been used to address the research problem for which it was obtained.

The third approach involves asking students to provide information about themselves. Under some circumstances this can be the most 'suspect' method of all. Children who are often victimised may be very reluctant to disclose what has happened because the victimisation may get worse and/or their reputation as a 'wimp' is further increased. Children who bully others normally do not advertise it too publicly, although a minority do. Clearly guaranteed protection is needed if this line of inquiry is going to be safe and useful. Therefore, the questions asked need to be answered anonymously. Under such a condition students do tell. They feel secure and, as we shall see, the data are reliable. Let us now look at this method in more detail.

The anonymous questionnaire

Students are asked to answer a questionnaire in which they can provide detailed information about bullying at their school, including self-reports regarding their own involvement in bullying incidents. The questionnaire is answered in a group setting; no names are required; and students are assured that the information they give cannot be traced back to them.

It is sometimes said that by not requiring students to put their names to their responses we are acknowledging and perhaps even perpetuating a sense of distrust between members of the school community. But this is simply an acknowledgement of reality. Children involved in bullying incidents, whether as bullies or victims, commonly do not want others to know about their involvement. If they are victims, as I have said, they are often afraid that teachers will make matters worse, and sometimes teachers actually do. Again, they may also be concerned about the stigma attached to having told a teacher that they are being bullied: that they 'dob' others in, that they are cry-babies. But they do want something to be done about it. They may have some faith that, if the truth does come to light, the situation can be changed. The protection of anonymity allows them to hope for this possibility.

Many children engaged in bullying will not normally want to reveal to teachers what is happening and especially the part they themselves are playing. But will they tell under conditions of anonymity? There are two reasons to expect that *some* of them will. Firstly, they may tell about it as part of the air of bravado often adopted by students who seek to dominate others. Secondly, as we shall see, there are some bullies who feel a great deal of anxiety about what they are doing, especially if they are part of a group that is doing the bullying. They may in fact like to see the bullying stopped. But they certainly would not like the others to know this. Again under conditions of anonymity the truth may come out.

A further objection sometimes raised to the anonymous questionnaire approach is that questionnaire answers do not provide accurate information. The critics of questionnaires rightly emphasise the difficulty of obtaining reliable answers to multiple choice questions. They stress the fact that many questions can be interpreted in different ways; that children misread questions and answer carelessly; that children will exaggerate and distort their answers; that they will tell you what you want to hear (or what you don't want to hear); that for them answering a questionnaire is a lark, not to be taken seriously. It is not my intention here to counter such arguments in detail—but to suggest two things: that before employing any questionnaire to assess bullying in schools the instrument be examined to see what has been done to reduce (not eliminate) the likelihood of these (and other) sources of error; and secondly, to consider the problems of getting accurate information that arise in face to face questioning. They may be greater.

Critics will sometimes assert that using anonymous questionnaires is un-ethical. It is argued sometimes that a case of serious bullying may come to light and if you don't know the students involved you cannot take immediate and necessary action. This is true. But under conditions of non-anonymity such information is unlikely to come to light at all. Further, it does not mean that you cannot act to help individuals on the basis of results from an anonymous questionnaire. You can invite students who have problems to speak with someone who can help them. Indeed, it is unethical to go further than this. The individual student must choose. The teacher's responsibility is to work *towards* providing a climate and a sense of trust in which the students can feel confident in getting the help they need.

Can we really trust questionnaire information ?

While we recognise that individual students may sometimes provide misleading answers, we need to bear in mind that the aim of the questionnaire approach is to obtain a reasonable estimate of what is going on. It is not intended as a means of providing individual diagnoses. At the same time, experience with the questionnaires indicate these things:

1 Students normally *do* take the questionnaires seriously. They provide considered answers, as is evident from the fact we normally obtain highly consistent information from them when answering closely related questions.

2 There is also close agreement between the results obtained in experiments in which have students have been asked to nominate others in their class who are victims of peer abuse (or are bullies) and self-reports obtained directly from the students who have been so nominated. In short, information from external and internal sources shows much agreement.

3 The questionnaires are very welcome if we may judge from the fact that many students indicate that they would like to receive help with the problem and would personally like to meet with other students to discuss ways of reducing bullying (see chapter 9).

I should stress again, however, that the value of the questionnaire data is dependent upon the quality of the particular instrument that is used. The *Peer Relations Questionnaire* (PRQ), which is now available for use by schools from the authors (Rigby and Slee, 1995), is one such instrument.

Bullying in schools

There is now abundant evidence on the nature, extent and effects of bullying in Australian schools. The bulk of it is from studies conducted by Rigby and

Slee and can be found in a series of research publications described in the reference section of this book. The most detailed and comprehensive account is provided in the authors' manual to the *Peer Relations Questionnaire* (Rigby and Slee, 1995). In that booklet results are described for over 8500 students from a wide variety of schools throughout Australia which participated in enquires between 1993 and 1994, and results are continually being updated as more schools become involved in the study. (In relation to some of the questions examined in this book, samples of up to 14 000 have been used.) The bulk of the questionnaires were answered approximately half-way through each of these years. The different types of schools were well represented, including, primary, secondary and all-age schools; coeducational, boys and girls schools; private and state schools.

The importance of preparing the respondents

The results of the surveys cannot be properly evaluated unless you are clear how the respondents understood the questions. What, for example, did they understand by the term 'bullying'? As I have said, the drawings provided by the children suggested that they generally had the same overall conception of bullying as the researchers: broadly that it was basically oppression, physical or psychological, by a more powerful person or group. But there was also a tendency among children (observable also among adults) to include as examples of bullying aggressive behaviour in situations in which there was no evident imbalance of power. Therefore it was important to insist, as did Professor Smith in the work done previously in Sheffield, England, that:

> *'it is not bullying when two people of about the same strength have an odd fight or quarrel.'*

Concrete examples of the kinds of behaviour that constituted bullying in situations of unequal power were provided. These included being called hurtful names, being teased in an unpleasant way, being left out of things on purpose, being threatened with harm, and being hit or kicked. In this way, physical and non-physical forms as well as direct and indirect methods were encompassed. Having carefully instructed students not to confuse bullying with other forms of conflict, you could confidently expect to get reliable estimates of the prevalence of bullying in schools based on individual reports from students on what had happened to them.

How often the different kinds of bullying were reported

The criteria used in the first estimation of the frequency of kinds of bullying were based on percentages of students who indicated that they had been bullied 'often' during the year in relation to each of five possible ways. The results are given below for over 6000 boy and 2500 girl students attending 16 schools located in South Australia, Victoria, New South Wales and Queensland during 1993 and 1994. Their ages ranged from nine to seventeen years (average age fourteen years).

Table 2.1 **Forms of bullying experienced 'often' during the school year**

	Percentages	
	Boys	**Girls**
Reported experience		
Being called hurtful names	12.6	11.5
Being teased in an unpleasant way	11.3	10.6
Being left out of things on purpose	5.8	9.5
Being hit or kicked	5.9	2.9
Being threatened with harm	5.4	3.2

These results showed that for both boys and girls verbal bullying was the most commonly experienced form of bullying with at least one child in ten saying that it happened 'often'. Physical bullying was experienced least. The figures suggested that on average we could expect one or two children in each class to encounter quite frequent physical abuse from peers. Being threatened with harm appeared equally prevalent. Indirect bullying in the form of being excluded was more common an experience than physical abuse, especially so among girls. (Gender differences inferred from these figures and others are considered in more detail on page 40.)

Bullying in general

Given the diverse forms bullying can take, can we reasonably speak of 'bullying in general'?

One way of addressing this question is to ask whether children who reported being victimised in one way tended also to be victimised in another.

The answer is that although one kind of bullying might well predominate, it was extremely common for a child who was being victimised to be treated badly in a variety of ways: verbal, physical, direct and indirect. If a child is being physically abused by peers, he or she will almost certainly be subjected to threats, verbal abuse and exclusion. The evidence for this statement is based in part upon intercorrelations between kinds of reported bullying and is given in detail in Rigby and Slee (1995).

We can therefore have some confidence in children's estimates of how frequently they are bullied in one way or another over a given time period. In a second assessment we asked students how often they had been bullied during the current year on a scale ranging from 'never' to 'every day'. The results are summarised below.

Table 2.2 **Incidence of reported victimisation among school children**

	Percentages	
	Boys	**Girls**
Every day	1.8	0.9
Most days	4.4	3.8
Once or twice a week	6.8	5.2
Once a week	6.3	5.1
Less than once a week	29.2	27.6
Never	51.4	57.4

From: Rigby and Slee (1995)

Two things are evident from these results: first, that for both boys and girls the distributions are similarly highly skewed: a large proportion of students are not bullied or hardly ever bullied at school *during any particular year*, and second, the proportion of girls indicating that they have been bullied is smaller.

For many students being victimised by peers at school is not a personal problem for them. Nevertheless, if we take the level of clearly unacceptable victimisation as 'at least once a week' we find the proportions in our sample are disturbingly high: for boys, 19.3 per cent; for girls, 14.6 per cent. We must remember, however, that these estimates are averages, and the major source of variation is the age of the student.

The age factor

The importance of age becomes clear when we look at the percentages of students who claim to be bullied 'at least once a week' according to age, as in the following table, based on results for students attending co-educational primary and secondary schools in South Australia.

Figure 2.1   Percentages of students aged 10 to 17 years in South Australian coeducational schools claiming to be bullied at least once a week

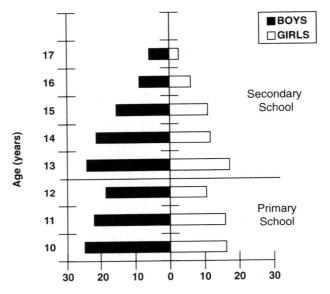

Percentages reporting being bullied by peers

Note: Percentages based upon samples of boys (N=2328) and girls (N=1901)

What we find is that reported victimisation is, on the whole, higher among younger students, and tapers off towards the end of secondary school. Although in the above sample children under ten were not included, our other studies have shown that it is often higher still among 8 and 9-year-olds. (Among younger children a questionnaire approach does not give such reliable results; but we know from direct observations that bullying can be quite a serious problem for some children as early as kindergarten.)

If we now take into account that our sample over-represented older students quite considerably (and older students are bullied less often) an adjusted estimated frequency of bullying in which the age groups are equally represented provides a revised estimate of about 20 per cent of males and 18 per cent of females in the 8 to 17-year-old age range being bullied weekly.

There is one further finding of particular interest to us. It is that bullying frequently increases markedly when students enter secondary school and find themselves among bigger, stronger students in what is often a relatively impersonal social environment. As we shall see this has important implications for preparing children for the transition from primary to high school.

Corroborative data from Kids Help Line

A further extremely useful source of information about bullying among young people is through statistics provided by Kids Help Line (KHL). This is a free service for children with problems who want to talk to a counsellor by telephone, and can be contacted by boys and girls in every state in Australia. During a twelve-month period in 1994 KHL received over 7000 calls from children about bullying. This constituted about 4 per cent of all calls received. A breakdown of *these calls* according to age group is as follows:

Table 2.3 **Percentages of calls about bullying received by Kids Help Line, according to age group**

5 to 9 years	16%
0 to 14 years	75%
15 to 19 years	9%

Kids Help Line Infosheet (1994)

These figures suggest strongly that the 10 to 14-year-old group is the one which has the most severe problems of bullying. As in the Rigby and Slee survey, it is evident that bullying is much less of a problem among older students. Unlike the data from our survey, those obtainable from KHL at first glance suggest that girls may be more frequently bullied than boys, since 55 per cent of callers about bullying were from girls and 45 per cent boys. However, more than twice the number of *all* calls come from girls, and, as we shall see, girls are much more inclined to talk to others about bullying, as indeed they are more inclined to talk about personal problems generally.

Changes in the nature of bullying with age

We have seen that bullying tends to be reported less often as children get older, especially in secondary school. This is true for all kinds of bullying: verbal, physical and indirect bullying. However, do the *proportions* of different kinds of bullying experienced change as a student gets older?

This question can be addressed by examining the relative frequency of different kinds of bullying experienced, choosing as categories (i) being called hurtful names (verbal); (ii) being left out of things on purpose (indirect); and (iii) 'being hit or kicked' (physical). In Figure 2.2 the relative proportions of the different kinds of bullying experienced are shown, based on a recent analysis of results from the PRQ for over 8000 boys and 4000 girls.

Figure 2.2 Relative proportions of three kinds of bullying reported 'sometimes or more often' by boys and girls in three age groups

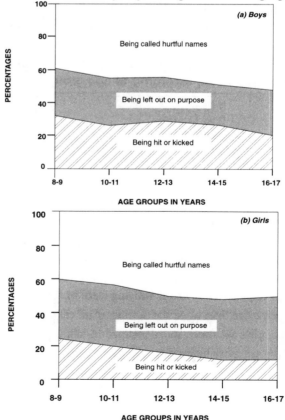

In interpreting this figure remember that in absolute terms there is a decline in the amount of bullying for every category with age, including being excluded by others on purpose and Figure 2.2 substantiates this. As both boys and girls grow older, there is a gradual increase in the proportion of bullying that is verbal and a general decrease in the proportion that is physical. The relative amount of exclusionary bullying, the indirect form, remains much the same from year to year. Despite these similarities for boys and girls, it is notable that for each age group indirect bullying forms a higher proportion for girls and physical bullying a higher proportion for boys. By the time they are 16 or 17-year-olds, boys are more likely to be bullied by being excluded than being hit or kicked. This is true of girls for every age group.

Who bullies whom?

Generally speaking bullies are somewhat older than the students they victimise. Whether the bullies tend to operate in groups or singly varies from school to school. Victimised boys more often point to an individual as the bully, but quite often the bully has a group of supporters who help to sustain that behaviour. There is a tendency for girls to report being bullied more by groups.

Table 2.4 **Percentages of children claiming to be bullied 'often' by (a) individuals and (b) groups in coeducational primary and secondary schools in South Australia**

	Boys Bullied by:		Girls Bullied by:	
School	*Individual*	*Group(s)*	*Individual*	*Group(s)*
Primary	6.9	4. 5	5.0	5.4
Secondary	4.4	2.8	2.8	3.6

Note: Based on samples of approx. 1100 primary school children and 3000 secondary school children.

Gender in bully/victim interactions

By asking students who had been bullied what gender the bully was, it became possible to make some generalisations about who was commonly involved (boys and/or girls) when bullying occurred. The following table summarises the results for students attending coeducational schools.

Table 2.5 **Gender of the bully or bullies: Percentages in each category**

| | Reported bullies | | |
	Always a boy	Always a girl	Sometimes a boy, sometimes a girl
Boys reporting being victimised	69.0	3.9	27.1
Girls reporting being victimised	24.1	24.5	51.4

From: Rigby and Slee (1995)

The first thing that strikes us is that both boys and girls are sometimes bullied by members of the opposite sex at school. About one-third of the boys indicate that girls are sometimes involved in bullying them; whereas about three-quarters of the girls say that boys are sometimes involved in bullying them. The contrast between the sexes is greater when we examine the proportions of boys and girls who say they are bullied exclusively by the opposite sex. Among girls a quarter are bullied *only* by boys; among boys being bullied by a girl only is rare: less than one in twenty say it happened.

Differences in the extent of bullying in coeducational schools.

It is clear that schools do differ according to the incidence of bullying, independently of the age and gender of the students. Given below are figures for eight coeducational schools at which substantial numbers of boys and girls (more than 100 in the same sex/age group) completed the PRQ.

The variations are quite substantial and they suggest that school factors can influence the extent to which students are bullied. Notice, too, that bullying can sometimes be high for one sex but not the other at the same school (see School F). We have not found that the size of a school has any bearing on the incidence of bullying. Although community factors, such as socio-economic status of families of the children, could conceivably affect the amount of reported victimisation in a school, there has so far not been any direct evidence in Australia supporting this suggestion.

Table 2.6 **Percentages of students aged 13-15 years reporting being bullied 'at least once a week' at eight coeducational schools**

| | Percentages | |
	Boys	Girls
School A	28.3	15.3
School B	26.5	19.5
School C	26.4	15.3
School D	23.0	18.7
School E	22.8	13.8
School F	20.8	5.7
School G	19.0	17.4
School H	17.1	13.8

Differences between coeducational and single sex schools

I am frequently asked whether there are differences between coeducational and single sex schools in the incidence of bullying. So far no *consistent* differences between the two types of schools have been found in the Australian survey results. Contrary to what is sometimes suggested, boys in boys schools do not report a significantly higher rate of bullying than boys in coeducational schools. Similarly, girls in coeducational schools do not, as we might suppose, report a higher level of bullying than girls in single sex schools, where, of course, there are no boys to harass them (Rigby, 1995b).

Children who bully others

Just as it is a minority of students who are frequently victimised, so it is a minority of students who frequently become involved in bullying others. These are not mutually exclusive categories, however—some bullies are also victims. Here we cannot be as confident in the estimates because it seems likely that some students may prefer not to admit their involvement as bullies, even under conditions of anonymity. Nevertheless, a surprisingly large pro-portion of students reported that they had engaged in bullying others 'more than once or twice' during the school year, either in a group or as an individ-ual. The percentages are given below, according to gender and age group, based on recent analyses of results from PRQ data for approximately 4600 girls and 8600 boys between the ages of ten and seventeen years.

Figure 2.3 Percentages of students claiming that they had bullied others 'more than once or twice' (a) as part of a group (b) alone as an individual

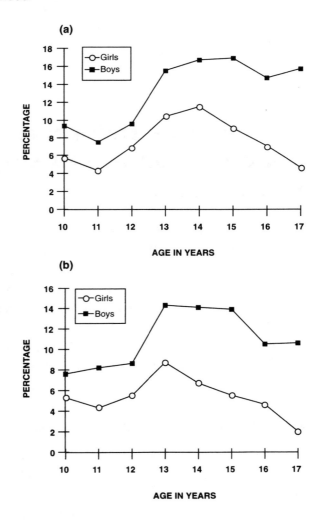

The trends are fairly similar for individual and group bullying. Bullying others increases as children get older from ten years old on, but declines towards the later teen years. For both boys and girls, bullying in this age range is perpetrated most by young adolescents between thirteen and fourteen years old. For every age group boys are much more likely to claim that they have engaged in bullying than girls, either as an individual or as a group member. We may notice, too, that bullying others as part of a group appears to peak later than bullying as an individual. Alternatively we can say that a decline in a one-to-one situation bullying tends to occur earlier.

Are schools safe places for children?

In the light of what has been written in this chapter, can it be said that schools are safe places for children? The Director-General of Education of New South Wales, Ken Boston, has given a clear affirmative answer. He has argued that compared with other places, such as the streets, such as the home, schools are safe. And in one sense he is right. In Australian schools we rarely find children carrying knives or guns; students are very rarely killed at school; they rarely suffer serious bodily harm and subsequent hospitalisation. This response from a spokesman for a school system is understandable, especially in the context of media hysteria about violence. But the discussion in the media so far has been based on a very narrow definition of what safety is.

I suggest that safety involves far more than physical security. Safety is jeopardised when there is a pervading fear or anxiety about being harmed by others. And if this anxiety is felt by, or on behalf of, a substantial minority of children at school (not everyone, many students can take care of themselves very well) then there is cause for concern. Such a state of 'unsafety' applies not only to a fear of bodily harm but also to psychological hurt. In discussions of safety we tend to focus on physical aspects. We forget that schools are (or should be) places where we deliberately (and at great expense) seek to induce the maximum cognitive and emotional development of human beings during the most sensitive period of their lives. This cannot be done for children who are fearful of the very environment that has been created for this purpose.

One of the advantages of the survey approach is that it enables us to get away from impressions or judgements of outside experts about what constitutes a safe environment. We can directly ask students whether schools are, in general, safe places—especially for young people who find it hard to defend themselves. We would expect a range of opinion, with some who have not experienced any bullying personally to underestimate the threat that others experience. *About four students in five believe that the school is, in fact, not a safe place for such children.* Here are the detailed results for boys and girls:

Table 2.7 **Perceived safety of the school for vulnerable students**

	Percentages giving judgement	
	Boys	**Girls**
Yes, it is a safe place for them	18.6	17.4
It is usually safe for them	65.7	69.6
It is hardly ever safe for them	12.3	11.3
It is never safe for them	3.4	1.7

Rigby and Slee (1995)

Among both boys and girls *less than 20 per cent* see the school as a 'safe place' for vulnerable students. To ascertain whether there was much variation between schools in perceived safety, I compared eight coeducational high schools for which there was data for practically the entire student populations, in each case, the numbers exceeded 200.

Table 2.8 **Perceived school safety at eight coeducational high schools**

Percentages of students judging their school as *not* always safe for vulnerable students

	Boys	**Girls**
School 1	94.0	97.1
School 2	93.2	96.2
School 3	93.1	94.0
School 4	89.4	93.9
School 5	87.8	90.4
School 6	87.1	89.3
School 7	81.5	85.1
School 8	71.9	77.5

When we look at the figures in Table 2.8, we may first be struck by the fact that the results for boys and girls put the schools in exactly the same order, with School 1 being the school about which there is most agreement that it is not safe, to School 8 about which there is least consensus to that effect. To the statistically minded the probability of this happening by chance is extremely remote. We may conclude that boys and girls do share similar conceptions of what environment is less safe. Yet it is also the case that girls are, in each school, rather more sensitive to a threatening environment. This is probably a reflection of their greater vulnerability. There is quite a range implied in these judgements given by boys and by girls; differences between schools are quite pronounced. But despite these differences between schools, it is fair to conclude that schools are perceived by a large majority of students as not always safe places for those children who find it hard to defend themselves.

The gender factor

We have touched here and there on gender similarities and differences in reporting the findings. Here we can summarise them:

1   The proportion of students reporting being bullied by their peers at least weekly is 18 per cent or over for both sexes in the eight to seventeen-year-old age range. It is somewhat higher for males; the differences are more pronounced at secondary schools; however, the differences depend upon the kind of bullying being considered.

2   For all age groups, girls are less likely to be bullied physically than boys, but more likely to be bullied by indirect means. The extent of verbal bullying encountered is generally similar for each sex.

3   Both boys and girls are bullied by individuals and groups, but group bullying is more likely to be encountered by girls.

4   Boys and girls are both bullied by members of the same and opposite sex. For girls, however, being bullied by the opposite sex in coeducational schools is much more common.

5   For both boys and girls there is marked diminution in the extent to which they are bullied as they grow older; physical bullying becomes less and less frequent compared with other forms of harassment; verbal bullying becomes comparatively more frequent with age; indirect forms of bullying as a proportion of all bullying remains much the same.

6   There is no evidence to suggest that the prevalence of peer victimisation is any different for boys and girls in single sex schools compared with coeducational schools.

7   Just as more boys than girls are victimised, more boys than girls identify themselves as children who bully others. Both boys and girls bully less often as they grow older in secondary schools, but the reduced tendency to bully occurs earlier among girls.

8   Although most students of either sex see their school as unsafe for vulnerable children, girls are consistently more likely to feel their school is not so safe.

How bad is peer victimisation?

The surveys do *not* provide grounds for supposing that bullying is a minor problem in schools in Australia, involving only small numbers of students. Although quantification of the basic features of the problem is obviously difficult, a proportion of approximately one in five children being victimised by peers on a weekly basis, as suggested by extensive survey results, is alarmingly high. True, we still have to examine the effects of bullying on children. It will be conceded that in many cases children are, thankfully, so resilient that many of them soon shrug off the misery that bullying can entail for some.

A further way of assessing the seriousness of the problem of bullying is to compare what we know about it with what is known about other problems children encounter. It is now widely accepted that child abuse by adults, especially parents, is an extremely serious problem in Australia, as in many other countries. How does the problem of peer victimisation compare?

According to a recent Canadian study when adults are asked to recall their childhood years, it is their peers whom they recall as the main abusers, not their parents (Ambert, 1994). Data from the Kids Help Line in Australia suggest that the incidence of sexual abuse of children (some of which is carried out by peers) is similar to that of bullying. Calls complaining about bullying are five times more numerous than calls about domestic violence or its effects on the callers. Calls from children with problems with drugs are disturbingly numerous, but they are not as common as calls about bullying.

Although comparisons with overseas countries are difficult to make because of subtle variations in the wording and context of the questions used in various surveys, it does, in fact, seem likely that Australian schools have comparatively high levels of bullying. The most extensive study of bullying in schools in Britain, led by Professor Peter Smith at Sheffield University, used comparable questions answered anonymously by 4135 students in both primary and secondary schools in Sheffield. That enquiry conducted in 1990 provided results indicating that in primary schools some 10 per cent of children reported being bullied 'once a week or more'; in secondary schools the figure was 4 per cent (Whitney and Smith, 1993). Compare these results with those from our more extensive Australian studies, for which analyses have been provided in this chapter for over 8000 students. The reported incidence in the Australian schools is about twice as high in the primary schools and four times as high in the secondary schools. It is also worth noting that it is claimed in the British study that the level of bullying in the English schools is considerably higher than that found in the Norwegian studies conducted by Olweus in the 1980s. It is impossible to draw precise conclusions from the existing statistics, but the large scale of difference between the results obtained in England and Australia does very strongly suggest that bullying is a more prevalent form of behaviour in the schools in Australia.

But, you may ask, could it be that children in Australia have tougher skins and that the bullying and harassment here does little or no harm? In the next chapter we examine this question in some detail.

Chapter 3

Consequences
of bullying

Scepticism and the need for evidence

For some readers it will be almost self-evident that bullying in schools has adverse consequences. Unfortunately this is not universally recognised. Some people regard bullying as a trivial problem, either because it seems to affect so few, or because its effects are seen as quite short term and readily shrugged off. In fact, some go further and claim that bullying has positive effects. It toughens people up, builds character, and prepares them for the real world. These claims cannot be dismissed as crackpot, or the views of the ignorant and unintelligent. I have heard such views expressed on occasions by teachers. One teacher, for instance, argued eloquently that it is the bullies of this world who achieve most, and that we do a disservice to children if we deprive them of the necessary qualities and skill to succeed. Therefore we must look at the case against bullying carefully and examine the evidence regarding its effects as dispassionately as we can.

What happens when children are bullied

As we have seen, the occasions on which more powerful students seek to hurt or intimidate other students are indeed numerous and at least 50 per cent of students each year, in a mild or more serious way, experience bullying personally. For some, in fact the majority, it is a fairly transient experience. For a day or two they have been the recipient of unwelcome attention from somebody who can and does make things uncomfortable. But the problem passes. They may have learned how to stand up to the bully or have got help from somebody or discovered how to keep out of the way. Or the bully may have turned to somebody else—or have given up bullying. Clearly many do as they become older. So that for some the episode has left no scars. It is seen as part of school life—it happened to many others. In retrospect they may claim not to have been bothered by it.

Now we might reasonably expect that the consequences would be more severe for students who are frequently bullied; say for students who report being bullied at least once a week. As we have seen, this comprises a substantial number of students, probably as many as one student in six on average across age groups. But we should bear in mind that some students are more resilient than others and may even come through experiences of fairly intense bullying relatively unscathed, physically and psychologically.

When students who report being bullied at least once a week have been asked how they felt about being bullied, a surprising number have indicted that they 'weren't really bothered'. This has been particularly true of boys. For example, 36 per cent of the weekly-bullied boys say this compared with 26 per cent of girls. Is this really how they feel or is there an element of 'denial' of reality in their response? In some cases almost certainly there is 'denial', in the clinical sense especially among boys whose status depends more on a show of toughness and stoicism. But it may very well be the case that many of these students are simply more resilient than others and are indeed little affected by their negative experiences.

Another factor that can influence the effects of bullying is the duration over which bullying has occurred. We know that some students have a long history of being bullied. In our survey 14 per cent of the boys and 12 per cent of the girls could recall being bullied by the same person or group for months, and over 5 per cent of boys and girls said that they had been continually bullied by the same people for over a year. Under such circumstances the effects are unlikely to be trivial, unless the victimised student is quite extraordinarily resilient.

When students admit that they are bothered by the bullying, they are likely to express either of two emotions: anger or sadness. Among the weekly-bullied boys who were 'bothered', 'anger' was the most common reaction (some 63 per cent report feeling angry); among girls there were far fewer (39 per cent). Some boys said they felt sad about it (37 per cent). For girls feeling sad was by far the most common emotional reaction; some 61 per cent of the girls who had been bullied said this is how they felt. These gender differences are quite large and strongly suggest that for girls depression may be a common outcome of serious and continued bullying.

Self-esteem

There can be no doubt that one of the common effects of bullying is to reduce the self-esteem of victims. Research in Australia (Rigby & Slee, 1993a) has supported that of others in showing that students who report relatively high levels of being victimised are relatively low in self-esteem. What is meant by low self-esteem can be conveyed by citing items from the Rosenberg (1986) measure of self-esteem that was used in our study. Students with low self-esteem agree with these statements:

> I feel I don't have much to be proud of
> At times I think I am no good at all
> I wish I could have more respect for myself
> All in all, I am inclined to think I am a failure

By contrast, non-victimised students agree more often with these statements:

> I feel I am a person of worth, at least on an equal plane with others
> I am able to do things as well as most people
> On the whole I am satisfied with myself

We may ask whether low self-esteem is a cause rather than an effect of being victimised. Children who are lacking in it may be advertising their vulnerability to bullying—and are duly bullied for it.

One way of answering this question is to ask students how they feel about being bullied *after* it has happened to them. Some 51 per cent of boys and 63 per cent of girls said they felt worse about themselves; rather less than half said they did not feel any the worse. Curiously, about 5 per cent said they felt better! Perhaps they felt that they had successfully come through some initiating rite; or perhaps they actually 'turned the tables' on the bully. Even ignoring the likelihood that some students lack insight into their feelings or prefer to deny them, a large proportion of students clearly feel that they are made to feel worse about themselves by being bullied.

Why being victimised lowers self-esteem

Why should being bullied have this demoralising effect on many young people? The truth is that a failure to stand their ground, to acquit themselves well, in any conflict situation with their peers, strikes deeply. The greater the emphasis placed in a school on position and status in the 'pecking order', the greater is the potential sense of loss and feelings of inferiority. Children soon learn that to be a wimp is to be despised by almost everyone. There is a further reason why feeling rejected should be especially hurtful to many children. As Storr (1988) has argued, unless they are prodigies, young children have not had sufficient time to develop the interests and skills that might enhance their sense of competence. They are therefore particularly dependent for their self-esteem on the quality of their interpersonal relationships, and in particular how their peers treat them.

Isolation

Children who are frequently bullied tend to have few (if any) friends. Many children have told us that they wouldn't be friends with a wimp. Here, as with low self-esteem, it is sometimes difficult to separate cause from effect. Children may be bullied in part because they have no friends. They are easier to bully than those who have supporters. It may also seem to some that their isolation is evidence of their appropriateness for bullying. But once the bullying has occurred the isolation deepens, and the victim may feel so depressed as to make little or no effort to make friends.

Absenteeism

Not surprisingly when bullying is serious and sustained a student may decide to avoid (if possible) going to school. This may require some deception. A parent may be informed that the child is not feeling well, which may, in part, be true.

Recently we gathered some facts about the extent of absenteeism from school from students themselves. Asked whether they had ever stayed away from school because of bullying, 5 per cent of boys and 8 per cent of girls said that they had, and a further 12 per cent of boys and 18 per cent of girls said they had thought of doing so. It seems likely that some students would be reluctant to admit this even in an anonymously administered questionnaire. This suggests that the figures understate the true incidence.

A child's aversion to going to school and meeting the bullies is sometimes so strong that the parents are virtually forced to try another school to get a 'new start'. Occasionally I have heard from parents who have become so devastated by the train of events and the absence of support from the local community that they have moved away from the area and entered their child in another school interstate.

The importance of a student's emotional reaction to bullying

Earlier we noted that children differ widely in how they respond to bullying: some do not appear to be bothered by it; others become either angry or sad. Hitherto researchers have not examined this extremely important variable. It has become clear that the effects of bullying do depend to a significant degree upon these alternative ways of responding or not responding.

First, those who are bullied frequently (at least once a week) and also say they respond emotionally to being bullied (either by anger or sadness) are generally less popular in their own estimation with their peers than those who are similarly bullied but say they are 'not bothered' by it (see Rigby, 1995a). They are also more likely to see themselves as unhappy people and to be absent from school. So by and large, those who are able to adopt a stoical attitude towards being bullied seem to be more fortunate. This suggests that their relative popularity is because they 'take it' and don't complain. But we should bear in mind that these 'stoics' are in fact less popular than those who are hardly bullied at all.

Secondly, where the reaction of a student after being bullied is one of sadness rather than anger the situation is generally worse for the victim. These 'sad' victims feel more incapable than others of offering resistance to bullies or, for that matter, bullying anyone else. They are much less happy in their everyday lives than the 'angry' victims. It is these students whose self-esteem is most likely to be reduced. In all these respects, boys and girls are similar: sadness after bullying is a less adaptive response for both sexes.

It should be recalled (see page 50) that girls are much more likely than boys to respond to bullying with sadness. One possible explanation is that girls are more inclined than boys to see themselves as being to blame when they are bullied, especially if, as is more often the case with girls, the bullying takes the form of exclusion from a group. Whatever the explanation, it would seem that because getting angry or indignant is often a more adaptive response girls may be, in a sense, psychologically disadvantaged. This could be because of the social conditioning to which girls have been long exposed. However, there are certainly signs that the times are changing as girls learn to be more assertive and non-accepting of domination by others.

Although the way a student reacts to bullying is a significant factor, it would be wrong to suggest that the negative consequences of bullying could be avoided by the victim cultivating a thicker skin. Students who are bullied frequently and say they are 'not bothered' by it nevertheless see themselves (probably accurately) as less popular and have fewer friends than those who are rarely bullied. Finally, like other students who are bullied a good deal, they are more likely than others to say that they have often felt a desire to hurt others. This suggests that their anger is really there but repressed.

A domino effect

A child who is being bullied continually at school by a more powerful peer or group of peers may be unable or unwilling to retaliate directly but may be motivated to take it out on someone else. He or she may feel very frustrated because that anger seemingly cannot be expressed safely through action directed at the source of the bullying. Displacement may occur; another innocent victim may suffer.

It is not unusual for bullying to produce a chain of events linked by a series of bully/victim interactions. We are reminded of Jonathan Swift's observations on the flea:

So, naturalists observe, a flea
Hath smaller fleas that on him prey;
And these have smaller fleas to bite 'em,
And so proceed *ad infinitum*.

We know from both self-reports of children who are victimised and results of peer nomination studies conducted in Australia that many children who are victimised frequently engage in bullying others. We call them 'bully/victims'.

Educational consequences

Whether academic work usually tends to suffer is a largely unexplored area. Certainly I have found children who have been unable to concentrate on their school work because of bullying, and absences from school have hindered their school progress. Equally, though, I have found bullied children who have become increasingly isolated from others, and have turned more and more to an introspective lifestyle in which reading and study have played an increasingly important part. Unfortunately this can and often does occur at the expense of adequate emotional and social development.

Health

It has become clear from a recent Australian study that the general health of children who are victimised by their peers at school can be seriously affected. In 1993 Dr Slee and I conducted a study in two large Adelaide coeducational high schools to ascertain whether there were differences in the health of children who were identified as frequently bullied at school compared with their peers.

It was assumed that a child was probably being bullied quite seriously if he or she reported being bullied 'at least once a week' in response to an anonymously answered questionnaire. The percentage of students identified in this way as 'victims' was approximately 15 per cent. These students also completed a standardised test for reporting symptoms of ill health: the General Health Questionnaire (Goldberg & Williams, 1988). This consists of twenty-eight questions. The respondents reported on their recent health by answering questions grouped in a number of areas: general; somatic complaints; anxiety; social dysfunction; depression and suicidal. For both boys and girls for every item a larger proportion of those categorised as victims reported that their health was worse than usual. On twenty-two of the items the differences were statistically significant for either boys or girls. Given below are some illustrative results.

Table 3.1 **Percentages of secondary school students indicating worse than usual health on General Health Questionnaire indices, according to self-identified status as victim (V) or non-victim (NV) of peer bullying at school**

	Boys		Girls	
	V	**NV**	**V**	**NV**
General illness				
Not in good health	25	13	42	22
Felt ill	34	18	47	26
Somatic complaints				
Hot or cold spells	20	10	43	19
Anxiety				
Lost sleep over worry	27	15	57	31
Constant strain	29	16	56	28
Panicky without reason	17	4	40	15
Social dysfunction				
Not keeping occupied	16	7	26	9
Not enjoying activities	22	7	26	13
Depression				
Feeling worthless	21	8	34	20
Life not worth living	23	11	40	16
Suicidal				
Wishing one were dead	23	12	40	21
Recurring idea of taking own life	23	11	32	15

Sample sizes: boys = 377; girls = 400

From Rigby: (1994c)

If we examine Table 3.1 we can see that the proportions of children who report 'poorer health than usual' are much more likely to be among those categorised as victims of peer abuse. We can see, too, that the indicators of ill health include both physical and psychological kinds. They reflect lower levels of well-being as indicated by poorer health generally, impairment in social functioning; anxiety and depression and perhaps most serious of all, through repeated thoughts of suicide.

We need to be cautious here, because we are dealing with results that come from self-reports only. It is true that children may know best whether they are being victimised, but it is certainly possible that those who tend to complain of being bullied could also be more predisposed to complain of ill health. It is also possible that physical weakness and self-pity may invite aggression from others and may be a cause as well as an effect.

To meet these objections a further study was conducted in which victimised children were identified according to nominations from peers in their class as well as by self-reports. In addition, children were asked not only to report on their health using standardised methods of assessment, but also to indicate whether in their opinion their health had been affected by any negative treatment they had recently received from their peers. The results (as yet unpublished) obtained from boys and girls attending three coeducational high schools in Adelaide gave some support to the earlier study. Both boys and girls identified as victims at school by their peers were more likely than others to claim that their health had been badly affected by peer victimisation at school and also to report a higher level of absenteeism from school. The relationship between being victimised and poor general health, as assessed by the General Health Questionnaire, was statistically significant for girls, regardless of whether self-reports or peer nomination measures of victim status were used. However, for boys the result was not replicated, suggesting that the relationship between being victimised and ill health is currently more firmly established for girls than for boys.

Suicide

There is some persuasive evidence of a link between suicide and peer victimisation at school. This is based partly on an examination of case studies of school children who have attempted suicide, and in some instances, succeeded in doing so. These have been reported in a number of countries, including Britain, Norway, USA and Australia. Establishing cause/effect relationships in this area is extremely difficult because many interrelated factors can contribute to a young person's suicide, including home background, failure in exams and disappointment in love relationships. Nevertheless the connection between peer victimisation and some cases of suicide seems very probable.

Some of the evidence for this connection is indirect. As indicated in the results of the Australian study of peer victimisation and health presented earlier, significant correlations were found between self-reported victimisation at school and what might be called 'suicidal ideation', that is, frequently thinking about suicide. We know from previous work on adolescent suicide that thinking about suicide often precedes the act.

The sheer number and plausibility of cases of child/adolescent suicide or attempted suicide seemingly related to bullying cannot be ignored. These studies have included young people widely differing in age and home circumstances. One account concerns an Australian youth who hanged himself shortly after leaving a school at which he had experienced many years of horrendous bullying. In a note discovered after his death the young man attributed his desire to die to a number of factors, including the repeated experience of being bullied by another student at his school.

A further case concerns an eight-year-old Australian girl who unsuccessfully attempted suicide at home after she had complained of being repeatedly harassed at school by a group of other girls. A rather precocious child, she had experienced considerable frustration from what she had seen as her inability to achieve at school what she knew she was capable of. Added to this, was the fact that she was seen as unusual in her behaviour at school (she was diagnosed as suffering from Attention Deficit Hyperactivity Disorder) and had great difficulty in gaining acceptance by her peers. Her suicide bid seems to have been multiply determined; the intolerant and bullying behaviour of other children was probably a contributory cause. Although we think of adolescence as the period of 'storm and stress' in which both internal and external factors can produce serious depression, here we have evidence that much younger children can be similarly vulnerable. There can be little doubt that bullying at school can contribute strongly to the desire students of all ages sometimes have to 'end it all'.

The buffering effect of social support

It was reported earlier that children who were bullied frequently report worse than average health. However, some children subjected to such stress do not appear to be affected. In part this may be due to their decreased personal vulnerability. As we have seen, the evidence from self-reports suggests that *some* children, like some adults, are remarkably resilient. But, in addition, it seems likely from our research that, for those fortunate enough to have it, social support can have a buffering effect preventing some students who are being victimised from experiencing the more extreme health consequences.

In one South Australian study a distinction was made between frequently bullied children who said that they thought they could get help from their mother or father if they had a serious problem at school and those who were similarly bullied but thought they would not receive help from their parents. It was found that the health of children who felt they could count on parental support if they had a serious problem at school was relatively unaffected by the bullying. The health consequences for those without support from either their mother or their father were far worse (see Rigby, 1994c). This finding must encourage us to believe that children can over-come the worst effects of bullying if they have strong parental support.

Long-term consequences of bully/victim problems

In examining long-term consequences of bullying at school we can focus on effects that concern (i) the victims; (ii) the bullies; and (iii) observers or bystanders, that is the vast majority who are not directly involved.

Effects on victims

It may be thought that the effects on a child being victimised by peers at school would be temporary. Recent studies have strongly suggested otherwise.

Follow-up studies have been conducted to examine possible effects on children who had been severely bullied at school. In Norway, Professor Olweus (1992) conducted a series of psychological tests with such children until they had reached their early twenties; in England, Professor Farrington (1993) has conducted longitudinal studies with bullied children into their thirties. The studies concur in suggesting that effects may be long-lasting. Self-esteem of people victimised at school tends to stay at a relatively low level, and according to Olweus, bouts of depression are not uncommon among adults who were badly bullied at school. Farrington's work indicates generational continuity: children bullied at school grow up to have children who are more likely than their peers to be victimised.

Retrospective studies in which adults have been asked to recall their schooldays and their relations with their peers at school have provided complementary evidence. In the United States, Gilmartin (1987) conducted such a study and found that men who were severely victimised at school by their peers were more 'love shy', as he put it, than others. That is, they were much less successful in achieving satisfactory intimate relationships with members of the opposite sex. In Australia, Dietz (1994) assessed the psychological well-being of men and women who were victimised at school and discovered that they were significantly more depressed than others and, as in Gilmartin's study, found difficulty in forming close intimate relationships.

The view that bullying can have destructive consequences for men and women's sexual life is strongly supported by the Australian poet and essayist, Les Murray (1994). He describes this group as 'almost certainly bigger than the gay population and all the sad victims of literal rape and sexual abuse put together'. They are, he writes, 'folk for whom the sexual revolution remains a chimera, the ones whose sexual morale was destroyed early by scorn, by childhood trauma, by fashion, by lack or defection of allies, by image.' Not all of them are unattractive, but all of them, he says, live and act in the belief that they are. They are described variously as 'wallflowers, ugly, wimps, unstylish, drips, nerds, pathetic, fat, frigid, creepy...'

According to Murray, this continual denigration should be seen as a crime because it all too often results in the sexual destruction of a person. It begins at school and is usually called bullying or harassment. The psychological scarring, he observes, may persist for a lifetime. But it is not only the taunting and jeering that is devastating. It is also, he argues, the 'abandonment that goes with them, the moral cowardice of fellow kids who don't jeer themselves but don't speak out either, or afford the tormented one support for fear of becoming victims themselves.' He adds that 'if the jeering or the avoidance come from the opposite sex, the results are apt to be severe and lasting.'

Letters from people reporting that they were victimised at school provide further support for believing that peer victimisation can have serious long-term effects. In the *Sunday Age* on 20 June 1993 there appeared a letter headed 'Schoolboy's life ruined by bullying'. In it the writer tells how as a boy he was assaulted and verbally abused nearly every day he went to his primary school and intensified, as it often does, when he entered secondary school.

The violence, he writes, was mainly physical, sometimes even occurring in the classroom. At times there were arranged bicycle 'accidents' when two of his classmates threw their bags at his front wheel as he rode past. However, it was the verbal abuse that really destroyed his self-esteem. 'Every infinitesimal fragment of my personality was ridiculed daily', he records. The situation did not improve when he finally in year nine 'escaped' to a Melbourne boarding school.

Reflecting on his experiences at school, the writer still cannot understand why he had been treated so badly. He desperately wanted to be popular. There was nothing unusual about his family. Now a 23-year-old, he finds himself 'still frightened of most activities and suspicious of affectionate people'.

In another letter written to me by an Australian doctor living in Melbourne the intensity and misery induced by peer victimisation is no less evident.

> Both in primary and secondary school I was subjected to serious and regular physical and emotional bullying from other schoolboys, and, in one case, from a teacher. At its extreme I would describe the bullying as persecution. This took place in the schoolyard, schoolroom and on the way home.

> The impact on my life at the time and into adulthood in particular was very powerful. I had deep feelings of anger, powerlessness, anxiety, distrust and preference for my own company and other avoidance behaviours. In my early adult years I was for a period dangerously depressed. In part, this may have related to my mistrust of people and loneliness stemming from this.

> In my mature years (I am now 46) and a parent of a young daughter (very socially skilled and well-adjusted) I often reflect on the root causes of my bullying. What were the temperamental and school circumstances that allowed it to occur and flourish unchallenged? Today I am a relaxed,

assertive and socially well-adjusted person, but still I wonder how some of my reactions to others are influenced by these circumstances so long ago. In the positive sense I have a very strong sense of justice for the 'underdog'. I also wonder about the adult persona of my persecutors.

When I see persecutory and bully behaviour on a large scale I wonder if these are not just mass manifestations of the immature power relationships of children.

In some respects this second letter is similar to the first. It contains an account of being the victim of sustained bullying at both primary and secondary school. Again, the experience is described as having far-reaching effects, inducing in the victim years of despondency and social isolation. In both cases the writers feel impelled to reflect upon what happened to them: why it occurred and what harm it did. But there is a difference. The second writer (twice the age of the first) has reached the stage in his life at which he has evidently come to terms with his school experiences, being now 'relaxed, assertive and well-adjusted', even though there are times, he admits, when he wonders how 'some of my reactions to others are influenced by the circumstances long ago'.

This second letter illustrates very clearly not only how an adult can be affected by school bullying for many years after leaving school, but also how some individuals can transcend social and emotional difficulties induced by school bullying—and indeed become motivated in later life to help other people to fight against social injustice.

Do victims become bullies?

Earlier it was suggested that children who are bullied at school, or for that matter at home, may be unable to retaliate and instead turn their hostile attentions towards another child who is more vulnerable. It has been further suggested that the experience of being seriously abused as a child may have long-term effects on some individuals, so that as adults they may seek to bully others. The possibility has been raised largely through findings from studies of domestic violence. The abused it seems quite commonly later become the abusers (Widom, 1995).

So far, this line of speculation has not been explored through social research in relation to peer abuse at school. But it has about it, a plausibility which has been captured in a short story called *Teacher's Pet* by James Thurber (1967).

An example from literature: Thurber's bully/victim

Thurber's story is about a depressed middle-aged man called Kelby who had begun to brood about an event in his childhood that happened some thirty-seven years ago. At school he had been the teacher's pet and had been mercilessly teased about it, especially by a thirteen-year-old boy named Zeke Leonard. One afternoon Zeke heard the teacher call Kelby 'Willber, dear'; after which Zeke began to follow him around after school calling out 'Willber, dear' in a high falsetto. Kelby eventually turned upon his tormentor, but Zeke was much the stronger, adding insult to injury by keeping one arm behind his back as he slapped and bumped and kicked Kelby around to the jeers and laughter of other boys. 'Look', said Zeke, 'both hands behind my back'. Kelby took flight in tears.

Kelby was still brooding about this incident many years later at a party when a woman asked him what he was thinking about. He told her: 'I was thinking of the time a boy named Zeke Leonard beat me up. I was the teacher's pet, and he beat me up.' 'What in the world for?' exclaimed the woman. 'What had you done?'

Kelby explained: 'A teacher's pet doesn't have to do anything. It is the mere fact of his existence that makes the stupid and the strong want to beat him up. There is a type of man that wants to destroy the weaker, the more sensitive, the more intelligent.'

The woman replied that she knew what Kelby meant. She had a son, Elbert, who was terribly sensitive; the older boys were always torturing him, particularly one boy called Bob Stevenson. Believing that she had found a helper in Kelby, she suggested that maybe Kelby could talk to her son's tormentor. She added that children who are treated in this way are not cowards. At least, she knew that Elbert wasn't a coward. Kelby, who by now had had several gins, replied that there were a lot of comforting euphemisms: 'Hypersensitive, peace-loving, introverted—take your choice!'

Bob Stevenson was, in fact, the son of the couple who were holding the party. Like his father, Bob was big and aggressive. Kelby could not help comparing Bob with Zeke Leonard. He imagined himself as thirteen again, squaring up to this big, ignorant boy. But this time smacking him on the point of the jaw and sending him reeling to the ground.

Two days later Kelby was out for a walk when he saw Bob Stevenson following Elbert along the street and periodically calling out 'Hey Ella' in a mocking voice. Eventually Bob overhauled his quarry, flipped off Elbert's cap and insolently asked, 'Do you want to make something of it?' When Elbert reached down to pick up his cap, Bob shouted 'Let it lay' and place-kicked it into the street. Then he took hold of Elbert's nose.

At this point Kelby rushed forward, grabbed Bob by the shoulders, flung him around and demanded that he pick up the cap and give it to Elbert. Bob glared back. 'Pick it up,' yelled Kelby, 'or, by God. I'll hold you over it by your ankles and make you pick it up with your teeth!' Bob collected it, spat neatly past it, and tossed it at Elbert who missed it. Then he called out to Elbert: 'So long, Ella, keep your nose clean.'

Throughout this scene Elbert had stood sniffling and whimpering. Suddenly Kelby turned on him and told him to shut up. But Elbert couldn't, and began to weep uncontrollably; whereupon Kelby seized him, shook him, and slapped him, shouting as he did so: 'You little cry-baby. You goddam little coward.'

A man passing by, with considerable difficulty managed to pull the grown man off the little boy. 'I've seen some bullies in my time,' he said later, 'but I never saw anything to match that'.

The story is instructive in several ways. Firstly, it illustrates the extraordinary persistence of memories of humiliation experienced at the hands of peers during childhood, and in some people at least, a hankering after revenge. Secondly, there is a generalising effect: it is not only Zeke Leonard against whom Kelby has such intense, undischarged hostility, but the whole world of Zekes: the big, the aggressive, the stupid. And combined with this, there is hatred of the self for having allowed it to happen. This, too, is generalised, so that he has come to hate and punish all those other selves who allowed it to happen to them: that is, the gifted and sensitive, in short (he would say in a fit of self-loathing) the cowardly.

Is this perversity fictional? Seemingly not. Research on abuse in families consistently shows that it is the abused who are more likely than others to become the abusers when they start their own families. Research on the effects of peer abuse at school on future abusiveness is sparse, but what does exist suggests that Kelby may not be exceptional.

Peer victimisation and attitudes to spouse abuse

Although no direct research as yet has been conducted to discover how children who were victimised often by their peers subsequently relate to members of their family, there is one piece of recent Australian research that suggests that there may indeed be a link between peer victimisation at school and subsequent spouse abuse. In this study, conducted with secondary school students, it was found that those boys who reported that they were victimised by peers relatively often were significantly more likely than others to be supportive of men physically abusing their wives (see Rigby, Black and Whish, 1994). The possible implications of this study for how such boys relate to their spouses in later life are serious. Somerset Maugham's aphorism reminds us: 'It is not true that suffering ennobles the character; happiness does that sometimes, but suffering, for the most part, makes men petty and vindictive'. (Maugham, 1919).

So it may well be that bullying is objectionable not only because victims suffer, but also because some may be motivated in later life to hurt others including those closest to them, that is their immediate family.

Consequences for bullies

We have been concentrating on victims, as if the effects on bullies did not matter. We must remind ourselves that the outlook for children who at an early age adopt a bullying lifestyle can also be bleak. Bullying at school is, as we might expect, associated with various forms of misbehaviour, for example, shoplifting, graffiti-writing, and trouble with the police generally. Bullying appears to be one aspect of an aggressive, impulsive, uncaring way of life. Not surprisingly, children who have been identified as bullies at school stand a much higher chance than others at a later stage in coming before the courts on charges of delinquency. A change in the orientation of children who are bullies at school can have extremely important implications for their future as law-abiding citizens, not to mention the trouble they could spare others.

Finally, among adults who have told us that they bullied others at school, there is more often than not, a greater degree of depression than is found among those who did not bully others at school (Dietz, 1994). Whether this derives from a sense of guilt, or a sense of wasted opportunities to work cooperatively with others, we can only speculate.

Bystanders

Although, as we have seen, schools differ enormously in the extent of bullying, children involved in bully/victim problems at any point in time are always in a minority. This is cold comfort, when we consider what it is like to live in a community in which individuals are being continually abused or harassed by their peers, often for no discernible reason. There are several reactions to be noticed among bystanders. Some are amused, some are sad and apprehensive, feeling that it may be their turn next. Some are angry; some feel ashamed or guilty for doing nothing; some simply don't care. But are there long-term effects?

Again we do not know, at this stage, how those who have stood by and observed bullying going on many times before their eyes are likely to be affected. We have little more than anecdotal evidence. I personally know of one man, now middle-aged, who was once much moved by accounts I had been giving at a psychology conference of how victims of peer abuse at school are sometimes affected. He recalled his own schooldays as we reminisced one evening. His school, a boys' boarding school, had been one at which there had been a great deal of quite violent bullying. He remembered vividly how some children had been savagely persecuted for no discernible reason. He had continually been afraid of being singled out himself as a victim. He had therefore deliberately identified with the bullies, had become friends with them, had cheered their exploits, had been one of THEM. He had kept safe. But what, he now wondered, had become of those boys who had been so relentlessly bullied. He still remembered their names. Could he find out what became of them? He was driven by a sense of guilt and shame to find out.

Some conclusions

There can be no doubt that for some children continual bullying or harassment at school can have serious short-term and sometimes long-term effects on their general well-being. I have stressed mainly the consequences for the victims and how the quality of their lives is reduced quite needlessly.

To some extent, it appears that the way the victim responds to bullying: by anger, sadness or general stoicism, can be a significant factor, and this may lead us to consider ways in which students may minimise some of the consequences. We have also seen that the provision of good support for children who are often victimised can reduce some of the adverse physical and psychological consequences. However, this should not detract from the fact that many students are simply not very resilient and some cannot access sources of emotional support.

We have seen, too, that there can be some less obvious long-term consequences of bullying: that being victimised can have the unfortunate effect of motivating victims to seek revenge, sometimes upon people who are weaker or less fortunate than themselves. And this induced vindictiveness can persist for years. But remember that, in others, the experience of 'persecution' can sharpen their sense of justice and individuals can sometimes learn to overcome the setbacks encountered in their early years at school.

Although our primary concern is, rightly, with those who are being victimised, and were victimised at school, there are others who may be affected too. We have seen how children who are bullies at school have a tendency to continue their aggressive, anti-social behaviour into adult years. They create distress among those they bully, but also spawn families which perpetuate the 'tradition' of abusing others. Finally, we should recall that bystanders may also be affected, too, in ways that we cannot predict.

Understanding
bullying

Is bullying understandable?

I have argued that before we can provide a remedy for bullying we must first make the effort of trying to understand it. If we do make the effort, we find a curious mixture of the understandable and the not-so-understandable.

Bullying begins with a desire to hurt someone. Indeed, bullying has sometimes been defined, though not in our view quite adequately, as the desire to hurt. This desire arises not unnaturally when we do not like someone. Sometimes the dislike is not easy to justify:

> I do not love thee, Dr Fell,
> The reason why I cannot tell;
> But this I know, and know full well,
> I do not love thee, Dr Fell.
>
> – Thomas Brown 1719

The feeling is not an unfamiliar one, and may under some circumstances translate into a desire to harm someone.

If we ask children whether they sometimes want to hurt someone, the answer is not uncommonly 'yes'. In one recent Australian study some 77 per cent of boys and 67 per cent of girls indicated that they did feel that way. It was found that responding in this way was to a small but significant degree a predictor of a child's actual engagement in bullying behaviour. However, many children who report having this feeling, very rarely, if ever, bully others. Some may express their hostility through occasional angry outbursts, often against people at least as powerful as themselves; others may simply keep it to themselves. The point is that dislike, anger, the wish to hurt others, even the carrying out of hurtful actions are normal, everyday occurrences, and, as such, not difficult to understand. We nearly all feel that way sometimes.

We may also find it in us to understand something of the satisfaction that the bully typically finds in dominating someone. Both in the animal kingdom and among people, the submission of others can be reinforcing. For some people it may signal a sense of victory over a rival. It may provide a sense of security in the knowledge that there are some people who will no longer provide an effective challenge. In the arena of politics this is quite familiar. Surely this enables us to come part of the way toward understanding bullying.

But let us recall what bullying is. The bully is not simply a person who dominates. The scenario is not that simple. In the classical case, the goal is not simply the glory of victory over a rival or a sense of security through the submission or acquiescence of another. The goal is the enjoyment of another's distress, because the experience of causing that distress is pleasurable. And the repetition of this experience continues to please. *This* is not easy for many of us to understand.

It is very puzzling to us. The questions we now ask are not easy to answer.

Why is the aggression of the bully evidently unabatable? Surely, we think, the anger, the hostility on the part of the bully would, sooner or later, be fully expressed and exhausted.

Why should there be this continual sense of enjoyment on the part of the bully in repeated 'victories' over the weak? Surely the pleasure must pall. It cannot be sustained, we think, by glory in achievement (what achievement?) or a feeling that justice is being done.

The victim's behaviour, like the bully's, may seem understandable—up to a point. When you are faced with an overwhelmingly powerful enemy it is natural enough to submit. Again we see this clearly among animals. Gestures of submission developed through years of evolution ensure that weaker animals are not destroyed. It is often so with us—the weaker submit, or at least defer to the stronger. Each person gets to know, more or less, his or her position in the hierarchy—the equivalent of the barnyard pecking order. The intrusion of new members may ruffle a few feathers; there is a time of instability perhaps; then things settle down, with everyone knowing his or her place.

But with bullying the situation really is different. The appeasement gestures do not appease. The torment continues, and so too the feeling of helplessness: a sense, as Simone Weil put it, of being somehow 'afflicted'. To the onlooker the situation may seem bizarre. Why, we wonder, is the victim so anxious to appease when it appears futile to do so? It is as if, in some strange way, the bully and the victim are locked together in a process of collusion. But to what end? The mystery of the victim's acceptance of the situation may be, at times, as baffling as the mad persistence of the bully.

Next, we may observe that bullying frequently goes on in schools and in other places with people around taking little or no notice of it. Yet again, we can understand some of that. If you interfere, you may be the next to 'cop it'. That is perhaps a cowardly but certainly an understandable consideration. But if we examine the situation in greater detail, we often find that real danger hardly exists at all. The bully may be of no great threat to anyone, apart from a victim who is unusual in being easily dominated. There are, commonly, many stronger, more powerful people among the onlookers, who are in any case in a large majority. Then why doesn't somebody do something to stop it? There is no justice—the suffering is all too real. Yet it goes on, and we watch it happen, or turn a blind eye to it. This too is a mystery.

Bullying as evil

We are sometimes tempted to see bullying as akin to the mystery of evil. John Betjeman (1960) in the poem,'Original sin on the Sussex Coast', recalls how the tormentors of his schooldays would lie in wait after school, to leap out and brutally assault and boot him, leaving him 'too out of breath and strength to make a sound'. He imagines them returning to the comfort of their homes and their indulgent mothers. He asks:

Does Mum, the Persil-user, still believe
That there's no devil and that youth is bliss?
As certain as the sun behind the Downs
And quite as plain to see, the Devil walks.

Much more recently in 1993 we were led to think again about the problem of evil by the horrific murder in England of the 2-year-old boy, James Bulger, by two 10-year-old boys. This case excited enormous public interest and outcry. The killers, Robert Thompson and Jon Venables, were widely regarded as inhuman freaks. They had not only abducted a toddler from a Liverpool shopping centre, but had dragged him 4 km to a railway embankment where they had doused him with paint and attacked him with bricks and an iron bar, leaving him dead.

An explanatory model

Whatever theological explanations we may propose to account for bullying, there are certainly conditions which make bullying more likely or less likely. I will now propose a model of how bullying behaviour arises and is sustained. We conceive bullying as the result of a combination of forces. To what extent our analysis will take the mystery or incomprehension out of bullying and lead to a strategy for countering it remains to be seen.

In this model we will make a distinction between the forces that operate *before* a child comes to school (and may continue to operate together with other forces thereafter) and those that are located in the school. The model can be summarised in the following diagram.

Model 4.1

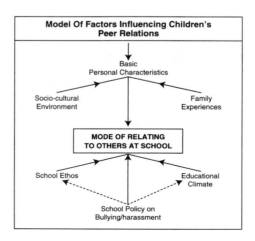

The model in a nutshell

It is proposed that during the first few years of life children develop in such a way as to make it more likely or less likely that they will bully other children or be bullied by them. This does not mean that a child on entering school is predestined to be one or the other. Many children are neither. Nor does it mean that we can set about labelling children the day they start school as a likely bully or a likely victim—what happens at school is of crucial importance. But it does mean that in the years before starting school, many children have already developed characteristic ways of behaving and reacting to events which will affect how they relate to others at school.

The model suggests that there are three major sources of influence on the child before he or she comes to school. The first we may call, with some trepidation, *genetic endowment*. Although we can say with confidence that children are born different, controversy still rages over what characteristics are inherited and, if any, how important they are compared with what is learned. I do not intend to debate this question, but simply to point out that children commonly differ widely from birth in their physical constitution, some being much bigger and stronger than others, and often these differences continue to place some people at an advantage and some at a disadvantage in physical conflicts. We can be less sure of psychological differences. But it is worth observing that some children are temperamentally more aggressive and more impulsive than others from a very early age, and again the differences are commonly maintained throughout life.

Aggressiveness is a highly stable characteristic over the life span. On some traits—for example, introversion—there is much less consensus. It is, nevertheless, probable that genetic and environmental factors interact in the formation of a child's personality and that a child's extroversion and sociability are affected by the outcome.

There is less controversy over the significance of *family background* and other *cultural influences* on the child. They certainly do affect the way a child will respond to others. Unlike genetic influences, we can do something about them. For example, families can sometimes be effectively counselled, and exposure to some aspects of the media may be enhanced or restricted. I will therefore concentrate on such factors as these in our explication of the model.

I have identified three major aspects of the school environment or situation. There is first of all the *school ethos*, which is conceived as comprising the predominant attitudes, beliefs and feelings that children have about how they should behave towards each other at school. Secondly, we have the *educational climate* which is the sum of influences which determine what and how children learn at their school. Finally, we have *school policy* as it relates to bullying. This includes not only what has been written down to deal with bullying issues, but also the rules (some unwritten) and practices followed at a school that impact upon bullying behaviour in some way.

In reflecting on the model, it will be evident that there are many pathways of influence, and various ways in which forces may combine in promoting or opposing bullying. For example, an uncaring family background, membership of a delinquent subculture and the possession of an aggressive personality, may each contribute towards a child using excessive force against others; the prevailing ethos at school may encourage the child to bully others; in addition, the educational climate may affect bullying by failing to foster and engage the interest of the child in study; and there may be an absence of any considered or consistent plan to deal with bullying when it does occur. All these influences may combine to produce a living hell for sensitive children who have been over-protected at home and have not learned to protect themselves. Let us look now at the model in detail.

Constitution/personality of the child

We can conveniently begin here. This is what we notice when the child begins school. These characteristics are more often than not found among children who bully others:

- Bigger and stronger than average
- Aggressive
- Impulsive
- Low in empathy and generally uncaring
- Low in cooperativeness

Contrary to the expectations of some, they do not tend to be lower than average in self-esteem; nor are they noticeably lacking in friends.

Regarding children who are more frequently victimised, the research findings are clear (see Rigby & Slee, 1993a; Slee & Rigby, 1993). These characteristics are commonly found:

- Physically less strong than others
- Timid, non-assertive
- Introverted
- Low self-esteem
- Few friends

Having labelled bullies and victims in this way, I am now anxious to assert that these are generalisations to which many exceptions can be found. Physical size and strength is more likely to be a factor among boys than girls. Where bullying is of a psychological or verbal kind, the capacity to ridicule others effectively can be more important than physical dominance.

I should also point out that the simple category of 'bully' suggests that all bullies are much the same. In fact, there are distinctions that can and should be made between bullies who tend to be generally anxious individuals and those who are typically very calm. Then there are bullies who are themselves quite frequently victimised, and others who are seldom, if ever, targeted.

Another important distinction is between bullies who commonly, or always, bully others in a one-to-one situation, and those who tend to bully in groups or gangs. In the latter case, the bully is likely to be more sociable and conformist. The motivations of the two kinds of bullies may be different.

Similarly, there are different types of victims. Some are, in fact, provocative—in the sense that they appear to deliberately antagonise others; some are non-provocative and do nothing, at least deliberately, to draw attention to themselves.

We should also distinguish between children who are victimised because of some social characteristic, e.g. they belong to a minority ethnic group, members of which may be harassed by others; and those who are bullied because of some individual characteristic they possess. Despite the difficulties that exist in maintaining generalisations about the personal qualities of bullies and victims (and the ever-present danger of stereotyping and labelling) it is useful to ask ourselves what kinds of influences are likely to contribute to the development of those 'types' whom we say are more 'at risk' than others when they do go to school.

Family background

There can be no doubt that, for nearly all children, the family is the agent of socialisation that, for better or worse, is most likely to mould their characters.

The social influence of the family is, for most children, continuous from birth to adolescence, and it is intense and pervasive. It is true that the composition of families has, in recent times, become less stable, with children becoming more exposed to changing home situations; that is, to single parenting, to new step-parents or foster parents. But the influence of families, especially of mothers and fathers, on the development of the personalities of children remains paramount. What is surprising, however, is that it is only in the last few years that psychologists have begun to consider how family background can influence peer relations at school.

The bully's family

Australian research into the family background of children who repeatedly bully their peers has now confirmed and extended the findings of overseas researchers, especially work undertaken in Norway by Olweus (1980) and Bowers, Smith and Binney (1994) in England. The Australian research has focused upon the families of adolescent schoolchildren. In a study reported by Rigby (1993, 1994b) of the 644 young adolescents attending South Australian schools, those children identified through psychological testing as 'bullies' were found to be different from others in the extent to which they saw their families as functioning. These are the sentiments more likely to be expressed by bullies in describing their families:

- My family does not sympathise with me and understand when I feel sad.
- Members of my family are not encouraged to work together in dealing with family problems.
- My family still treats me like a child and not a maturing person.
- My father does not care about me or accept the sort of person I am.
- Honesty is not important in our family.
- My parents are not very interested in my future job and career.
- We do not feel free to express our opinions in our family.
- We do not consider each other's feelings.

What was called 'poor family functioning' as indicated by the expression of such sentiments, applied equally to the families of both male and female bullies. *It may be concluded that, regardless of gender, the child in a badly functioning family is more likely to bully others.*

How families may promote bullying

There are several ways in which this can happen. First, a dysfunctional family does not help in the development of empathy in the child. Quite the reverse. Parents are seen as not caring, not accepting the child for what he or she is, not considering the child's feelings. That element in the bully's make-up, an absence lack of empathy, is strengthened. Such children are not cared for; why should they care for others?

Secondly, there is little or no encouragement in the family for the child to cooperate with others. Family members go their own way. As we have seen, a tendency not to cooperate with others is another mark of the child who bullies others.

Thirdly, the adolescent in a badly functioning family is likely to be dismissed by the adults, by parents or older siblings, as a child and not a maturing person. Therefore, there is a sense of inferiority, and resentment at being dominated by others. Why should such a child not, in turn, dominate others?

Fourthly, there would appear to be no encouragement to develop positive social values, such as honesty. A cynical attitude to human relations is likely to develop.

The picture emerges of forces emanating from the bully's family which are inclining the child to become uncaring and uncooperative, with a desire to dominate others and a cynical disregard for the well-being of other children.

But not all families of children who become bullies fit this mould. The research we have cited does indicate a statistically significant relationship between family functioning and a tendency to bully others. But it leaves a good deal still to be explained. I have met children who commonly bully others who come from families in which parents do care a lot about their children, and are proud of them. Of course the pride may be misplaced, as when parents actually admire and encourage aggressiveness in their children. The following cartoon is an example.

It follows that we cannot attribute the pernicious influence of families in creating bullies simply to pathological aspects of their functioning. We must also understand that the values and attitudes of some families endorse toughness and dominance, and, in effect, may encourage bullying.

"I just heard the most wonderful news from school – my son's a bully."

The victim's family

A good deal less is known about the families of children who are victimised by others, probably because our society is so concerned with the perpetrators of aggression and violence. This is seen as a higher priority than understanding victims. However, it must not be forgotten that, if there were fewer children who were not easy targets for rampaging bullies, aggression in schools could be greatly reduced.

What has been suggested in the literature on families and the bully/victim problem is that, just as the families of bullies are insufficiently cohesive and supportive, families of victims may go to an opposite extreme: that is, they may be too 'wrapped up' in each other, resulting in a failure to learn to interact effectively with the external world. Such families are often referred to as being 'enmeshed'.

In such families, children are apt to be over-protected. Stephen Spender captures this feeling of being protected—and the sad consequences:

My parents kept me from children who were rough
And who threw words like stones and who wore torn clothes.
Their thighs showed through rags. They ran in the street
And climbed cliffs and stripped by the country streams.

I feared more than tigers their muscles like iron
And their jerking hands and their knees tight on my arms.
I feared the salt coarse pointing of those boys
Who copied my lisp behind me on the road.

They were lithe, they sprang out behind hedges
Like dogs to bark at our world. They threw mud
And I looked another way, pretending to smile.
I longed to forgive them, yet they never smiled.

Gender differences in family effects

So far no distinction has been made between factors that influence boys and those that influence girls. And, in fact, the similarities, between the sexes, for example in personality correlates of bullies and victims, are more evident than are the differences. However, recent research has suggested that dysfunctional families may affect girls in a way peculiar to them. In the South Australian study mentioned above, it was evident that female victims of school bullies also tend to come from families which function badly. For example, in families where there is little warmth and poor communication between family members, girls are inclined to become *either bullies or victims,* as opposed to not being involved at all in bully/victim problems. This is true of girls only. Boys in such families tend to become bullies; there is no tendency for them to become victims.

It has been suggested by Noller and Callan (1991) that poor family functioning has a particularly devastating effect on the self-esteem of girls. As we have seen, low self-esteem is a crucial factor in deciding who will be the chosen targets, and this may be the explanation.

Cultural influences

Although it is likely to be the dominating one, the family is not the only influence on the child's interpersonal behaviour. We should take into account both the broader cultural forces, deriving from social class and/or ethnic identity, and the effects of fortuitous associations with individuals and groups encountered by the growing child. Generalisations are dangerous and often hard to establish—the context must always be specified.

In Britain there is persuasive evidence that bullying is more common in schools in working-class areas, particularly where physical bullying is concerned. This is consistent with research indicating that physical forms of punishment of children is much more frequent in working-class homes in England (Newson & Newson, 1976). Whether this is the case in Australia has yet to be confirmed. Ethnic group differences have been suggested in the use of physical aggression, again without clear evidence. These possibilities cannot be discounted and may be found to have considerable local significance.

Less questionable is the view that children do, from time to time, become involved with groups of children who engage in seemingly mindless violence. The need for peer support and the attractiveness of becoming a member of an admired group may outweigh an individual's better judgement. Having become a member of such a group, attitudes conducive to bullying and associated behaviour patterns can develop, and become an even more potent factor in the genesis of bullying than parental or family influence. And clearly these influences should not be seen as mutually exclusive. They interact with each other. The family is permeable, each member is capable of being influenced through the relationships each forms with others outside the family.

A further cultural factor of considerable importance in the lives of many young people is, of course, the visual media. The glorification of violence and frequent demonstrations by 'attractive' characters that ascendancy can be gained over others by the use of force is unfortunately not an uncommon feature of many TV programs. There can be little doubt that the viewing of violence on television can lead to the practice of aggression against others (Eron et al, 1972), and that unregulated exposure to violence shown in an attractive light can play a part in the development of a bully. It is easy to see how programs glorifying violence in wrestling, however clumsily staged, or, more recently, aggression in gladiatorial combat, could lead to some (not all) children seeking out weaker children to hurt them. To the influence of such TV programs we should add violent videos and also some computer games.

I have here emphasised factors which seemingly encourage bullying behaviour. We should bear in mind, however, that some community organisations, including some churches, and indeed some television programs, seek to counter the use of gratuitous violence by speaking up against it and promoting more constructive activities. To some degree, this may reduce any tendencies to harm others, but, at the same time, we may question the wisdom of bodies that promote the notion of not responding angrily or even assertively to personal abuse; that is, the notion of 'turning the other cheek'.

Subculture and harassment

Harassment is an aspect of bullying that involves social stereotyping and prejudice. Where there is a combination of sadistic hatred looking for a target and social prejudice, which seems to legitimise directing that hatred towards a particular group, the consequences can be particularly appalling. This is evident in the group in Australia known as National Action, a neo-fascist organisation, which not only attracts people who enjoy violence but has a platform that promotes discrimination against such groups as Jews and Asians.

Over the last ten years the fear of AIDS has, in some places in Australia, intensified prejudice against gays, resulting in the cruel harassment of people, including children, who are thought to be homosexual. Perceived grounds for discrimination and consequent harassment in a school can be almost limitless. In the Australian context sport may feature largely, for example—in one class of Year 12 students subgroups were identified by students acccording to whether they were Footballers or non-Footballers, and the latter group further divided into Fats (girls who were seen as overweight) and others who were dismissed as Faggots.

The school ethos

We sometimes see a school as the creation of teachers and sustained by teachers. In fact, a school has an ethos that has developed, sometimes over many years, that is largely independent of the influence of educators. The attitudes, expectations and norms relating to student behaviour at a school, which constitute the ethos, can vary widely between one school environment and another and may change radically over time.

Let us take an example of how the school ethos may affect bullying behaviour. At the Grammar School in England that I attended as a schoolboy there were clear expectations about how newcomers should be treated. There were a number of initiating practices. For those travelling to school by train, the instrument of torture was the leather strap which served to adjust windows in the railway compartment. This was used by the older boys to strap the new kids. For those who not surprisingly complained about this initiation, the answer was that, in due course, they too would have the opportunity to use the strap. In this way a bullying tradition was maintained. Not all senior students were happy about it, but for those to whom bullying came naturally, as it were, the opportunity couldn't be missed.

Such institutionalised bullying can only continue in a school in which there are values and attitudes held by dominant interests which are seldom, if ever, seriously challenged. But, apart from what is institutionalised, there may flourish many other forms of bullying, ranging from repeated teasing and name-calling to serious harassment and physical assault. These are likely to be carried out by individuals and groups who feel that the ethos is one that supports or, at least, does not oppose, such activities.

What then are the values and attitudes that are central to support for bullying? This is my list:

Might is right

It is good to be able to dominate others

To be dominated by others is shameful

You should never complain about ill-treatment by others

You should learn to take it

You should never sympathise with wimps

To be gentle and compassionate is to be weak

Now although these values are more likely to be embraced by male students, there are schools in which they are strongly held by girls also.

Macho is gender-neutral. We will see later when we come to examine the school ethos in greater detail that macho-values are embraced by substantial numbers of students, especially in secondary schools.

Bullying as a conforming response

When a student is exposed repeatedly to pressure from students who have extreme macho attitudes, bullying may be viewed not as a deviant act but rather as a conforming response. The dynamics then relate much less to any predisposition to aggression in the child (although that is not irrelevant) and much more to the character of the peer group. This may help us to understand how a student who comes from a home in which he is treated with respect and kindness and is liked by many students might nevertheless resort to bullying others. Finally, because I believe that the attitudes that children have towards bullying are of very great importance in understanding and in dealing with bully/victim problems in a school, I propose to examine this issue in greater depth in the next chapter. For the present, I am content to illustrate what I mean by a school ethos and to view it as part of the number of influences that incline children to bully others.

The educational climate

By this I mean the nature and quality of the school environment as it pertains to the what and how of formal instruction and learning. It therefore includes the curriculum, but goes beyond that. How knowledge and understanding are mediated are at least as important as the content of school subjects. The perceived character, enthusiasms and aversions of teachers towards their subjects and their students may be as important to a child's moral, social and intellectual development as the brand of pedagogy they practise. We may now ask: what kind of an educational climate is most conducive to bullying?

Boredom

'Of course, boredom can lead to anything. It is boredom that sets one sticking golden pins into people.' That was Dostoevsky's opinion of boredom. Many children are very bored at school and it should not surprise us the lengths some go to overcome it. What is boring to one student may be vitally interesting to another. But there are some generalisations which are worth considering:

(a) There are large numbers of children for whom subject content is inappropriate—either because it is not challenging, or because students are unable to make the required effort to understand it; or because its relevance to the student's needs and aspirations cannot be demonstrated, is not clear. In a period of considerable unemployment in Australia in which there are few jobs available for school leavers and more and more children stay on at school longer, the task of devising relevant, interesting and motivating curriculum content becomes ever more difficult. But we should remember that one of the consequences of failing to do so is increased boredom among students and concomitant restlessness, leading often enough to a child bullying others.

(b) Where content is appropriate, the teaching methodology may still be inadequate for the students in question. This may arise through a mismatch of student capability and mode of instruction, or more simply a failure of pedagogic skill. In any case, the result may be non-involvement of students—and boredom.

(c) Finally, boredom may develop because staff may be poorly motivated to interest students. This can, and does, happen when teachers are stressed and confronted with students who are uninterested, uncooperative and disorderly.

If we are correct in suggesting that boredom at school may be an important cause of bullying, any analysis of what a school can do will include an evaluation of the curriculum, teaching methods and staff morale—and inevitably the factors that impinge upon these.

Teacher behaviour

G.K. Chesterton once suggested that the main purpose served by a school, apart from getting children out of the home, was to provide examples of adult behaviour under stress. This would afford them with all the material they needed to study human character. The modelling effect of teacher behaviour is potentially very great indeed. Much of teacher behaviour is unavoidably directed towards getting people to do what the teacher wants, and this does not always coincide exactly with what a student might like to do. How the teacher copes with this situation is of great importance.

The student soon learns that teachers employ different means of getting (or failing to get) their way. Some employ an authoritarian style. In effect, they are saying: 'Do as I say because I, THE TEACHER, am telling you'; with varying degrees of success, ranging from instant obedience to hilarious disobedience. Others behave in a more permissive laissez faire manner, following whatever it is the children want to do at a given moment. Depending on the maturity of the students this may result in anarchy or inspired spontaneity. Then there is the authoritative approach. Here the teacher has a firm idea of what needs to be done and is, in this respect, like the authoritarian. The difference is that the teacher will normally give reasons for what is to be done, and may, under some circumstances, decide to take a democratic course.

The potential bully may well identify with some of the teachers. Like teachers, bullies often feel a need to impose their will on others. The democratic and especially the laissez faire teacher may seem contemptible. The authoritative teacher has some appeal perhaps, but the giving of explanations will be interpreted as a weakness. The failed authoritarian is an object lesson on what not to do. The teacher who attempts to quell others by force, physical or verbal, but is a laughable flop, and worse still is actually bullied by others, may leave a lasting impression. (We certainly do remember them!)

The potential bully may see one way of avoiding this disgrace by fiercely imposing his or her will on somebody who is much weaker. This may help to account for the ferocity with which bullies attack the people they victimise. How disastrous, the bully thinks, if this miserable wimp (whom everyone despises, who couldn't hurt a fly) should somehow turn the tables on me. He (or she) must be thoroughly crushed. The potential bully will sometimes view the effective authoritarian teacher as a positive role model. This is not mere conjecture. Teachers who were bullies with their students are often remembered with a mixture of admiration and awe. One man told me that his admiration for the teacher-bully was the main reason why he began as a student to bully others.

Occasionally you come across an example of a teacher who deliberately leads children into bullying others. A recently reported case was provided by a teacher who during in her childhood had been diagnosed as dyslexic. Her own teacher, she recalled, at primary school had in fact encouraged the class to ridicule her for her slowness. She would ask: 'Who's the slowest person in the class?' to which the class would reply in chorus gleefully: 'Rebecca'. Bullying here was legitimised. While this is an extreme case, the use of sarcasm and subtle forms of ridicule by teachers is not uncommon and can contribute substantially to classroom bullying. Of course there are many teachers who effectively model a democratic style of interacting with others. Here we are concerned with the occasional teacher who provides a model for bullies to follow.

Competition

Competition, as part of the educational climate, can sometimes be a positive, spurring some children on to develop skills and acquire knowledge that is recognised, admired and rewarded. It may bring the best out of some children, providing they are successful or that disappointment in one area is compensated for by achievement in another.

The extent to which a school should employ competitive methods to promote educational aims is a contentious one, and in this book we do not intend to provide a settled verdict. But it seems likely that the consequences of an undue emphasis upon competition in schools may have a harmful effect on some children and contribute to bullying behaviour.

We can see this happening in several ways:

(a) It can produce in some children who are particularly unsuccessful across a range of valued school activities a sense of being 'losers' who will never succeed in doing anything well at school. This may be highly frustrating and, given a capacity to bully others, in this they might choose to excel.

(b) Alternatively, in another child, failure in a range of competitive activities may result in a loss of self-esteem that cannot be compensated for by bullying others. Deeply discouraged, such a child may become a target of peer abuse.

(c) Among the 'winners' success in competitive activities can produce a brand of arrogance that delights in demonstrating superiority at the expense of others who are less capable. A good deal of bullying involves the systematic, continual belittling of others.

The above analysis suggests that the effects of competition at school are complex and may be extremely difficult to predict. The influence of competition interacts with other factors, especially the personality of the child, but also with the general ethos of the school. In some schools there are children who succeed in competitive activities who become targets for harassment!

On the irrelevance of ideology

In his *Guide for the Perplexed* Schumacher (1977) examines the answers given by social scientists to the question of what is the best educational system. He considers the claims of educationalists from the Right who insist that the key to success in educating children in schools is discipline, order, control; and then, in contrast, the views from the Left, where the catch cries are self-expression, spontaneity, freedom. He concludes that the question of which is better is not really capable of scientific resolution, as is, say, the question of how to make a two-wheeled vehicle propelled by your feet. (The answer is a bicycle.) No, the correct ideology is not the point. Somehow to educate children in school, he says, you must somehow do the impossible. You must love and respect all of them. In short, attitudes and relationships may be seen as the things of real importance in working with children. It is these that help to create an ethos in which people do not bully each other.

For the potential bully, whom we have already seen to be a person who has, for whatever reason, a good deal of hostility and, more often than not, a history of neglect and no little frustration, there must be respect. Not, it must be emphasised an acceptance of bullying behaviour; rather, acceptance of him or her as a person worthy of respect. For the child who is victimised, likewise—and, it must be added, this is not easy. For some it is particularly difficult to feel respect for a boy or girl who has little or no respect for himself or herself, which is the condition of many children who are continually victimised. For the habitual bully it is even more difficult. How can we respect a person who does not respect others? And yet, as Schumacher says, it has got to be done; and done, we may add, not only in the counselling room of the caring psychologist, but in the hurly-burly of the teacher's classroom.

Policy regarding bullying

Policy consists of rules and guidelines about what should be done on a defined matter. Different schools may have different definitions of bullying; some prefer to use different names to describe the same phenomena. In many Australian schools there is a preference for the term 'harassment'. So, if we are looking for evidence of relevant policy in practice, we may need to look for it under a variety of headings.

Here are some:
- Anti-bullying Policy
- Bullying and Harassment Policy
- Behaviour Management Policy
- School Discipline Policy
- Sexual Harassment Policy
- Social Justice Policy
- Pastoral Care Policy
- Protective Behaviour Policy

The important thing is not, of course, where the policy lies. What matters is what it says and what, if anything, people do about it. We should also recognise that a policy is not always written. There may, nevertheless, be principles which are generally understood and in accordance with which people actually act. We might also find the reverse case: a written policy document that is entirely disregarded. A policy on bullying under whatever heading or form (written or unwritten) can be invaluable. In Chapter 8 details are given of the kinds of things that may be included in such a policy.

In relation to the model which we have been exploring, we can see policy as being directed towards two ends. The first is ensuring that the *ethos* of the school is as far as possible not conducive to bullying. This means that it is directed towards the development of positive attitudes and values that are inimical to bullying. From this may flow a number of initiatives and responses which may involve disciplinary action, counselling practice, and parent and community education. The second is influencing the nature of the *educational climate* so that it becomes more effective in educating children both academically and socially. Again a number of initiatives may flow concerning how teachers can effect improvements in children's social behaviour and their interpersonal relations in the course of planning and providing the conditions for learning.

'Big Bully Billy'

Let us now look at an actual case study of a bully and ask whether the model that has been proposed can help us to understand bullying behaviour a little better. The case is taken from an account given by the English researcher, Tony Parker (1990), in the form of a transcription of an interview with a man who had recently been released from prison after a 'life' sentence. Billy (Willam Davenport) is described as a massive man in faded T-shirt and jeans, six foot four in height and weighing nearly twenty stone; so big that he had to sit awkwardly sideways on a tiny two-seater sofa in the small front room of his terraced house. Billy was thirty-two. This is what he said:

'When I was a lad at school, it was almost like I were royalty. Already by twelve or thirteen you know, I wasn't just the biggest boy in the class, I was the biggest boy in the whole school. It didn't bother me whether I was educated or not: the way I looked at it I didn't need to be, not with the status and reputation I had. I was big, heavy and powerful: I could knock anybody over just by giving them a shove. The whole school knew it and I did too, and I kept up my reputation by demonstrating it at least two times a week. I'd go up to one of the lads in the top class, anyone, it didn't matter who, just to pick a quarrel with him and provide the opportunity for having a fight with him. I kept a sort of mental list as to whose turn it was next, and if they'd not done nothing to me I'd accuse them: somebody had told me they'd said something nasty about me. 'Big Bully Billy', that was my title; and I did, I liked it. There was one day I remember when another lad's parent, his father, came up to the school to see the Head, to complain to him his boy'd said I'd been bullying him. The Head sent for me, and when I went in his study this bloke stood up, I think with a mind of telling me off. He wasn't all that small and he was quite well set; but on me he only came up to about here. So all he did was look at me and keep his mouth shut and sit down again. After he'd gone the Head said to me 'Davenport', he said, all reasonableness you know, 'Davenport, you don't want to get yourself the reputation of being the school bully do you?' I said, 'Oh no sir, no I don't', trying as hard as I could not to sound as though that was exactly what I did want.'

The first and most obvious feature in this account of a school bully is Billy's obvious capacity to bully: he was big and strong. Let us not neglect the obvious. But equally important is the school ethos. He was admired. He kept up his reputation by giving a practical demonstration of what he could do well at least two times a week. What of his family? How, if at all, had they predisposed him to be a bully? Evidently, from Billy's account they were straightforward decent people:

> 'My dad's an honest, hard-working man in light engineering. I've a brother who's completely straight and my older sister's married with two kids. Neither of them as far as I know's ever done a thing wrong in their lives. And my mother's the sort of woman who'd go straight back to a shop if she thought they'd made a mistake and undercharged her...'

So far, no hint at family problems. Then he adds:

> 'About the only unsettling thing in my childhood was my brother and sister was both clever at school, and I wasn't up to their standard and I knew I never would be.'

This brings us to the classroom climate. We are not told what happened there. Billy could not do the work that brings praise from teachers. As we learn from him later: 'I was ... not very clever in the sense of school education or things of that sort, but', he adds, 'with a good head for business work'. This he was to demonstrate by making money buying and selling at local markets and 'paying my mum and dad for my keep and a bit over'. But at school he was a dud; it rankled as he compared himself with his successful brother and sister. Still Big Bully Billy could do one thing well, as other kids discovered to their sorrow. And the school was not able to find a way of competing with this terrible, compensatory joy of being 'cock of the school'.

And what of the school policy for dealing with bullies? Here we see, on the part of the headmaster, softness masquerading as tolerance as the two of them collude rather than collide. The moral impact of the school was nil. There was no grappling with the problem. When Mr Davenport was nineteen he was sentenced to nine years in prison for a brutal assault.

Many, if not all, the elements to which the model draws our attention are there: the physical predisposition of unusual strength; a school ethos that rewarded the conqueror; a classroom climate (we surmise) that did nothing for this uneducated, though intelligent, dud—except add more weight to the chip on the shoulder of a boy already resenting his siblings' easy success at school. And finally the reaction of the school in the person of the headmaster: 'You don't want to get yourself a reputation for being a bully do you?'

James Bulger

Much has been written about this horrific case in 1993 involving the cruel victimisation and murder of a young two-year-old by two ten-year-old boys in Liverpool. There were clearly many 'risk factors' in the family backgrounds of both of the bullies who killed James Bulger. In both there a was a broken home, the children being raised by a mother; in the case of Thompson constant resentment at being a woman alone, 'victimised' and without support. So starved of affection was Robert Thompson that he was reported by the police as 'not being used to being touched'. Jon Venables was depicted as a 'follower' rather than a leader, troublesome both at home and at school; the subject of intense disciplinary pressure from his mother; largely friendless. Together, the two boys could join forces against the world. Having been hurt, they could together, with responsibility diminished, enjoy the terror of someone else in pain.

Writing of this case in *The Australian* (1st December 1993), Margot Prior, a clinical psychologist at La Trobe University, comments:

> 'Imagine for a moment if the two young British boys, Robert Thompson and Jon Venables had been identified as in need of help at the pre-school level; if their families had been assisted in managing their behaviour problems in both the short term and on an on-going basis; if intervention to facilitate a more successful school experience had been available; if consistent and predictable supervision of their behaviour had been in place; how different their story could have been.'

Again we can see that a number of factors contributed: involving family, school and, one may add, the community in not responding to the need for help when it should have been all too evident.

Is bullying understandable?

At the beginning of this chapter I raised the question of whether bullying was understandable, and argued that up to a point it certainly seemed to be. The desire to hurt others, it was contended, is not that uncommon, and probably all of us at some time have felt the impulse to hurt someone and on occasions given way to it. We might also admit to a sense of satisfaction in a demonstration that we could dominate someone through the threat or use of force.

But when we recall the nature of highly destructive malign bullying, in which a person continually seeks out and enjoys the distress of another, the limits of understanding through introspection may be soon reached. We need to call upon what we can learn from cases which we label 'pathological'. We need to recognise that conditions which are severely adverse to children's moral and social development can produce disastrous consequences, as in the killing of James Bulger.

Although most of us can identify with being a victim at one time or another, and recognise the commonsense or even the necessity of submission in the most adverse circumstances and against impossible odds, we may still find it hard to comprehend why some children appear never to put up a fight at all when they are cornered. Why do they crumple rather than try to fight back? Finally, although we can easily understand the need to intervene when a child is being seriously bullied by others, we are perplexed as to why so often people merely observe what is happening and do nothing about it.

As we come to the end of this chapter we can ask whether we are any wiser. Is bullying then part of an impenetrable mystery of evil? Or are there explanations which allow us to understand it better? Malign bullying *is* hard to understand because, for most of us, the circumstances that lead to the development of extreme frustration and hostility, and also the apparent legitimising of its expression through hurting others, simply do not apply. Further, bullying in schools is particularly difficult to account for because we typically underestimate the pressures that exist for schoolchildren to impose themselves on others and to prevent others from imposing on them. We have mostly forgotten what it was like at school. We know that the desire to hurt others is for some people largely responsible for the act of bullying others.

To understand bullying we should first inquire why the desire to hurt others is so extraordinarily strong in some children. The answer often lies in what has gone on for many years in a child's family. In some cases no sense of secure attachment had ever developed between the child and its parents. Such insecurity can lead to a generalised sense of hostility. By contrast, in other cases, an expectation is developed in the first few years of life in the child that he or she will be loved by the parents and accepted in the family. Unfortunately, this expectation is not always fulfilled. Studies show clearly that a substantial proportion of children simply do not experience a sense of belonging and acceptance. Instead of love, there is continued hostility in the air. Examples set by members of the family are overwhelmingly negative.

Under such circumstances a child is likely to grow up with a deep sense of frustration which will, if possible, be vented upon others.

We also know that some children in the most adverse of family circumstances do not grow up to be bullies at school. They are perhaps fortunate in meeting others who care for them. But for those who find themselves repeatedly exposed to negative examples through association, perhaps with delinquent groups, or even, in some cases, continual exposure to media violence, frustration is indeed likely to be converted into action, and the child becomes a bully.

If we are to understand bullying fully we must make an imaginative effort, by rolling back the years to the first days of primary or high school, and seek now, as an adult, to grasp and identify those forces that lead many children to feel that, as far as peer relations are concerned, the chief imperative is to conquer or be conquered. In the next chapter we will help you to do this by examining how children think about their peers at school.

Have we yet understood why a wimp is a wimp? Again, we have identified those conditions and pressures (which many of us fortunately do not experience): forces which often seem to produce a personality and set of reactions which at first sight seem bizarre. We have emphasised 'over-protection' in the family, and seen this as the starting point for the career of many a child who is subsequently bullied. The world of the 'over-protected' child, continually prevented from experiencing a range of human types and life situations, is not unlike the agoraphobic, who is afraid of leaving the security of the home. The 'wimp' goes forth with extreme trepidation unprepared for what is to come.

Throughout I have stressed that bully/victim behaviours are multiply determined. Many children who are over-protected triumph over their initial disadvantage. But for the child who is a born introvert, the struggle is more difficult—every threat is magnified and acts so as to sap the resolution. The result, all too often, is that the anxiety of the child serves as a signal for children looking for someone to bully. If the child cannot adequately defend himself or herself, the consequence is almost invariably a loss of self-esteem which is already low. Inevitably this is a further magnet for potential bullies. To understand the incapacity of many victimised children to resist aggression, we need go no further than considering the effects of extremely low self-esteem. The belief develops that you cannot resist aggression from anybody. There is a kind of death-wish.

Finally, if the child is in such distress, again, why does no one intervene? Part of the answer lies in the psychology of bystanders. The situation can easily be seen as ambiguous, at least if viewed briefly—as one hurries past. Maybe it's a game; maybe some 'rough and tumble'. As a clincher: but if it was important, if it was as bad as it might seem, wouldn't somebody intervene? The paradox is that the more people are present, the less likely is intervention to take place. It was estimated that as many as thirty-eight people saw the baby boy, James Bulger, distressed and crying as he was being roughly handled by the two ten-year-olds on the way to the place where he was killed. But no one intervened. Each person might say: among so many people, there must surely be somebody more competent than I am to stop it? Thus responsibility is diffused and no one acts. It is much later perhaps that it begins to dawn on the person hurrying past that it was, after all, a serious situation, and a good reason for hurrying past was that they didn't know what to do.

A conclusion

This chapter has attempted to show how what happens outside the school (both before and after a child begins school), and what goes on within a school can affect the way children ultimately relate to each other. The focus has been on 'bullying behaviour'—but it should now be evident that this behaviour cannot be adequately considered in a vacuum, and solutions applied, such as 'punish, suspend, expel', or, for that matter, 'counsel and comfort' as if it were a discrete condition for which there was available a neat formula or remedy. We have still to consider a variety of things that have been suggested in the growing literature on 'what to do about it'. I hope, however, that in picking and choosing what to do, you do not lose sight of the complexity of the issue, nor its enormous importance to children.

The school
ethos

It has been proposed that the ethos of a school is of very great importance in determining whether a child engages in bullying at school. We have already considered the view that the ethos may operate differentially on children. Upon those who are already predisposed by nature or as a result of learning experiences to be aggressive or to want to hurt others, the effect may be crucial.

To a large extent the ethos of the school exists independently of what teachers and parents think and do. It seems to have a life of its own. Unless a school is a quite recent creation, it was there long before many of the children and teachers came to the school. It will be there after they leave. The quality of life that is sustained at the school and contained within that ethos may have a long history, and this will not be easy to change.

'Ethos' sounds nebulous and vague. But if we conceive it as the cumulative effect of individual attitudes and related beliefs about how children should behave towards others, it becomes easier to grasp. We can then identify some attitudes and beliefs as particularly relevant to bullying. We can enquire into how widely and strongly such attitudes are held. Much of the research in Adelaide was directed towards this end.

It was suggested through the work of Askew (1989) in England that children in schools are often pressured by others into acting the part of tough guys with their fellow students. This may lead some children into bullying others to prove their toughness. If they are victimised by another student, they will feel that they should not complain but 'take it like a man'. The root of the bullying problem might conceivably be found in the stereotypically masculine or macho images children have of themselves.

Attitudes to bullying

One approach to assessing the ethos of the school as it relates to bullying is to inquire into what children think about it. This was done in a recent large-scale study conducted in 1994 by Rigby and Slee in South Australia by asking students in primary and secondary schools to say how strongly they agreed or disagreed with a series of statements made about bullying. Each of them suggested a tough macho view of bullying. The results are summarised below for boys and girls attending mixed primary and mixed secondary schools.

Table 5.1 **How bullying others makes schoolchildren feel: Percentages of students endorsing selected statements about bullying**

Statement: Bullying other students:	Primary		Secondary	
	Boys	**Girls**	**Boys**	**Girls**
1 makes you feel good about yourself	6.7	4.8	15.4	9.6
2 gets you admired by other children at this school	13.9	9.5	23.4	14.5
3 prevents you from being bullied	27.1	22.3	35.6	26.8
4 shows them you are tough	36.6	32.7	39.3	31.2
5 makes you feel better than them	33.2	30.0	47.1	40.3

Number for sample: Primary schools: Boys=843; Girls=541
Secondary schools: Boys=2158; Girls=1884

The results indicated that a substantial proportion of children really do admire bullies and may think that bullying is a sensible way of behaving; that is, it gets you admired; it shows you are tough; it makes you feel better than others. It has the advantage of preventing you from getting bullied yourself. A minority (but as many as one in seven in the secondary schools) indicated that it makes you feel good.

You will notice that the proportion of children with an admiring attitude to bullying is greater in the secondary school; also that it is rather more prevalent among boys than girls. There is some comfort in thinking that the pro-bully group is in a minority, but you should bear in mind that some students were simply neutral or preferred not to commit themselves. These figures do suggest that many children do see positive qualities in bullies.

Attitudes to victims

Now it is possible to feel that bullying has something to be said for it: for example, it stops you from being bullied and shows you are tough, but at the same time feel that there is much unfairness in victims being picked upon or bullied by others. In one study we were keen to discover how children in general feel about those children who are frequently bullied by others. Would they, we wondered, tend to be supportive or would they tend to despise and reject victims as 'weak people', and perhaps even approve of bullying? We began by conducting a survey of 667 children between the ages of eight and fifteen years to find out (Rigby & Slee, 1991).

As expected, a wide range of opinion was found. Between 10 and 20 per cent of children reported that they felt negatively towards victims of school bullying. About one child in five agreed that they 'would not be friends with kids who allowed themselves to be pushed around', and one in seven agreed with the statement, 'Soft kids make me sick'. A similar proportion felt that 'kids should not complain about being bullied'. Here then was evidence of strong macho attitudes involving a rejection of children who get bullied at school.

Similar proportions of children expressed approval of bullying. About 15 per cent endorsed the statement that 'kids who get picked on a lot usually deserve it', and about 10 per cent thought that 'it is funny to see kids get upset when they are teased'. That children should express these views even in a questionnaire is depressing, and provides confirmatory evidence that tough-minded and unsympathetic attitudes of children do help to form a school ethos. But at the same time we should not forget that we are talking about a minority of students. The notion that nearly everybody in a school rejects and despises the wimp is not supported.

Indeed, if we look at the extent to which children want to see victims supported the result is more cheering. Approximately three children in five agreed that 'it is a good thing to help children who can't defend themselves', and four out of five expressed admiration for people who take action in endorsing the statement, 'I like it when someone stands up for kids who are bullied'.

In some ways then, the survey results were reassuring. They suggest that a teacher can count on the support of the majority of children in a class to oppose bullying and support ways of helping victims. At the same time, we can see how a child who finds it congenial and attractive to bully others can find plenty of support. In any class there will be a handful of children who will support a bully and reject a victim. Many more will be non-committal, and act as mere bystanders. This then is the problem for a teacher who wishes to get a class to stop bullying happening: How to keep the majority of children who are 'on side' actively engaged in opposing bullying, and how to negate the influence of a minority of 'tough guys' who are decidedly unsympathetic and probably antagonistic.

Gender and age as factors in determining attitudes of students

We were not surprised to find that girls, as a rule, have more positive and supportive attitudes towards victims of school bullying. Some researchers have suggested that females are by nature more empathic than males. Others have argued that females can identify with victims of unjustified attacks more readily in a society in which women are much more likely to be the target of spouse abuse than are men. Whatever the explanation it is clear that opposition to bullying tends to be stronger among girls than boys, although it is important to recognise that there are many individual exceptions.

There are girls who enthusiastically support bullying of people they dislike, and boys who do not. But the trend is quite clear—you can normally count on more support from a group of girls to end bullying than from a group of boys.

Less expected, however, as children became older between eight and fifteen-years-old, they tend to become *less and less sympathetic* towards victims. Dr Slee and I were surprised at this because there is much evidence from developmental studies of children that with increasing age the capacity of a child to take the perspective of another person, and therefore to empathise, becomes greater. This strongly suggests that the socialising process at school towards more macho values overcomes any tendency for a child to grow in sympathetic understanding. It follows that it becomes increasingly difficult for teachers to gain support from children to counter bullying as the children become older.

In a later study, Dr Slee and I examined the question of whether the trend towards less and less sympathy for victims of bullying continued into late teens. Older children were included in another sample drawn from twenty-five schools in South Australia. Each responded to a questionnaire and answered ten items in a reliable or internally consistent measure of Attitudes to Peer Victimisation. Examples of the items were: 'It's funny to see kids get upset when they are teased' and 'It makes me angry when a kid is picked on without reason'. Children scored as pro-victim if they agreed to statements like the second one; and disagreed with the first one. A mean score was calculated for each age group for boys and girls independently. In total, 2689 girls and 4061 boys provided data for Figure 5.1.

Figure 5.1 Relationship between students' attitudes to peer victimisation and age

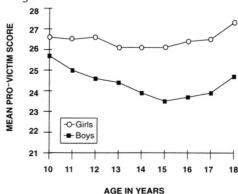

As in our earlier study, large differences between boys and girls were found: girls in each age group were more supportive of victims. But when we examined the age trends with older teenagers included, it was clear that the trend towards less and less sympathy for victims, most striking in the case of boys, did *not* continue beyond the age of fifteen. In fact among the older students there was a tendency for them to be more pro-victim, that is, more supportive of victims.

In summary, developmental psychologists were wrong who believed that when children became old enough to see the other person's point of view, they would become more sympathetic to victims at school. The relevant cognitive capacities surely increase as children go from eight to fifteen-years-old, but sympathy for victims does not increase; for boys especially sympathy becomes less and less. This means that there is an increasing number of students who are more likely to exacerbate the problem than help to solve it. But those also were wrong who believed that with continued exposure to the school milieu or ethos young people would become more and more unsympathetic to victims at school. Maturity seemingly comes late, but for increasing numbers of children it does come—eventually.

Complaining

When children feel free and safe to tell others when they are being seriously bullied, at least half the battle against bullying has been won. If it is acceptable to tell, there is much less hope among bullies that they will 'get away with it'.

Yet we know that many children are extremely reluctant to seek help when they are being bullied, even in circumstances when help is desperately needed. One of the questions asked in the Rigby and Slee surveys using the PRQ is: 'If you were bullied every day by someone stronger than yourself, would you tell somebody about it?' The results are worth examining in detail:

Table 5.2   **Whether students would tell if bullied daily**

	Percentages	
	Boys	**Girls**
Definitely yes	30.6	40.4
Yes	28.5	27.9
Can't say	30.2	26.8
No	7.1	3.1
Definitely no	3.5	1.7

Rigby and Slee (1995)

As we can see, over 40 per cent of boys and 30 per cent of girls either would not, or feel they could not, say whether they would tell. Under the stress of continual bullying: 'every day by a stronger person' large numbers of children prefer to tough it out. Further analysis showed that it was in the thirteen to fifteen-year-old age group that this 'macho response' was most entrenched. As we have seen, if help is asked for, it is generally from a 'friend', not an adult, not a teacher, and more especially not a counsellor. That really would be an admission of weakness.

What children think of complainers?

A further study was conducted to examine the question of how children feel and what they think about children who do tell others about it. In total 280 students, of whom 49 per cent were boys and 51 per cent girls, from a high school answered another questionnaire. This study was carried out in a secondary school in Victoria with the assistance of a school teacher, Garry Black. Children were asked to complete a sentence which read: 'Children who complain about being bullied...' The questionnaires were again completed anonymously, this time by students in the first and third years of the secondary school; their ages ranged from twelve to fifteen-years-old. The sentence was completed by 93 per cent of the students receiving the questionnaire; these consisted of 82 boys and 82 girls. A full report of this study is given in Rigby and Slee (1993b).

We were able to categorise the responses according to whether they reflected positive, neutral (or mixed) or negative attitudes towards those who complain about being bullied. An example of a 'positive' sentence completion was '... are very sensible'; a negative one, '... are a pain'. Neutral responses consisted of those that could not be classified as above, either because they did not imply an evaluative judgement, e.g. '... are smaller and not in the in-group', or involved 'mixed' content, e.g. '... are mostly right, but get a bit too complaining'.

As in our previous studies the positive, supportive responses far outweighed negative ones for boys and girls in both age groups. Again, too, there was a tendency for fewer positive and more negative responses to be made by students in the older age group.

Blaming the complainer

We will now examine some of the things children had to say about the people who complain. First we will look at the negative things. (In the results that follow the gender of the student is given as 'm' for male and 'f' for female; ages are also provided.)

Denigration

Some simply abused or denigrated the kind of person who complained. These were typical comments.
They were:

'losers' (m,13);   'wimps' (f,12);
'poo-dicks' (m,15);   'pussies' (m,15);
'stupid' (m,13);   'a pain' (f,12).

They were also described as people who:

'often complain too much' (m,12);
'have little self-respect' (f,14);
'[are] little kids who don't know anything' (m,14);
'normally ask for it' (m,12);
'bring it on themselves usually' (f,15);
'are often wimps trying to get other people in trouble' (f,14); and
people who 'should take it with a grain of salt' (m,14).

Self-defeating

Some students saw complaining about bullying as self-defeating. According to one student, complainers were 'stupid because they just get bullied more' (m,14). Others added:

'they get bullied more for whingeing' (f,15);

'they get teased' (m,12); and

'often get into more trouble from the bullies' (m,13).

In need of better advice

Then there were students who merely passed judgement on the complainers as being blind to better alternative forms of behaving. They should, for instance:

'look to themselves to see if they can do something to prevent it' (f,14);

'not tell the teacher but find another way to deal with it' (m,14);

'go to self-defence lessons' (m,15); and

'at least do something about it than complain' (f,15).

Some saw fighting back as clearly preferable. Complainers should:

'Stick up for themselves and not let themselves be pushed around' (f,14);

'face up to the people bullying them' (m,14); and

'bully the bullies back' (f,13).

Approving of the complainers

As against those students who blamed the victim, there were, as we have seen, a larger number who in fact said positive things.

Supporters

According to some, complainers were:

'very sensible' (m,13);   'all right' (m,12);

'smart' (f,12);   'strong' (m,13);

'pretty courageous' (m,12);   'good' (f,13); and

'normally nice inside' (f,13).

Their complaining was seen as justified:

'Is fair enough because you would if you were being bullied' (f,12);

'is good or it will keep happening' (m,12);

'are usually telling the truth, I feel sorry for them' (f,13);

'are trying to protect themselves' (f,14);

'something should be done' (m,15);

'need to be helped to have their self-confidence restored' (m,14);

'should be listened to and believed by people who will do something about it' (f,14);

'should have the bully stopped' (5,12); and

'should be helped by you' (f,13).

Victims' rights

A number of those approving of 'complainers' insisted upon the rights of victims.

'They have a right to complain to people if they are bullied' (m,14); and

'shouldn't feel scared to do so' (f,14).

Rights mentioned included:

'the right to speak up' (f,13);

'the right to be listened to' (m,13; f,13); and

'the right to be protected' (f,14).

'Complaining', commented one, 'is not dobbing' (m,13).

'No child should be bullied' (f,14) added another.

Good advice

Some provided positive advice:

'Should go and tell someone to help stop bullying' (m,14);

'go and tell a teacher' (m,12); and

'should tell their parents or teachers and then they can deal with it' (f,13).

Some expressed a personal readiness to help:

'I help as much as possible' (f,14);

'I would go and help them' (f,13).

Being neutral about complainers

Then there was a substantial minority of students whose sentence completions could not be classified as 'positive' or 'negative'.

Detachment

Some appeared detached or objective. Running through the things they wrote provided almost uncanny echoes of what research psychologists have been saying about bully/victim problems. Those who complain were described as:

'usually smaller and not in the in-group' (m,14);

'sometimes very quiet and don't like coming to school' (f,12);

'don't have much confidence' (f,14);

'usually used to warm friendly people around them' (f,15);

'are people who should make more friends, get into a group of kids' (m,12);

'some bully other kids in return; some don't' (f,15);

'usually keep it [bullying] to themselves' (f,13).

Other 'neutral' comment included straight advice:

'should stay away from bullies' (m,12);

'should move schools' (f,13);

and pure detachment:

'I would not really care unless I was involved' (f,12).

Ambivalence

Other students expressed mixed feelings:

'I feel sorry for them, but sometimes they deserve it' (f,12);

'sometimes they're over-reacting and want attention and maybe sometimes some kids need help with this' (f,14);

'are sometimes right and sometimes want to get other kids in trouble' (f,12);

'I pity them but laugh with everyone else' (m,12);

'are people I feel sorry for, although I hate to admit that sometimes I just don't care and I'm glad it's not me' (f,14).

It was clear from this later study that children have a wide range of opinion about children who complain, some negative, some positive and some mixed. In short, the student population is much divided, Not only that, but many school children are clearly divided in themselves, struggling with contradictory impulses—feeling sympathetic at times, but also derisory and cynical; sometimes wanting to help but equally determined to follow a self-preservatory impulse to steer clear and thank their lucky stars they were not involved.

Differences between schools in student attitudes

We have seen that schools do differ markedly in the amount of bullying that goes on there. If the school ethos does make a difference we would expect that schools would differ on the indicators of children's attitudes to bullying and also to their attitudes towards the victims of bullying. This is, in fact, what we found, but more especially among boys. Some schools appeared to have relatively high proportions of children who admired bullies and despised victims.

This can be illustrated by the results we obtained at two coeducational high schools in Adelaide. From each of them we obtained responses to questionnaire items from over 100 children of either sex in identical year groups. The schools contrasted in the amount of reported bullying, especially among the boys. At School A, some 22 per cent of the boys reported that they were being bullied at least once a week; at School B there were 11 per cent. We then examined the responses of the boys to questions relating to the school ethos. In School A a significantly higher proportion indicated that (a) bullying gets you admired by other children at this school (29 per cent against 21 per cent); and (b) prevented you from being bullied by others (48 per cent against 33 per cent). On every one of the ten indices of attitudes to victims there was greater sympathy expressed towards victims by children at School B. For example, at School A 15 per cent of the boys thought that one should *not* complain about being bullied, compared with 9 per cent at School B; and 26 per cent at School A thought it 'funny to see a kid get upset when teased' compared with 16 per cent at the other school. Comparison after comparison between the two schools indicated that the school ethos was different at the two places, and suggested that the pressure to bully others and not to care for victimised children was greater at the school where more bullying occurred.

Teachers' contribution to the school ethos

So far in this chapter we have focused on the attitudes of students towards bullies and victims. But teachers may also contribute and we will understand the school ethos better after we have explored *their* attitudes.

As we have seen, students differ a good deal in their attitudes towards bullying. Although a majority of students appear to be clearly on the side of victims and dislike bullying, there are substantial minorities who provide support for bullies and increase the sense of isolation for those who are often victimised. Is this true of teachers also?

There have been two studies conducted in Australia concerned with what teachers think about bullying. In one of these (Rigby & Slee, 1991) thirty-two teachers from primary and secondary schools in South Australia completed questionnaires anonymously and gave their personal opinions on the problem in their schools. Five described the situation as 'severe'; twenty-six said it was 'somewhat of a problem'; and one thought it was 'no problem'. On the question of how many children in their classes they thought were being continually victimised, the teachers gave a somewhat lower estimate than that provided by the students in their classes. Nevertheless, it is fair to say that in 1990 when these data were collected teachers were generally acknowledging that bullying was a problem for them. Subsequently, in seminars and workshops conducted in schools and elsewhere with teachers, there was overwhelming evidence that many teachers did care a great deal and wanted to see something done to reduce the problem.

But were they any more concerned and motivated to act than students? In a further enquiry in Victoria (Keogh & Rigby, 1995) ninety-nine teachers from primary and secondary schools were questioned about their attitudes to bullying in schools. Like the students who had been questioned earlier, they answered questionnaires anonymously. It was found that where teachers answered the same questions as those answered by the students, teachers were decidedly more pro-victim and anti-bully than the bulk of students. Teachers were almost unanimous in believing that children should indeed complain if they are being bullied; about one third of the students had thought otherwise. Practically all teachers felt that kids who got picked on a lot did *not* deserve it; half the students thought otherwise or were undecided. These differences suggest that teachers are, at least in theory, more supportive of victimised children than the students themselves. Further opinions expressed by teachers (not asked of students) indicated that nearly all of them believed that bullying was not inevitable. It was not something that just had to be accepted. More than 90 per cent of the teachers believed that something could be done about it.

So far so good. But when the teachers were asked about their personal capacity to act effectively with actual cases of bullying a surprisingly large proportion (one in three) agreed with the statement 'bullies make me feel intimidated'; and quite a few (one in five) felt that somebody else, not themselves, should be dealing with it—the principal, the year coordinator, but not the classroom teacher.

Judging from these results, which currently are the only ones upon which judgements can be based, teachers *are,* as a group, different from students in feeling practically unanimously that victims should be supported, that victims are not to blame, and something should be done to solve the problem of school bullying. Unlike students there is not a substantial minority who think otherwise. Yet it is now also clear that for many teachers, probably more than were prepared to say in responding to the questionnaire, there is a personal fear of intervening and a wish to avoid the responsibility of taking personal action.

Is this hesitancy to act on the part of teachers communicated to students? Survey results from over 8000 students answering the Peer Relations Questionnaire in 1994 and 1995 strongly suggest that it is. According to both boys and girls in this sample, over 30 per cent saw teachers as either 'not interested in stopping bullying' or 'only sometimes interested' (Rigby & Slee, 1995). This is not intended to blame teachers: many situations, as we shall see, are not at all easy to deal with. But it is true to say that the uncertainties of teachers in this area must encourage some bullies, produce dismay in victims, and help to explain why many students do not inform teachers even when they are being seriously victimised by individuals or groups.

Parents and the school ethos

As part of the school community, parents also affect the school ethos. We already know that they can have an effect, for good or ill, through the attitudes and behaviours they inculcate (or allow to flourish) in their children. But as yet there has been no study in Australia to allow us to reach a judgement of their attitudes based on empirical research. However, from interactions with parents at numerous meetings concerned with issues of bullying, this seems to me to be the situation:

1 Like teachers, parents in general feel that bullying is a vicious and entirely undesirable practice that should be stopped. Where the parent has a child

who is being bullied, the attitude is commonly one of anger and outrage. Such a parent is much more vehement about it than the teacher.

2   Parents whose children are bullied are more likely than others to adopt a punitive attitude towards bullies and to pressure the school to take punitive action—often to the despair of counsellors who believe that bullies can be persuaded to change their ways.

3   A minority of parents (we can only guess how many) actually admire the bully, especially if he or she is a son or daughter. They can act as a counter-force to plans to reduce bullying.

The influence of parents has so far been largely indirect through their parenting in the family; in some cases it has been extremely positive in promoting pro-social attitudes and behaviours; in some cases, unfortunately, the opposite. Currently we need to know more about what parents think, for they too can contribute powerfully in the formation and modification of the school ethos, through what they do in the home, and what they can do at the interface of school and family as they interact with teachers and attend parent/staff meetings at the school.

School and society

We must be careful that we do not regard the kinds of attitudes that flourish in schools, which can result in people who need help being denied it, as specific to schools—as if in the wider adult world people invariably ask for help when they need it, regardless of what it might do to their 'tough guy' image.

As I write, one of the tough guys of Australian sport has just died. He was Ted Whitten, widely admired as a great footballer, but also a man enormously revered by many Australians because of his resolute toughmindedness and larrikinism. He died of prostate cancer at the age of sixty-two. The former Adelaide Crows football coach, Graham Cornes, had this to say of him:

'The tragedy is that Ted didn't have to die so prematurely.
The qualities that made him a great footballer and a good bloke
contributed as much as any to his early departure. The Australian
male ethos of 'she'll be right, mate' and the belief in our own
indestructible masculinity masked the early warning signs of prostate
cancer. He told us that the warning signs were there but he didn't go
to a doctor about them.'

In short, misplaced stoicism is endemic in Australian society, as in the schoolyard. But it would not be accurate to describe this simply as a gender issue.

We should bear in mind that it is an issue and a problem for many women and girls also.

What can
be done

Chapter

Linking
understanding
to practice

We now come to the part of the book where we turn our attention to 'what
can be done about it'. How we start will depend upon the understanding we
have developed of the bully/victim problem in schools, and also on our
motivation to act. We have seen in Part One that, despite early vehement
claims to the contrary, bullying is a real problem in all our schools and not
the invention of hypersensitives and do-gooders. It is now clear that it was
not the invention, either, of Scandinavian and English educators. Bullying
in schools in Australia is at least as pervasive as in the schools overseas
where the earlier research was done. Survey results derived from thousands
of school children throughout Australia should convince us that bullying is
indeed a significant social problem. It is only just being recognised for what
it is, and at last being seriously addressed—in some schools.

I hope by now you are convinced of the far-reaching consequences that bullying at school can have for many children and how their subsequent development as adults can be affected. But, in dwelling on the dark side of school life and the psychopathology of human development, I fear that some readers may feel quite pessimistic, perhaps even discouraged. If so, this will be an unfortunate starting point for Part Two. Are there good reasons to believe that the problem of bullying can be overcome? I think so.

Grounds for optimism

The evidence for believing that schools can take effective action against bullying has been gradually accumulating since Olweus (1989) detailed and substantiated his startling claim that a 50 per cent reduction in bullying had taken place in Norwegian schools as a consequence of a well-planned and intensive intervention programme. Subsequently, a most rigorous and sophisticated enquiry into the effectiveness of interventions to reduce bullying has been carried out in Sheffield, England, by Peter Smith and his team (Smith & Sharp, 1994). The conclusions of this study are worth quoting at this juncture, as we prepare to consider what might be done in Australia.

> 'In general, schools improved on most measures of bullying—relating to reports of being bullied, bullying others, not joining in, telling someone if you were bullied, having someone to talk to you if you bullied others.' (Smith and Sharp, 1994, p. 53)

In their report they show that the reductions in the amount of bullying being reported over a two-year period in the twenty-six schools where interventions took place varied a good deal between the schools, being greater where interventions had been most thorough in terms of time and effort. The changes were generally greater in primary schools (where bullying is more common) but significant reductions were also found in the ten secondary schools involved in the project. These results, in my view, are very important because they clearly show that if schools are willing and able to put time and effort into a thoughtful, comprehensive anti-bullying program, peer victimisation can definitely be reduced.

Is there a simple answer then?

It has been said that for every complex problem there is a simple answer. To which the cynic replies: 'And it's always wrong'.

Bullying certainly is a complex problem to which there is no effective simple answer. It is true that peddlers of simple solutions do abound, three of which regularly appear in some such form as these:

- Crack down on the bullies so hard that they will not dare to bully anyone again.
- Show the victims how to stand up for themselves. Give the bullies a taste of their own medicine. A bully is really a coward.
- Be kind to the bullies. Help to raise their self-esteem and they will not want to bully others.

Would that it were so simple! At best these are quarter truths; at worst, do more harm than good.

Appreciating the complexity

Earlier a model of factors affecting children's peer relations was presented and examined in order to develop an appreciation of the multiplicity of potential causes of bullying behaviour in a school (see p. 70). It is worth revisiting as we prepare to consider what schools can do about bullying.

It will be recalled that a variety of factors were seen to be operating, each with the potential to turn a child into a bully (or a victim), long before he or she comes to school; moreover, these factors were seen as continuing to have effects while the child was actually attending school. These 'early originating' or home-based factors were identified as:

(i)   basic personal characteristics, such as size, strength, and personality, of which aggressiveness, impulsivity, low empathy, introversion and poor self-esteem are perhaps the most relevant.

(ii) family experiences which were seen as not only contributing to the formation of a child's personality but also predisposing some children to bully or be victimised; and

(iii) the socio-cultural environment, a milieu in which the activities and attitudes of a student's habitual companions and the nature and quality of what is provided by the media can together play a part in determining how a child will treat its peers.

Other factors, it will be recalled, were seen as operating within the school. These included the school ethos, that is the views and attitudes of teachers and students towards bullying. Depending on its nature, this ethos might encourage or discourage bullying behaviour especially among those most susceptible to its influence. A further factor was identified as the educational climate of a school—which might promote absorption and enjoyment in study and also cooperation with others, or alternatively give rise to boredom, frustration and the hindering of others, that is, to conditions in which bullying behaviour can thrive. Thirdly, we noted the potentially key role of the School Policy on Bullying, the means by which the attention of the school community could be focused and its energies harnessed to counter bullying in the school.

The first question we might ask ourselves about the model is: How fixed or alterable are the factors it suggests? I think we would agree that each one of them is susceptible to change, including, within limits, even the physical and personality characteristics of children. The next question is more difficult to answer: How can changes be made?

Once the 'causes' of bullying are viewed as the model suggests, the folly of expecting a single, exclusive answer to this question becomes obvious. There are many ways in which actions may be taken to reduce the likelihood of bullying behaviour: in family life, through community action, and by what schools can do themselves. We have seen how dysfunctional families can produce bullies. We need therefore to consider as a society how we can improve their functionality, especially through educating individuals to be more effective parents. Violent videos and computer games have been identified as contributing to aggressive behaviour among young people. How can these be countered? In schools we have seen a variety of contributory influences, central to which is the school ethos. How, we should ask, can this be changed from one that encourages macho values and dominating behaviour to one that promotes cooperation and empathic concern for others. Perhaps most clearly in the hands of schools is the potential for improving the educational climate. How can this be achieved? All these must be considered before we come to the question that is uppermost in many minds: What shall we do to the bully?

It may be comforting to think that there is just one simple answer to a problem and that other answers are wrong, irrelevant and even to be disparaged. Yet in this area, as in many others, it is unwise to think of exclusive solutions. There is a story by Abraham Maslow of a mother who gave her son two ties for his birthday. As he put one of them on to please her, she asked sadly, 'And why do you hate the other tie?' He might have replied, as we should to single-pointed proposals to solving the problem of bullying, that it is not a matter of either/or, but both this and that. In the following chapters we will explore a variety of ways in which the problem of bullying can be countered.

Getting
started

However desirable and urgent a solution to the problem of bullying might seem to the reader, whether he or she is a principal, deputy, counsellor, teacher, administrator, parent or student, it is unlikely that it will be tackled very effectively unless certain conditions are present. These are as follows:

1   A general recognition by the school community (staff, students and parents) that bullying is, in fact, occurring at the school on a significant scale.

2   A widespread belief in the school community that peer-victimisation at school can have serious consequences.

3   Optimism regarding the outcome for a school of applying new policies and practices directed towards substantially reducing the problem.

If we now review these conditions, we will see that each one of them is essential; the absence of any of them could be a fatal stumbling-block to taking effective action at a school. For example, it might be conceded that bullying at a school is rife, but the consequences are seen as trivial.

Alternatively, it could be widely accepted that bullying is rife and the consequences serious, but that *no conceivable action* on the part of the school could reduce it. Optimism regarding the possibility of reducing the problem is essential.

Therefore in addition to finding out the extent and nature of bullying in a school and how it is affecting those who are engaged in it, you must also explore the perceptions and attitudes of members of the school community: what *they* think of the situation. All this must be done before direct steps can be taken to counter bullying in a school.

How this is to be done next depends in part on what may be called broadly the school's current position on the matter. 'Bullying' is unlikely to be a new issue. It may have been talked about a lot. Already there may have been some reactions and judgements expressed at the school about the need for policy, some positive, some not. The school may have received directions or guidelines from its educational authority. A growing number of educational authorities in Australia are currently (end 1995) preparing or providing policy statements or guidelines for schools on bullying, including the South Australian Department of Children's Services and Education and the New South Wales Education Authority among others. In most cases schools will not therefore be starting from scratch. However, it is one thing to receive directives or recommendations from above and another to generate your own response and 'own' the problem.

Informally assessing the school ethos

To the person who wants to get things moving at a school the first piece of advice I would give is to proceed with caution and be patient if things do not happen quickly. We know that policies and programs that are most effective are generally those that have wholehearted support from a large proportion of members of the school community—ideally everyone. It is best to start with an attempt to get a 'feel' for the nature and quality of interpersonal relations at the school; in essence, how people, children, staff and parents associated with the school actually treat each other on a day-to-day basis. At the same time, try to gauge people's reactions (if any) to what is happening in relations between these people. In short: assess the school ethos.

It is in some respects easier to appraise a situation if you are an outsider observing people's behaviour at a school for the first time. If you have grown used to the school, the habitual way in which people treat each other will appear 'normal'. 'That is the way,' we might say, 'students talk to each other; that is how teachers talk to students. This is what happens when parents and teachers meet. Each is playing a role.' You need to make an effort to take a fresh look at what is going on as an outsider would.

As an example, take the matter of how people use each other's names when they are together. At a very early stage in our lives we become aware of the sound of our names. We hear them first, as a rule, spoken lovingly by our parents and family. We learn to identify with the sound and later the letters that form our names. Gradually, as we hear the name spoken by others and see the name in writing, our self-esteem somehow gets built into it. Whatever is said about the name is said about us. How it is said expresses an attitude, one of acceptance, admiration, love, pity, kindness, respect—or of rejection, contempt, hatred indifference, cruelty, disrespect.

In the video, *Only Playing, Miss!* (Neti-Neti Theatre Company, 1990), when the school identifies with the victim they sing in chorus:

I've given up trying to say my name
My name has just become a game
They kick it around and laugh at what they've found.
If I show that I care
They just copy me and stare.

It is very instructive to reflect on how names are being used by staff as well as students. In the video 'Only Playing, Miss!', the victim is a boy about thirteen-years-old whose name is Eugene Hickey. When he is discovered by a teacher, beaten up and in distress in the schoolyard, he is addressed unsympathetically as 'Hickey'. 'Grow up, lad', says the teacher, 'it's a hard world out there.' To his mother he is 'Eugene'. To the boy who is continually bullying him, he is 'Little Euge' spoken in a mockingly kind and derisory manner.

Now although the choice of name to be used at school is sometimes a matter of custom (in some schools *not* being called by your surname by a teacher would be distinctly embarrassing!), the tone of derision that enters into the pronunciation of your name is unmistakable. Listen to how people use each other's names. It is a good indicator of the quality of interpersonal relations in a school.

I have begun by drawing attention to what may be a sign of verbal abuse because it is by far the most common form of school bullying. As we have seen, it often accompanies other forms of bullying such as deliberate exclusion from groups and physical assault. Some of the latter may have come to light during the school's recent history and may be well remembered. But we should always bear in mind that evidence of quite serious bullying frequently remains hidden and only a small proportion of the bullying becomes public knowledge. We know that most students are reluctant to inform teachers, even when they have been bullied continually and severely. Nevertheless, school records and the experiences of counsellors in particular can provide useful preliminary data. So, too, can records (if they are kept) of parents coming to school or phoning to complain of their children being bullied at school.

A caution

It is often unwise for a parent or teacher to go on a One-Person Crusade about bullying, especially if you can anticipate significant opposition. The 'agitator', so-named, can in some circumstances become quite isolated and consequently disregarded. It is better to find out unobtrusively what staff members think about bullying at the school and to identify those who will support doing something new about bullying—seek to work with them. Consider together how the school as a whole can become motivated to tackle the problem.

It isn't going to be all that easy, especially if there is going to be a 'Whole School Approach', which is really needed for maximum effectiveness and for the maintenance and continuation of the drive against bullying. It has been wisely suggested that you need to consider what is needed in the short term to get things moving, that is, arousing interest and awareness in the staff; then, what must be done in the medium term to provide a reasoned and justified case for an anti-bullying policy that will convince and involve not only the whole staff, but children and parents as well; and next, what is needed in the long run, namely agreed methods for preventing bullying and intervening in cases of bullying, and especially methods that are maintained and even improved over time. An excellent analysis along these lines by

Australian researchers and practitioners, Hyndman and Thorsborne (1994), provides the steps that a school must take to achieve and sustain effective action against bullying. It is important not to be cowed by this task. As Margaret Mead put it: 'Never doubt that a small group of committed people can change the world. Indeed, it's the only thing that ever has' (cited by Sue Gordon, 1995).

At the staff meeting

Sooner or later the subject of school bullying will be raised at a forum, probably a staff meeting, in a formal manner. Someone will speak to the staff about it, someone (let us hope) who is assured of support from some others in the group. It is very useful to be able to anticipate the concerns that will be raised. Here are some:

A
Those who honestly think that there is very little (if any) bullying going on in the school.

For these people you need to gather and marshall the evidence.

B
Those who accept that bullying occurs but believe it does little harm.

Again evidence is needed, but this time of the effects of bullying. Case studies often provide the most persuasive arguments.

C
Those who accept that bullying occurs but feel that it is not their responsibility to do anything about it.

Here it must be pointed out that legal action has been, and is being, taken against some schools in Australia that have not taken reasonable steps in cases of serious bullying. The best way of preventing this from happening is to develop sound policies and defensible practices.

D

Those who believe that children should learn to defend themselves against bullies, rather than be 'wrapped in cotton wool'.

Often it is sensible to concede that victimised children should be encouraged to defend themselves (and this can be part of an anti-bullying policy) but question whether in some cases it is a realistic option, especially where group bullying is concerned.

E

Those who accept that bullying occurs but believe it is best to deny it—to protect the school from adverse public and media judgement.

This is understandable, and not at all uncommon, especially among senior staff. However, it can be pointed out that it is now widely accepted that bullying goes on in all schools, and kudos accrues to those schools who can show that they are actually doing something about it.

F

Those who accept that bullying is a problem, but think it must be viewed in the context of other issues of higher priority and shortages of resources.

Query what are the matters of higher priority. Then consider how an anti-bullying policy would complement and advance other objectives the speaker may approve of. Whether resources are available will depend on the support that can be mustered to deal with the issue.

G

Those who strongly deplore bullying and would like to see it stopped but see it as a part of human nature that cannot be altered.

Here the answer is to provide the sceptic with the evidence from well-researched studies, such as those conducted by Olweus in Norway and by Smith in England which show that bullying can be substantially reduced.

H

Those who admit the problem but believe (or want to believe) that all the relevant policies are in place and the school is already doing what is needed. These people may list the policies that exist to counter bullying in the school, such as: Anti-Harassment, Sexual Harassment, Social Justice, Discipline, Pastoral Care, etc., etc.

Here you need to be very careful. There are likely to be vested interests at stake, not to mention some understandable ego involvement in promoting and continuing policies that have been started. There may be leadership positions at risk, and groups or cliques that are threatened if a new policy and any consequent restructuring is agreed to. It is therefore vital that the contribution of those whose work has been concerned with any aspects of bullying is fully recognised, and their further contributions warmly welcomed.

Forewarned is to be forearmed. It is unwise to steamroller any opposition. A combination of hard evidence, tact and reason is likely to win over many, if not all.

But beware of one source of apparent support that may have a quite counterproductive effect. This may come from staff who take an extreme view about the desirability and achievability of eliminating *all* aggressive thoughts and actions. This view is to be found in one popular definition of bullying originating with Delwyn Tattum in Wales and adopted by the Scottish Council for Educational Research:

'Bullying,' (they say) 'is a wilful, conscious desire to hurt or frighten someone else.'

This is an ideal that many people would like to achieve but the realists (and cynics) on the staff will not want to identify with a cause that equates bullying with hostile thoughts or wishes. There is no need to convert people to a crusade against all aggressive feeling or even to the elimination of all aggressive acts. Bullying, we should remind ourselves, is essentially an abuse of power: that is, aggression that is unjust.

Is bullying funny?

A common reaction to talk about bullying is to find it funny. At seminars I have often observed people laughing and joking about it. Pretending to look about them in a mock-scared way: 'Who,' they ask, 'is bullying whom at our school?' There are at least two reasons for the hilarity. First, as is well known, humour is often a cover for what is embarrassing and painful to think about. It is sometimes painful to recall incidents or episodes in which you have been humiliated by a bully. It may also be unpleasant to face up to existing situations at school or at home in which you are under the thumb of a petty tyrant. But, like all human activities there is often a funny-sad side to it. Don't get intense if people start laughing. 'Yes,' you might concede, 'bullying can be funny but it also has its dreadfully serious side.'

Outcomes

Positive outcomes from staff meetings on the issue of bullying are increasingly common. It is likely that a group of people at the meeting will be nominated and asked to go away and examine the problem in more detail and make recommendations. In some cases, it may have been decided at the meeting that steps should be taken to educate the staff (and possibly parents as well) about the problem of bullying in schools. Possibly, too, it has been agreed that a speaker with expert knowledge of the subject be invited to a future meeting. Finally, it might have been agreed that facts and figures be systematically collected at the school to discover the extent of the problem and an individual or group directed to start the process.

Finding out what is going on

Let us assume now that with the blessing of the staff (or most of it) some of its members can now go ahead and make plans for obtaining a more precise picture of bullying in the school.

The pros and cons of different ways of collecting useful data about bullying at school have already been considered in Chapter 2. Here let us briefly re-capitulate the major points and some practical issues to be confronted.

The question of definition

This may seem, initially, to be a somewhat theoretical matter. In fact, it is a very practical matter—there must be a clear definition of what is being researched to which there is general agreement; otherwise, the purpose of the enquiry will be confused. Discuss the definition employed by Rigby and Slee in their work, and the reasons why it was chosen. You might wish also to consider the distinction we made between 'bullying' and 'harassment', and how you see this as applying to your school. You will certainly need to consider the distinction between 'conflict in general', which includes fighting and quarrelling between people of about equal strength or power, and 'bullying' which presupposes an imbalance of power. I think it is important to preserve this distinction, for this very practical reason. Many people will not agree that we should try to put an end to all conflict (some may even defend the practice of physical fighting between equals to settle a dispute). Practically everybody, however, would like to see an end to bullying. But don't be swayed by those whose definition reflects a plan to end all human hostility in the school. It won't happen. We are concerned with preventing bullying behaviour, not changing human nature.

But whatever you conclude, it really is necessary to be explicit: *to have an agreed definition down in writing*. This will provide the focus for your investigation.

Choice of method of data collection

A variety of methods may be used, including self-administered questionnaires, interviews and direct observations. With young children (under-eight years-old) or children with marked learning difficulties, a questionnaire approach may *not* be suitable, and interviews will be necessary.

I have already expressed a clear preference for the self-administered questionnaire completed anonymously by children. This is primarily because children commonly do not want to be identified personally as providing information about either being bullied or about bullying others. In addition, interviews often introduce a greater degree of bias and raise problems of objective interpretation. But this does not mean that supplementary sources of information about bullying should not be tapped. Questions should also be asked of fellow teachers and parents. Group discussions or Focus Groups are frequently useful, especially at an early stage in the enquiry.

You may wonder whether to use a questionnaire that has already been developed or to develop your own. The case for developing a questionnaire at the school is as follows. It can be related to your own preferred definition of bullying, which may be unique to your group. It can be used to examine issues that are particularly relevant to your school. The work involved in developing your own questionnaire may result in a better understanding of the problem of bullying. Finally, working together to design a good question-naire can help to produce enthusiasm and commitment.

An alternative is to make use of a standardised measure of peer relations. This ensures that a reliable and well-tested measure is used that enables comparisons to be made with other schools, such as the *Peer Relations Questionnaire* (PRQ), developed for use in Australian schools with Australian norms provided (Rigby & Slee, 1995). The use of an existing questionnaire economises on time and effort. Additional questions can be added to suit the needs of particular schools.

These are some of the questions that teachers often want answers to:

1 How often are children bullied at school by their peers?
2 What is the frequency with which different forms of bullying occur?
3 Where, when, and in which years or classes does bullying take place most often?
4 How often are children bullied by individuals; and how often by groups? Are there bullying gangs operating at the school?
5 How 'safe' do children feel at the school?
6 How often do children take part in bullying others?

7 How do children react to being bullied? What are their feelings after being bullied?
8 Do they tell others? Whom do they tell?
9 To what extent do children want help with the problem of bullying?
10 What proportion of students *want* to talk together about what can be done about bullying?

You might like to add (or subtract) from this list. Teachers generally want to know about gender similarities and differences and how bullying differs between years and classes. Therefore results need to be cross-tabulated for this purpose.

Analysing the questionnaire data

It is most important that any enquiry into the prevalence of bullying in a school should lead to a careful summary and presentation of the results to those who are interested. This needs to be done well. Criticism of the way the results are presented, or the interpretations put upon them, can severely reduce the chances of others making a constructive response. Arithmetical errors and the use of tables and figures that unfairly represent what has been found must be avoided at all costs. For this reason, it is usually wise to involve teachers with training and skills in quantitative analysis, especially those with a background in mathematics and statistics in the analysis of the results. Criticism from this quarter could be devastating.

Educating about bullying

If it has been decided that a systematic attempt is to be made to educate the staff about bullying, it is best to allocate a half-day or even a full day for the purpose (tacking it on to the end of a staff meeting, especially at the end of the day can be disastrous). The meeting can provide a useful context in which the results from the survey (if any) are presented and considered in the light of what has been learned about the problem.

Sometimes it is useful to invite a speaker who has carefully examined or researched the problem and is familiar with the literature on bullying in schools. Already in Australia there are a number of people with a good background of understanding of the issue. I have listed those I know about in the Resources section of this book on page 289. Sometimes a staff member who has examined the topic carefully may be encouraged to make a presentation. But remember the prophet in his own country. The outside expert may know no more but in some schools may be more acceptable. Videos, too, can be useful as means of raising awareness. The video, *Bullying in Schools* by Rigby and Slee (1992; available through the Australian Council for Educational Research) can be helpful in this way.

There is much to be said for preparing a group of people to listen to a talk about bullying by asking them first to recall events when they personally experienced bullying in their own childhood, either as a victim or as a bully or as a bystander. They can be asked to talk briefly to one or two other people near them, and to say how they felt about it at the time. I have found that this simple exercise will sensitise participants to the issue and enable them to 'tune in' and make constructive contributions to the talk which will follow.

It is essential, however, that there is a clear understanding of what role the speaker will play. It may include the giving of information about bullying such as is contained in the first part of this book. It may include a brief overview of what schools are doing about bullying nowadays.

These points, I feel, should be emphasised:

1   Bullying in schools is now being regarded in many countries around the world as a pressing social issue.
2   This is so because it goes on in all schools and the consequences are being recognised as serious for many children, in both the short and long term.
3   Positive and effective steps *are* now being taken in some schools to reduce the incidence of bullying.
4   Schools need to make their own decision about intervention and do it in their *own* way.

The speaker should keep within strict time limits to allow the audience to hear about what is happening in their own school and to discuss what to do next. But—and this is important—the results from questionnaires should be introduced only after some careful preparation in which the general context of bullying has been provided. This should be done in a matter of fact manner by the member or members of the team who carried out the study.

Presenting results of the survey

The following is the advice Rigby and Slee (1995) give to users of the *Peer Relations Questionnaire* in their manual for use in schools. It can be adapted for use with other survey methods, if desired.

A short verbal presentation of results with a few clear 'overheads' summarising results is desirable. It is easy to go on too long, give too much detail and lose the audience. In addition to the presentation, a short written report should be provided for staff and for students. These may differ according to what is seen to be of primary interest to each group.

How the facts are presented is important. They should be presented in a clear and unambiguous manner. Heated discussion about what the so-called 'facts' mean at the beginning of the presentation can be damaging to a constructive discussion of their implications. Try not to overwhelm the audience with masses of data. It is generally wise to make a few key points supported by clearly presented results; for example:

(i)   bullying is being reported by substantial numbers of students in this school;

(ii) there is evidence of negative consequences for some students;

(iii) a good number of students have expressed a wish to get help with this problem.

For each proposition quantified support should be provided. At the same time, the use of some direct quotations from what students have said in the open-ended questions can be complementary—and very compelling!

The presentation should lead into a discussion on what can be done. Although the presenter may have strongly preferred solutions, it is unwise to present them as *the* answer. It is best to canvass opinion and invite suggestions. Generally speaking, approaches which have wide staff support are really the ones to develop.

Ending the meeting

Try to ensure that the meeting ends on a positive note, with further action being planned. It is a good idea to have a small group of staff agreeing to meet to formulate suggestions for policy and practice. They might be encouraged to undertake some focused reading on approaches to countering bullying in schools (see Resources). Ensure that the selected members include stakeholders who are already involved in relevant activities in the school, such as behaviour management, counselling and sexual harassment policies. It is desirable to agree to co-opt student representatives and parents at an early stage in the development of a planned response to the bully/ victim problem. Finally, plan to have a further general meeting at which progress can be reported.

School
policy
on bullying

Ideally a school policy, or its finalisation, emerges out of a process of education about bullying and discussions and consultations involving staff, students and parents. In practice, responsibility is apt to fall upon a small group of dedicated people, mainly staff, who must drive the policy, the educational program it necessitates, and its implementation. They need to be well organised and highly sensitive to the views of others. It can be a slow process, but this is better than a quick fix or a token gesture. The resulting policy should be one that the staff as a whole can enthusiastically embrace with the positive support of students and parents. This cannot be achieved overnight.

It is sensible to begin with an examination of policies that actually exist in the school which are relevant to the prevention and treatment of the problem of bullying. You will need to evaluate these carefully in relation to both their rationale and effectiveness. The maxim, 'if it ain't broke, don't fix it' may well apply. Perhaps existing policies can be improved or built upon.

You need to distinguish between policies that are in written or document form and those that are unwritten or not locatable. The latter may sometimes determine practice more than the former. It may be that bullying incidents in a school are treated in a particular way without anyone being able to point to a corresponding policy statement. There may be policy statements which are in effect 'dead letters', ignored or generally not known about, irrelevant to practice. Some policy statements may contradict or be inconsistent with others. In some cases you might find unnecessary duplication. There may also have developed within the school different ways of responding to bully/victim problems, each reflecting the philosophies and interests of different staff members. The group delegated to begin the development of a common policy on school bullying will need to examine what has been happening in the school by scrutinising documents and talking to staff and students.

For those schools which receive directives or policy guidelines from centralised educational authorities, it is, of course, essential that intended school outcomes be linked to certain formal external expectations. Details of key documents currently being provided by State educational authorities to help in addressing problems of bullying and harassment are given in Resources and guidelines section (p. 292).

Target groups or oppressive acts?

In the course of examining policies relevant to bullying or harassment you may be struck by the multiplicity of groups that have been identified as potential targets for 'unacceptable discrimination' and consequently in need of special consideration. These may include the disabled, the aged, ethnic minority groups, Aborigines, females, people from disadvantaged areas, gays and lesbians. An example of specially identified groups is contained in *Guidelines for Developing the Students Code of Conduct* provided by the Victorian Directorate of School Education (1994) in which it is stated that suspension from school could follow harassment towards another person based on 'sex, race (including colour, nationality and ethnic or national origin), marital status, the status or condition of being a parent, the status or condition of being childless, religious beliefs or physical or mental disability or impairment' (p. 23).

While the enumeration of groups towards whom there exists prejudice in our society can be useful in increasing community awareness and corresponding sensitivity, you may question the wisdom of extending the list interminably. The social characteristics of people who may become the targets of bullying are almost infinite. They often include middle-class, male, white Australians who are heterosexual and able-bodied. The policy makers might decide to focus more on acts of oppression rather than the social characteristics of the oppressed which can, in fact, at different times include everybody.

In drawing up a draft policy, you will be continually confronted with the question of what precisely the purpose of the policy might be and how it will be used. In an atmosphere of cynicism about 'one more piece of paper'— 'don't we have enough policies?'—you can easily become discouraged. Is it going to be just another piece of rhetoric, more political correctness? Will it have a real impact upon practice in schools?

Features of an anti-bullying policy

These may be considered the chief features:

1 The school's stand in relation to bullying.
2 A succinct definition of bullying, with illustrations.
3 The rights of children with respect to bullying at school.
4 The responsibilities of children who witness incidents of bullying.
5 What the school will do to counter bullying on the premises.
6 An undertaking to evaluate the policy in the light of its effects.

Clearly some parts of the policy are likely to be agreed upon more readily than others. Let us consider each in turn.

1   The school's stand in relation to bullying

This requires a strong statement regarding the unacceptability of bullying in the school. It seems straightforward, a matter of choosing strong words to make a serious impact. Almost inevitably at this stage there will arise the question of whether to include both 'bullying' and 'harassment' in the statement. The distinction is a fine one (as we have pointed out) and more to do with current and local usage than semantics. The overall impact is little affected by including both words. But if a strong statement is to be made, do avoid the use of the prim and proper, 'Bullying is inappropriate behaviour in this school...' Words should reflect the abhorrence you feel.

We should add, too, that the school's stand against bullying need not confine itself to bullying between peers. Indeed, if the document is developed (as I strongly suggest) through a consultative process involving teachers, students and parents, it is almost certain that it will be suggested that the bullying of teachers by students will be included; so, too, will bullying of children by teachers (students will see to that); and the bullying of teachers by other teachers cannot be ignored. These suggestions can be anticipated. If they are incorporated the document will have a higher level of acceptability to the school community.

2   A succinct definition of bullying with illustrations

I have continually emphasised the importance of definition. In my view the essence of bullying is continual negative behaviour (not merely thoughts) by a more powerful person in a situation where there is an imbalance of power (not in any situation) and the weaker person is really hurt. How this is expressed is a matter of judgement.

Here is an example from Xavier College in Melbourne, taken from their policy statement:

> 'Bullying is an act of aggression causing embarrassment, pain or discomfort to another; it can take many forms: physical, verbal, gesture, extortion and exclusion. It is an abuse of power. It can be planned and organised or may be unintentional; individuals or groups may be involved.'

Notice that the definition deals with behaviour and consequences for the students who are victimised. It makes it clear that bullying is 'an abuse of power' and that it can be intentional or unintentional. To expand on this, the Xavier School Policy goes on to give illustrations. The full version is given on pages 136 to 138.

3   The rights of children

Because the primary purpose of an anti-bullying policy is to protect vulnerable people, especially children, from being bullied or harassed, a statement of the rights of children on this matter should be prominent. The James Busby High School in New South Wales in its Anti-Harassment Policy in 1993 (in citing Brandeis, the American judge) put the matter strongly:

> 'The right to be let alone is the most comprehensive of rights and the right most valued by civilised people.'

In the school context you may properly state that students have a right to a safe environment. This implies that the school is *on the side of students* in helping to make its environment safe for children who might otherwise be endangered by the aggressive intent and actions of others. 'Safety' is to be understood as extending beyond avoidance of physical harm. It encompasses psychological harm that comes from continual verbal abuse and discrimination.

This does not, however, mean that the school must ensure that every student always feels safe (it cannot), but rather that the school recognises an obligation, derived from the rights of students, to take steps to do what it can to prevent bullying and assist students when their safety is threatened.

4   The responsibilities of students who witness bullying

This is extremely important, indeed crucial, to the success of any anti-bullying policy. Unless students, in general, feel that they themselves should (and can) take action to reduce bullying, policy statements and teacher-directed responses to bullying are unlikely to have much effect. However, in asserting that students who witness bullying have a responsibility to act in some way, we should be aware of the situation from the student's point of view.

Some students will not feel that they have such a responsibility. They may wish not to be involved. They may say: 'It is none of my business.' Some may actually feel loyalty and respect for the bully and despise the victim. Some may sense the injustice, but be afraid to do anything, even to show displeasure at what is happening. Some may not care and feel 'glad it's not me'. They may feel responsible only for their own safety.

If you do assert that students have a responsibility to act, for example by informing teachers, then two considerations must follow. The first is that the school must seek to develop in students the moral judgement that bullying ought to be stopped. This is not self-evident to some students. This is a matter of moral education for the school. Secondly, the school must recognise that it may be putting demands on some students that may make the school *less* safe for them as individuals. The school must undertake to make it easier for students to discharge their 'responsibility'. We will return to this point.

5   What the school will do to counter bullying

This will depend upon what the school has decided are the best and most acceptable means at its disposal. Much of the remainder of this book is devoted to exploring methods of prevention and intervention, some of which will be more attractive to some schools than others. The Policy Document is generally not the place to spell out details. However, the specific methods to be used may well affect the generalisations that *can* appear in the document. Therefore, in formulating policy, it is extremely useful to know what the alternative practices are and to have evaluated them carefully.

There are some things that all schools who have thought about the bullying problem will, I think, readily agree upon.

The first is that staff in the school must be open to talk with students who seek help on any problems that may arise through peer-bullying. This is a more radical statement than it might first seem. It has been common-place for staff in some schools to actively discourage students from talking about such things, either because they despise students who would wish to do so, or because they would rather not be bothered. A statement of openness and acceptance of the legitimacy of talking about being personally bullied or having observed bullying can be an important step.

Equally important, parents are to be encouraged to discuss matters of suspected bullying at school with staff. This, too, has rarely been made explicit. Sometimes schools have, in practice, sought to deter parents from raising such a question. Parents need to be reassured that *it is acceptable to talk about bullying*, and that the school will listen.

Given traditional attitudes, some teachers may be alarmed at the prospect of students and parents speaking with them on these matters, and it must be conceded that it is not always easy—complications and dilemmas do arise. We will return to the question of how such interviews might be conducted later.

6   Undertaking to evaluate policy

Although the immediate concern may be to get things moving, there are good reasons why a policy document should include a promise to review and evaluate policy in the not-so-distant future. We might say after a year. Countering bullying is not easy, and it would be surprising if a school got it completely right first time. What seemed likely to succeed may have run into unanticipated difficulties, and no longer seem useful. New ideas are continually emerging in this area—what appeared radical and odd in one year (and not acceptable) may be seen as an excellent idea later.

Other considerations

The process by which the policy has been developed can be as important as the content. Consultation with interested groups, though often time-consuming and sometimes frustrating, is needed if the policy is going to be broadly supported and effectively implemented. Remember that the document must be acceptable to students and to parents as well as staff. Remember that within any staff there are diverse elements and interests that may need to be reconciled. Remember that there are likely to be other policies and programs that are relevant to a policy on bullying. The new policy must articulate with, or replace, the old.

The style of the document is important. Make sure that it is not pompous or full of politically correct jargon. The language should be simple and clear, readily understandable by children as well as parents and teachers. Versions may need to be written in community languages for people of non-English speaking background. Once finalised, the policy should be disseminated widely by means of booklets, newsletters, posters, notice-boards, parent meetings, by whatever means can reach the entire school community.

An example of an anti-bullying policy

Xavier College in Melbourne began to develop a school policy on bullying in schools in 1994. They began by discussing the issue with staff members, students, ex-students and parents. They were encouraged to find out more about what was happening in the school by carrying out a survey. They agreed to administer the *Peer Relations Questionnaire* (PRQ) to all students in the school. Subsequently the results were analysed at the University of South Australia and a report provided for the school. Following this, a working party was formed to develop a draft policy against bullying. This was revised in the light of feedback from the College Community to produce the following document which has since been widely disseminated.

A policy against bullying

Xavier College does not tolerate bullying in any form. All members of the College Community are committed to ensuring a safe and caring environment which promotes personal growth and positive self-esteem for all.

1   What is bullying?
Bullying is an act of aggression causing embarrassment, pain or discomfort to another:
- *it can take a number of forms: physical, verbal, gesture, extortion and exclusion*
- *it is an abuse of power*
- *it can be planned and organised or it may be unintentional*
- *individuals or groups may be involved*

2   Some examples of bullying include:
- *any form of physical violence such as hitting, pushing or spitting on others*

- *interfering with another's property by stealing, hiding, damaging or destroying it*
- *using offensive names, teasing or spreading rumours about others or their families*
- *using put-downs, belittling others' abilities and achievements*
- *writing offensive notes or graffiti about others*
- *making degrading comments about another's culture, religious or social background*
- *hurtfully excluding others from a group*
- *making suggestive comments or other forms of sexual abuse*
- *ridiculing another's appearance*
- *forcing others to act against their will*

3   If we are bullied:
- *we may feel frightened, unsafe, embarrassed, angry or unfairly treated*
- *our work, sleep and ability to concentrate may suffer*
- *our relationships with our family and friends may deteriorate*
- *we may feel confused and not know what to do about the problem*

4   What do we do to prevent bullying at Xavier College?

As a School Community we will not allow cases of bullying to go unreported but will speak up, even at risk to ourselves.

a) *This requires Staff to:*
   i) *be role models in word and action at all times*
   ii) *be observant of signs of distress or suspected incidents of bullying*
   iii) *make efforts to remove occasions for bullying by active patrolling during supervision duty*
   iv) *arrive at class on time and move promptly between lessons*
   v) *take steps to help victims and remove sources of distress without placing the victim at further risk*
   vi) *report suspected incidents to the appropriate staff member such as Homeroom/Class teacher, Year Co-ordinator, Deputy Head-master, Pastoral Care Staff, Chaplain who will follow the designated procedures*

b) *This requires Students to:*

i) *Refuse to be involved in any bullying situation. If you are present when bullying occurs:*
    (a) if appropriate, take some form of preventative action;
    (b) report the incident or suspected incident and help break down the code of secrecy.

If students who are being bullied have the courage to speak out, they may help to reduce pain for themselves and other potential victims.

c) *the College recommends that parents:*

- *watch for signs of distress in their son, e.g. unwillingness to attend school, a pattern of headaches, missing equipment, requests for extra money, damaged clothes or bruising;*
- *take an active interest in your son's social life and acquaintances;*
- *advise your son to tell a staff member about the incident. If possible allow him to report and deal with the problem himself. He can gain much respect through taking the initiative and dealing with the problem without parental involvement.*
- *inform the College if bullying is suspected;*
- *keep a written record (who, what, when, where, why, how);*
- *do not encourage your son to retaliate;*
- *communicate to your son that parental involvement, if necessary, will be appropriate for the situation;*
- *be willing to attend interviews at the College if your son is involved in any bullying incident;*
- *be willing to inform the College of any cases of suspected bullying even if your own son is not directly affected;*

When staff, students and parents work together we create a more Christian environment at Xavier College.

Reflections on policy

The policy of Xavier College has many strengths. It begins with a strong statement about the unacceptability of bullying at the school. But, wisely, it immediately puts bullying in the context of a school philosophy that is concerned with providing 'a safe and caring environment which promotes personal growth and positive self-esteem for all'. It does not begin by sounding like a witch-hunt to get the bullies. It is concerned with achieving positive goals. It then provides a thoughtful and sound definition of bullying, with plenty of illustrations of what is meant by the term. From then on we know what is being talked about. It recognises the sad effects of bullying: what happens if 'we' are bullied. Next it describes, details and emphasises the responsibilities that everybody in the school community has to act to prevent or deal with bullying when it occurs, beginning with the school staff, next the students and then parents. We see clearly that each has a part to play. Finally it places the matter in a wider context; as befits a Catholic school it calls for cooperation in the community to create a more Christian environment.

We find this emphasis upon positive goals a recurring feature in good policies to counter bullying or harassment. At Prince Alfred's College (a boys' school in Adelaide) the Anti-Harassment Policy includes a strong statement of a school philosophy that centres upon respect for others. The document asserts the value of caring for others—and three Cs that have caring as their basis, namely Courtesy, Consideration and Cooperation. Clearly acting in accordance with these values precludes bullying or harassment.

How far should a school go in detailing what to do about bullying in its policy statement? Schools differ widely in how much detail they provide about actions that can be taken and the process of dealing with cases. At Prince Alfred's College a series of steps is outlined in the Policy Document for students to follow if they are harassed, beginning with:

(i)   ignoring it, showing that it doesn't upset them;
(ii) confronting the harasser and stating that the behaviour is unwanted and unjustified;
(iii) talking it over with others, such as friends or parents who may help to make plans;
(iv) taking the matter to a class or tutor group meeting where public disapproval of the harassment may stop it;
(v)   reporting to a class teacher who may deal with it effectively;
(vi) taking the matter to a higher authority, if necessary the principal, with support from teachers or parents.

But what will the authorities actually do ? Sometimes we see in documents the dark but unclear threats: consequences will follow. Prince Alfred's College is explicit. The policy states: *The School will punish bullying.*

But not all schools are committed to resolving the problem of bullying in this way. At James Busby High School there is, as at Prince Alfred's, a complaints procedure, and at each stage it is hoped that a resolution will be achieved. However, it is made clear that the 'person accused' will be 'counselled by appropriate personnel'. Then he or she may be 'disciplined where appropriate'. Pembroke Secondary College in Mooroolbark, Victoria, has adopted a similar approach. It proposes in its Bullying Policy to begin by providing first offending bullies with the 'opportunity to modify their behaviour'. The Method of Shared Concern is employed for this purpose, as outlined by the author of the policy, the School Counsellor, Bronwyn Harcourt. If this method is not successful, traditional 'consequences' are to be employed, leading to parents being interviewed and the possible expulsion of the student. In its policy statement Xavier College, as with the other schools, urges complainants to report incidents to the school author-ities who will then follow 'designated procedures'.

What we find, then, is that while there is broad agreement on the rhetoric of policy, there can be significant differences on what schools say they will actually do. In some cases schools are either unsure, not in full agreement, or think it wise to keep the detail to themselves. But it may indeed be sensible sometimes for a school not to 'show its hand' entirely in its policy statement, to allow itself some flexibility in how it deals with some aspects of bullying. But we would hope that it does not refrain from doing so because it does not know what to do.

Chapter

Gaining
student
support

An anti-bullying policy will not be very effective without the positive support
of students themselves. From a staff point of view this may require the
mobilisation of student support for the policy, which must become essentially
'theirs'. Teachers have a special responsibility to do what they can—unaided
by students if necessary. But the chief benefactors of an improvement in peer
relations through a reduction in bullying are the students themselves. The
greater the degree of positive student involvement, the more achievable is
the goal.

From a practical viewpoint, bullying behaviour is difficult to reduce if it
is continually being reinforced by the approval of a significant number of
students. As we have argued, changing the school ethos from one in which
there is widespread admiration for dominating and aggressive behaviour to
one of concern and compassion for victims of school bullying is needed if an

anti-bullying policy in a school is to succeed. Students are often far more influenced by other students than by teachers in their social behaviour; indeed, as authority figures teachers not uncommonly have a counter-productive effect when they seek to influence student behaviour directly. As we shall see, the nature and quality of peer relations in schools may be quite dramatically affected by positive actions by a handful of students who know what they are doing.

What can you expect of students?

I have already provided in this book a detailed examination of student attitudes towards victims and bullies (see Chapter 5). We recorded there how students responded to questions about bullying at school. From this it was clear that students differ widely among themselves in their acceptance or tolerance of bullying in the school community. Some openly admire it; some are appalled by it; some are indifferent. On the whole, however, our conclusions were positive and encouraging. Most students do feel that victims should be supported, and that bullying should be opposed. But will the students act? Do they want to get involved in countering bullying at school? Survey results are again instructive on these questions.

Student views on becoming involved

On the whole, students do accept some responsibility for trying to stop bullying at school. They mostly (about 80 per cent) think that both teachers and students should be concerned about bullying. About two out of three students agree that students should help to stop bullying. Less than half, however, say that they normally do try to stop it. Consequently, we have the familiar gap between what people believe they ought to do and what they do in practice. There are reasons for this: a feeling that others could intervene more effectively, as well as prudence and fear, and—we suspect—sheer inertia. But the important thing we have gained from these enquiries, based as they are on replies from over 8500 students (see the PRQ Manual for further details) is that most students recognise an obligation, a responsibility to help to stop bullying, and we can build on this.

When it was asked whether 'teachers and students should work together to stop it (bullying)', a majority agreed: 58 per cent of boys and 64 per cent of girls. We were, of course, in the world of what is 'socially desirable': what ought to be the case. Then came the crunch. When they were asked whether each would personally be interested in talking about the problem with other students, the percentages fell to 30 per cent for boys and 38 per cent for girls. There was, in fact, no tendency for those who were being victimised more than others to be more (or less) in favour of group discussions.

Therefore while two out of three students believed that students should help to stop bullying, only one in three was evidently prepared to talk with other students about how this could be done.

As you might expect, the proportions of students who wanted to talk changed with age—as the following figure shows:

Figure 9.1 Percentages of students interested in talking about the problem of bullying at school with other students according to age

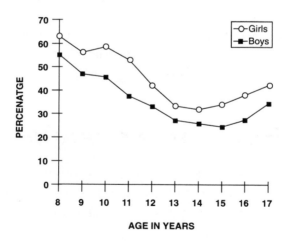

What is striking is that the numbers of students who are positive about talking about bullying dwindles up to the age of fourteen or fifteen years; then it begins to increase. Girls, we should add, always outnumber boys in their readiness to talk; age trends are similar, except that the increase in interest around mid-teens begins somewhat earlier for girls

The generalisations that have been presented are based upon a large number of schools from different parts of Australia. They should not blind us to the fact that there are quite large differences between schools. If we take, for instance, that age-group when there is greatest reluctance to engage in group discussions about bullying (the thirteen to fourteen-year-old), we find that the percentages have ranged from 14 per cent to 37 per cent among boys; and from 23 per cent to 41 per cent among girls. Schools do make a difference. We should also bear in mind that many students are 'on the fence' about this issue. There is something to build upon in all schools, although it will certainly be tougher to do so in some.

To summarise:

1 Although most students do feel that they should help to stop bullying (and work with teachers to do so) there is a reluctance among many students, including those who are victimised a good deal, to bring the issue out into the open and to discuss what can be done to stop it.

2 You can generally count more on a readiness to discuss the issue with younger students in primary school and older students (over the age of fifteen) in secondary schools. Young adolescents constitute a greater challenge.

3 Schools differ widely in the extent to which students are prepared to discuss the question of bullying in a group. Nevertheless, there is something to build upon in all schools.

How can we begin?

If we want students in a class to talk constructively about bullying at school, it is often necessary to plan carefully—and be prepared to abandon or modify the plan if necessary. But let us begin in a cautionary manner with *what not to do:*

1

Don't begin with an indignant tirade in which students are being blamed (directly or indirectly) for bullying others.

This will immediately antagonise the bullies and their supporters and produce a highly charged atmosphere in which victims are cowed and thoughtful discussion is impossible.

2

Don't begin with a description of a bullying incident which has happened at school and then identify the victim(s) and bully or bullies, and ask the class for support.

This will antagonise some, frighten others and polarise the group.

3

Don't raise the matter of bullying if the class is very unsettled or being silly.

Choosing the right time is not easy; but there are times when the question of bullying will not be considered seriously and a constructive outcome will be unlikely.

4

Avoid extremes in the way the subject is introduced.

Don't treat it flippantly, almost as a joke (there may be some encouragement to do so); don't make a really big thing of it either. Let the class determine how important it is for them—with your guidance.

Timing is important. If there has recently been a serious incident of bullying in the school, involving and perhaps dividing class members as to its justifiability or the justice of the response by the school, the time may not be ripe. Unless the teacher is confident that she or he can get students to discuss the issue in a constructive manner (and this will depend very much on the teacher's relationship with the class) it is better to wait for a more opportune time, when the students are less emotional or less confrontational. On the other hand, if a bullying incident has occurred about which the students want to talk, and there is already a strong feeling of disapproval of the bullying and concern about the person victimised, then the teacher may rightly decide that the issue can be openly discussed.

Normally the question of school bullying will be introduced at a time when it is not a burning issue for most students, but it will be for a few. The problem is how to raise the awareness and concern of the bulk of the class without upsetting those children who are often victimised. It is well to bear in mind that most of the students are likely *not* to have been involved directly in serious/bully victim problems. Most of them will have been by-standers, and their active support is especially valuable.

Alternative methods

Different teachers will have their preferred ways based, in part, on their experience with the class. Here are some possibilities.

i   Introducing 'bullying' as a social problem' in the context of other similar problems that are now being discussed in the community

This may set the scene for a relatively objective discussion. But examples will be needed. Provide case study material or examples that can be invented to illustrate what you mean by bullying. Seek student opinion on such questions as these:

Why does bullying happen?

What effects does it have on people?

What sorts of things do bullies do?

What can students who are bullied do about it?

How can bullying be stopped?

As far as possible, a neutral opinion-gathering approach is needed, without personally blaming anyone or attacking particular viewpoints. Because a range of opinions is almost certain to be found within the group, it should be possible to elicit positive and constructive suggestions rather than make them up yourself.

It is important to bring the discussion to a constructive end if at all possible. This may take the form of general agreement on certain proposals or principles. An example of the kind of thing that can emerge from classroom discussions has been provided by the Swedish psychologist, Dan Olweus, through his work with Scandinavian children. He has suggested that these rules may be formulated and agreed to by the class.

• We shall not bully other children

• We shall try to help students who are bullied

• We shall make a point of including children who are easily left out

The teacher's role here is emphatically not to *propose* rules. It is much better if they arise, seemingly spontaneously, out of the class discussion—with teacher encouragement.

In Australia students can respond in a similar way, as was shown at the Mount Barker South Primary School in South Australia. *They* addressed the question of why harassment is wrong, and gave their answer:

WHY IS HARASSMENT WRONG?

NO-ONE WINS

It is unfair and upsets people

Makes people feel bad, scared or angry

It teaches people to harass

Makes people hate each other

People don't trust each other

They also provide a belief statement, which is given below:

We believe that harassment is wrong and shouldn't happen

We believe that we must try to stop harassment

We believe that we should have the right to learn in a safe environment

We believe that we should be able to play and mix freely with other students in a friendly way

We believe that students have the right to walk to and from school safely

BELIEF STATEMENT

1. We believe that harassment is wrong and shouldn't happen.
2. We believe that we must try to stop harassment.
3. We believe that we should have the right to learn in a safe environment.

4. We believe that we should be able to play and mix freely with other students in a friendly way.

5. We believe that students have the right to walk to and from school safely.

ii   The use of videos and plays

If the subject matter is appropriate, this can have the desirable effect of enabling the students to become emotionally involved in the question of bullying without the teacher having to appear as a 'bleeding heart'. The teacher can then promote reasoned discussion.

A particularly effective educational video is one produced in Britain called *Only Playing, Miss!* (Neti-Neti Theatre Company, 1990). It runs for sixty minutes and is an engrossing and powerful examination of a bully/victim problem in an English Comprehensive School. The video is particularly popular with secondary students. It focuses upon a boy who is being bullied by another boy and his supporter or 'hanger-on'. It explores some of the reasons for the bullying, the reactions of other students, some positive and some negative, and the roles played by teachers in helping, or not helping, the situation.

Sometimes it is possible to bring live theatre to the school. The Neti-Neti Company in Britain which made *Only Playing, Miss!* began their work by visiting schools and performing their play. In Australia, a play called *The Demolition Job* by Graham Gordon, an Australian author, has also been performed in schools, as well as publicly. It examines the longer term consequences of a student being continually bullied at school. It centres upon a chance reunion of victim and bullies years after they had all left school at a demolition site—and there the wounds, which had never properly healed, are re-opened. Another Australian play of considerable relevance to bullying in schools is *Sticks and Stones* by Paul Johnson (see Resources on Bullying). This, too, has been performed in many schools in different states in Australia. It deals with issues of harassment, violence and conflict resolution in the life of a young boy who is being made miserable by another boy at school. A live performance can have great impact, especially if students can discuss the play with the actors afterwards.

iii Role playing of bullying situations

This method can be very powerful but of course it requires a readiness and capacity on the part of the teacher to initiate it. This is often more within the province of drama teachers and can be done more easily, as a rule, with younger students. The teachers must shape the role-playing so that the story line is positive, that is, supportive of victims. Successful role-play can create an unusual degree of involvement as students put something from their own lives into it and will increasingly volunteer information about what is happening in their school. Subsequent discussions can be very revealing and provide an ideal occasion for a constructive examination of the problem.

iv Essay writing

As described earlier, one approach suggested by Anatol Pikas is that students be asked to write an essay about conflict between students at school as a preliminary step towards an examination of the issue in class. This can be part of the requirement of an English lesson and some guidance is needed for students doing the exercise. It is stressed that what is required is an 'eye-witness' account of conflict between students that the essay-writer has actually observed at school. This is not to be a fictional or fantasised account. Secondly, it is explained that the essays will be discussed in class afterwards, but that if anyone wishes his or her work not to be made public, that is acceptable. This is a necessary precaution because some incidents might not be recorded if they are seen as likely to get some students into trouble with other students in the class. This method depends upon there being a trusting relationship between teacher and students. The essays can subsequently be used to promote discussion about bullying.

First, the essays can be read out in class and used to raise awareness of the kinds of conflict that are occurring in the school. This can be done by the students themselves. This is so much better than relying upon an incomplete and less credible account provided by a teacher. And they give the teacher something to build upon for the next stage of the method.

How the discussion is to be developed will depend upon what the students have written and the style of interaction favoured by the teacher. But here are some ideas suggested by Pikas:

1 Help the students to make a distinction between conflict as it occurs between students of equal strength or power and the sort of aggressive behaviour which is really an abuse of power, that is, when the target of the aggression is unable to resist.

2 Focus upon this latter category, bullying. Sooner or later, the question will be raised as to what can be done about it—and discussion can begin.

3 Because some students (the more introverted and quiet) will not be able to participate easily in the discussion and will not be heard, especially if the discussion is heated, the students can be asked to write down what they think might be a way of solving the problem of bullying.

4 The 'solutions' can next be summarised on a white-board for the students to see. Then they can be categorised according to the favoured approach. These are likely to include exhorting the victim to stand up to the bully, getting help from teachers or other authorities, and having other students participating in resolving the conflict. The pros and cons of these approaches can be explored with the students.

This approach takes us further than 'awareness raising' and, according to Pikas, can result in students being trained (importantly at their request) in methods of peer mediation and conciliation. We will take up this theme again at a later stage.

v Students as researchers

In some classes it may be possible to encourage students to research the issue of school bullying, using interviews and questionnaires with other students and teachers. The attraction of this approach is that not only can it develop student skills in social research and questionnaire design, but it also provides a source of information about the phenomena that those involved in the research are unlikely to dispute. It may also act as a strong motivator for students to examine means of taking action to reduce bullying.

What can be achieved?

What can you hope to achieve from the class meetings? The first consideration is to avoid a negative outcome. This can easily occur if the students feel they are being accused of bullying or blamed for not having intervened. Our first concern is not to make matters worse.

In general terms, we would hope to have strengthened the tendency for students to behave in such a way that bullying is actually discouraged and the children who are victimised to be more effectively supported. We would hope to have made some impact on the school ethos so that the implementation of the School Policy on Bullying can become a more realisable goal.

We can list desired behavioural changes in a hierarchy according to the degree to which students have been positively influenced:

1 When bullying occurs:
   (a) fewer children will join in, for example by offering to 'hold' the victim; acting to prevent him/her from escaping; making suggestions about what can be done to the victim; or volunteering to act as a 'look-out';
   (b) fewer children will smile or show approval;
   (c) fewer students will promote the status of the bully or victim by writing graffiti about either of them or spreading stories or malicious gossip;
   (d) more children will be prepared to express dislike of what is going on;
   (e) more students will volunteer information about what has happened rather than keep it to themselves.
2 More children will include those students who are commonly victimised in their play activities.
3 More students will make constructive suggestions about how peer relations can be improved so that bullying can be reduced.

4   Students will undertake to receive special training in methods of peer mediation and conciliation to resolve conflict between fellow students.

Educating about bullying through the curriculum

In advocating the use of the curriculum to counter bullying, we are making several assumptions, which should be carefully examined before we go any further.

1   Bullying is not simply an issue of 'behaviour management', that is the prevention and control of an inappropriate behaviour to which schools object. It is that, in part, but it is much more than that.

2   Bullying is a central issue for the community at large. Essentially bullying is the abuse of power. The success of schools in countering the all-pervasive tendency for the powerful to oppress the weak can have far-reaching consequences for the quality of life not only at school, but also in the home and at work—for everyone.

3   Schools can make a significant impact on the problem by systematically promoting moral values and social sensitivity, both in the content of what is taught and the manner in which learning is encouraged.

What can be done in lessons

Let us be clear about one thing. It is not proposed that lessons be given over regularly to the topic of bullying. 'Not bullying again', we might hear the students groan. It must be more subtle than that. It is proposed that knowledge and ideas that help children to understand bullying better and be motivated to help deal with it be continually explored—where and when the context permits

Concepts that help us to understand bullying are these: 'power'; 'oppression'; 'violence'; and 'prejudice'. They are pertinent to many questions and issues in history, literature, and social and contemporary studies.

Take History: it is filled with examples of how groups of people used their superior power to oppress, exploit and sometimes enslave others—the ultimate form of bullying. We can see it at work in the history of ancient civilisations, among the people who occupied the Greek islands where much of our civilisation began. We can trace the rise and fall of many diverse groups who conquered, oppressed and at times enslaved their predecessors; among these were the Minoans, the Myceneans, the Macedonians and the Romans; and in more modern times, the Franks, the Ottomans and the Germans under Hitler. We see this form of inter-group bullying at work today in Bosnia and Rwanda in the policy and practice of 'ethnic cleansing'. Nearer home, relations between white settlers and Aboriginal people have been marred by dispossession and oppression on the part of the colonists. What, the teacher can ask, made it possible for such things to happen. How did the oppressors gain their power? Why did they use it as they did?

History also contains innumerable examples of individuals who achieved enormous power only to abuse it by persecuting and torturing others, from the ancient Roman emperors like Nero to modern dictators such as Hitler, Stalin and Idi Amin. Why is it, we might ask, that the powerful so often abuse their power by oppressing others. Is it true, as Lord Acton proposed, that 'Power corrupts and absolute power corrupts absolutely'?

Tyrants, it might be pointed out, are not only mighty public figures. They occur frequently in literature, as they do in everyday life. Novels like *Lord of the Flies* by William Golding and *Tom Brown's Schooldays* by Thomas Hughes have the capacity to raise the basic questions of the nature of power and its abuse in the lives of young people themselves.

Ideas that are most pertinent to bullying can be discussed with children in classes dealing with contemporary social issues, drawing upon reports from the printed and electronic media. This approach has been pursued recently by Christine Forsey (1994) in a thoughtfully considered and well-presented publication for use in schools called *Hands Off*. The focus here is on violence and prejudice. A similar contribution has been made by Jean Jenkin (1996) from the University of Western Sydney. Her work is directed towards secondary students and examines ways in which problems of violence can be resolved through education.

As part of a program of raising awareness and developing understanding of such issues, students can be asked to collect examples from media reports that highlight perceptions and attitudes of people that will be of interest to the class. Some may be taken to show how violence and aggression are often encouraged in our society through the glorification of sportsmen and women who dominate others by fair means or foul. Australian political life can also provide a rich source of comment that a class can discuss. Recently (August

1995) it was reported that the ex-premier of New South Wales, Mr. Fahey, had given the Federal Opposition leader, Mr Howard, then beset with problems of in-fighting in his party, a piece of advice that he could use when he became Prime Minister: 'Be a bully'.

Moral values and bullying

If we are to counter bullying in all its public as well as private manifestations, schools need to promote moral values and modes of moral reasoning that are incompatible with oppressing others. But we must be careful. Too much preaching and laying down the law about right values and actions can be counterproductive. Moral values tend to be 'caught' from others with whom we habitually interact and feel respect, rather than 'taken in' from authority figures who hand them down. Teachers can have a role in facilitating this good contagion. How can this be done ?

The philosopher-psychologist, Kohlberg (1984) identified various stages of moral reasoning which he believed held true for many different societies, and they are highly pertinent to bullying. These stages are discussed in Phillip Slee's (1993) useful Australian text on *Child, Adolescent and Family Development*. First, there are low or immature levels of moral reasoning that are concerned only with the physical consequences of an act or whether it satisfies your personal needs; then somewhat higher levels at which an action is seen as justified if it produces approval from others or is consistent with the norms or legal requirements of your group; and a higher level still, at which you are motivated to act by ideas of justice, regardless of whether other people like you or reward you for what you have done.

Kohlberg argued that, under favourable conditions, as they get older children normally employ increasingly higher levels of moral reasoning. How can a teacher help to provide these favourable conditions? One way is seek to engender a secure environment in which children feel free to speak their mind. Children can then be helped to think about moral dilemmas to which people are often exposed, such as whether to intervene in situations in which an innocent victim is being oppressed by a person who is also your friend, or by a group to which you belong. By hearing the expressions of different opinions in an environment in which everyone's view is respected, there are good grounds for believing that the level of moral reasoning of individual children will indeed rise.

Education of feelings

While changes in thought and behaviour can be engendered through an increase in knowledge and an improvement in reasoning, changes in values can also come about through improving the sensitivity of children to others. This can be done within the school curriculum through repeated exposure to cultural products that evoke sympathy for a wide range of people and animals. The collection and selection of such resources in the form of novels, plays, poems, videos and films is an important part of a strategy that can discourage bullying. This work has become increasingly necessary to counteract the effects of many violent videos which are available in many homes. These blunt sensitivity and by presenting violence in an attractive light may increase the appetite for more and more violence in real life.

Promoting cooperativeness

It is almost a platitude that the more cooperative children are in their relations with others the less bullying there will be. This has led some people to suggest that steps can be taken to deliberately increase the extent to which children engage in cooperative behaviour in their work and other school activities and that this will have a positive spin-off in reducing school bullying.

But first what is cooperativeness? Following Argyle (1991) it can be defined as follows:

'acting together, in a coordinated way, at work, leisure, or in a social relationship, in pursuit of shared goals, the enjoyment of the joint activity, or simply furthering the relationship'

A recent survey of children's attitudes towards cooperating with others in a large coeducational school in Adelaide provides an estimate of how students (N=750) from years 8 to 11 felt about cooperation (Rigby and Cox, 1994). Results for selected items from a 21 item scale are given below.

Table 9.1   **Attitudes towards cooperation among high school students**

| | | Student responses: | | |
		Agree	Uncertain	Disagree
Team work is the	Boys	56	32	12
best way to get results	Girls	57	34	9
I like to cooperate with	Boys	80	12	8
others on projects	Girls	89	9	3
Friends ought to be concerned	Boys	76	19	5
about each other's wishes	Girls	88	11	1
Friends usually can't agree	Boys	18	34	49
	Girls	12	28	60
Committees are a waste of time	Boys	20	34	46
	Girls	8	27	65
I prefer not to share my	Boys	16	18	66
ideas with others	Girls	8	21	71

Although most of the students appeared to have cooperative attitudes, on some items almost half were either unsure or negative about the value of cooperation; for example, many felt that committee meetings were a waste of time and that friends usually can't agree. The more negative responses tended to come from boys! These results show that the student body is by no means of one mind on the matter of being cooperative, and that there is a lot of room for change in developing more cooperative beliefs and attitudes among adolescent students.

Teacher perceptions of student cooperativeness

We have just seen that although students, by and large, see themselves as cooperative in their behaviour with others, substantial numbers do not. If we examine teacher perceptions, as did Johnson, Oswald and Adey (1993), we find that discipline problems at school seem to centre very much upon students acting in ways that are *not* cooperative. In their survey of discipline problems, as reported by 777 teachers in South Australian primary schools, Johnson et al. found that in class the major discipline problem was 'hindering other pupils': the exact antithesis of cooperation. Over 35 per cent of the teachers reported that this was happening on a daily or almost daily basis. Around the school the main problem was seen as 'lack of concern for others' encountered at least once a week by over 95 per cent of teachers. These results show very clearly that, according to teachers, uncooperativeness of schoolchildren with one another is indeed a major problem in Australian primary schools.

Lack of cooperativeness of bullies and victims

The survey conducted by Rigby and Cox (1994) also included self-report measures of engaging in bullying behaviour and being victimised by peers. As you might suspect, those identified as 'bullies' were significantly less cooperative in their attitudes than average; so, too, were 'victims'. The reasons for bullies and victims being relatively uncooperative are different. For bullies, it appears that their uncooperativeness is often a consequence of low degrees of empathy and a generalised hostility towards others; among victims it seems more likely to be a consequence of lower levels of sociability (victims are usually more introverted than average) and their non-acceptance by others.

Why are children not more cooperative?

The advantages of cooperation seem so obvious. The survey showed further that the more cooperative children were generally happier and more popular. Before suggesting remedies for uncooperativeness, it is as well to ask ourselves why some students tend not to want to cooperate with others. These are some of the reasons:

1   Cooperating with others has not been rewarding in the past;
2   Cooperative behaviour has not been encouraged or modelled by the people they have been with;
3   They lack the necessary skills to cooperate with others;
4   Others will not let them cooperate;
5   They prefer to be alone.

Now the last of these reasons cannot be discounted. It is not fashionable to prefer solitude to social engagement and interaction with others. Nevertheless, there are individuals who often like to be alone, to work on their own and to have minimal interaction with others. But they are rare and account for a very small proportion of those who do not wish to cooperate. For the most part, the reasons for low levels of cooperation on the part of some schoolchildren are the first four given above.

Much of the problem of uncooperativeness stems from the home background of students. We have already seen that dysfunctional families, in which cooperation and communication between members is poor, are much more likely than others to have children who bully others. In such homes cooperative behaviour is little valued or encouraged. The norm of reciprocity which is understood and operates in most families has not been set, or is seen as having limited application, perhaps operating between close friends but not between people generally. A suspicious attitude towards others, especially strangers, is likely to develop. Such a child may be generally distrustful of the intentions of others, believing that no one would wish to be cooperative without some ulterior and possibly sinister motive. To help such children you must face the fact that uncooperativeness may have a long history of development and cannot be undone overnight.

Sometimes individuals simply lack skills to be able to cooperate with others. Here we should distinguish between generalised social skills, the lack of which would prevent you from interacting successfully with most people, and a lack of particular skills which would prevent you from gaining acceptance by groups of people who have themselves developed the necessary relevant skills. We may think here of participating in dancing, drama, chess and football, for which technical knowledge and skill are obviously needed.

When children cannot cooperate because they are not being allowed to do so you must again distinguish between:

(a) situations in which a change in behaviour or the acquisition of new skills is needed on the part of the child who is being prevented from joining; and

(b) situations in which the child is the victim of prejudice and discrimination that simply cannot be tolerated.

Increasing cooperativeness

It is clear from the above analysis that children may be relatively uncooperative for different reasons, and these may call for different strategies. Generally, however, the school can increase cooperativeness to the degree to which it is able to provide experiences in which cooperative behaviour is rewarded.

Direct reward in the form of praise from a teacher for behaving cooperatively with others is likely to be more effective with younger children, but even here it must be provided subtly; otherwise it is apt to be seen as gratuitous and perhaps manipulative. Of greater importance is the arranging of situations in which students work together on a problem—the solution of which benefits all the members. The teacher's role is largely to create a cooperative context.

How this can be done has been explored by a number of educationalists and psychologists, among whom two brothers, David and Roger Johnson at the University of Minnesota in Minneapolis, have been the most influential over the last two decades. They reason that:

> 'For cooperation to exist there must be mutual goals that all parties are committed to achieving. I am not successful unless you are successful. The more successful you are, the more I benefit and the more successful I am. In a cooperative situation students work together to accomplish shared goals. Students seek outcomes that are beneficial to everyone involved. They are committed to each other's, as well as their own, well-being and success.'

Johnson and Johnson (1991) 2:3.

Creating a cooperative classroom is clearly an art that needs to be developed and can never be free of difficulties. It can involve not only the assigning of students to groups in which they can work together on problems in an environment that is conducive to productive interaction, but also the devising of questions that lend themselves to group-problem-solving methods. Materials may need to be provided that need to be shared and information exchanged. One useful technique is known as 'jigsaw classroom'. Material needed for the completion of a task is subdivided into units so that individuals need to share their part of the solution with others to solve a problem. The pre-existing differences between children may be forgotten in their absorption in a common task and finally overcome in their celebration of a joint success.

Another approach to developing cooperation between students is through group-problem-solving, employing a method known as Quality Circles. Originating as a means of developing ideas to promote efficiency in business and industry, it has been adapted for use in some schools. Typically the process has these features:

- Forming a group to solve a problem
- Brainstorming to elicit possible solutions
- Investigating the problem through gathering relevant data
- Identifying causes
- Suggesting solutions
- Presenting the solutions for appraisal—to the Management
- Monitoring and evaluating the outcome

The 'Management' in this case would consist of the principal and other staff; possibly also senior students and parents. Once an outcome has been reached and evaluated, it may be that the problem will be revisited, perhaps by another group, who will seek new and better solutions or improvements.

The Quality Circles approach has many strengths. It enables individuals in a group to take part in a cooperative problem-solving exercise that can have a real and valued social outcome. It provides the opportunity for students to develop qualities of imagination, creativity, logical thought and inference, the ability to present conclusions in a persuasive way and, above all, the capacity to work in a team. But, of course, much depends on the leadership, the setting of realistic goals and a careful monitoring of the process.

Although there have been some striking demonstrations of the success of co-operative learning strategies in improving both academic skills and improved interpersonal relations, sometimes between children of different races, the difficulties in overcoming bully/victim problems, in particular, by this method should not be underestimated. In one recent study in England the impact of cooperative group work on social relationships in middle schools was examined over a two-year period (Cowie et al., 1994). Although some children who had previously been victimised by peers were more accepted in their class after cooperative learning had been introduced, overall the extent of bully/victim problems in the school was, unfortunately, no lower than that found in the control group which had received no training at all in cooperative learning. The authors suggest that the failure of the intervention may have been due to a number of factors, including the reluctance showed by some of the teachers in 'letting go' or 'sharing power' with their pupils. There was, they report, an anxiety on the part of some teachers about 'lifting the lid for fear of what might happen to school discipline'. In addition, they report that some classes contained very 'difficult' children with whom teachers found it difficult to cope. From this it seems likely that successfully reducing bullying through cooperative learning is by no means assured. The approach needs considerable dedication and commitment—and probably needs to be started with younger students.

Social skills training

The capacity to interact with others in such a way as to produce the desired effect is one way of describing social skills. There are clearly many difficulties that arise in everyday life when children are having to interact with others and either don't know what to do, or are unable to do what is needed, in order to satisfy their personal goals. It is often proposed that training in social skills can be very helpful

The components of social skills, as first proposed by Argyle (1983) include perceiving a situation accurately (and especially the intentions of others); making an appropriate plan on how to respond; carrying out the planned action; noting its effects on the other person(s); then modifying your subsequent perceptions, plans and actions accordingly. The development of the capacity to do this is uneven: some children acquire good social skills early; some later, some never. The question is how can these skills be developed to a higher degree in more children so as to reduce the incidence of bullying?

One suggestion is that the whole class be instructed so that they will be able to give more appropriate responses in a variety of social situations. This can be done by a teacher modelling certain appropriate ways of acting or reacting in social situations, such as being introduced to someone or engaging in conversation; next, asking the child to practise the skill, perhaps in a role play and then providing constructive feedback about the performance. It is assumed that skills developed in this way will generalise to real life situations. A greater level of social confidence is expected to result enabling the child to be able to handle situations that may have previously caused problems, including being threatened by a bully.

As with cooperative learning, again there have been some reports of success with the method in increasing the social competence of schoolchildren. And again, the path has not always been rosy. For example, a recent application of social skills training in Sydney with kindergarten children failed to produce any significant changes in assessed social competence (Brown and Richardson, 1994). These authors concluded that social skills training can be better employed by targeting children who have specific needs. How does this apply to bullying?

I think it requires us first to make an analysis of how social skills training may apply to children who are involved in the problem. If we turn first to 'bullies' we find that in many cases their behaviour cannot be traced to inadequate social skills. It is true that some bullies do misperceive situations and attribute malicious intent to others, and some use force to get their way when there are easier socially skilful ways of achieving the same goal. In these cases, social skills training can be useful. But many bullies simply prefer to use the bullying skills they have developed because they are pleased with the effects they are producing.

We have evidence from some studies, including studies conducted in Australia, that bullies are not notably different from others in the numbers of friends they claim; nor, according to recent American research, are they more peripheral than others in the subgroups or cliques to which they belong (Cairns and Cairns, 1995). For some forms of bullying the bullies may be *more* socially skilled than others. In a Finnish study, the social intelligence of children who bullied others indirectly (a common method with girls) was judged to be higher by peers than that of other children (Kaukiainen et al., 1995).

Social skills training should not be regarded as a panacea for the treatment of anti-social children, such as bullies; yet in some schools it has been common practice to refer 'difficult children' for social skills training. The inadvisability of this procedure has been confirmed by a recent study conducted in schools in New South Wales. It was found that students who had been identified by teachers as anti-social in their behaviour and therefore candidates for social skills training possessed at least average social skills. As indicated by the accuracy of their perceptions of social situations and their capacity to make friends, they were no different from other students in the class (Snow, 1992).

In some areas, however, social skills training can be valuable in addressing bully/victim problems. We can identify two areas. First, social skills training can be used to help children who are persistently being victimised by their peers primarily because they lack the capacity to act assertively (how this can be taught is examined in detail in Chapter 14). Secondly, social skills training can be useful for some children who find it difficult to gain acceptance by their peers. Being 'outsiders' they are isolated and often vulnerable to bullying. Sometimes (not always) their difficulties may stem from a lack of appropriate social skill. They may simply not know how to join in with groups in an acceptable way.

One approach to help children to join in and interact more effectively with others is through the Stop Think Do program pioneered successfully in Australia by Linda Peterson (1994). In this program children are encouraged to consider the traffic light symbols: to STOP (on red) to clarify a problem, identify feelings and consider goals; THINK (on yellow) to consider solutions, evaluate consequences and DO (on green) to choose a plan of action and act! Thinking may very well lead to cooperation as we see in the following illustration.

As we look at the way in which the two donkeys solved their problem (see p. 164), it becomes evident that cooperation may be impossible without the exercise of social skills and that such skills may have a vital cognitive component. But we should not forget that to make a positive contribution in a school social skills must be linked to the promotion of agreed values. Social skills may be used to hurt other people. They are the means by which positive and negative goals can be reached, not ends in themselves.

We have concentrated in this section on the help that may be provided for individual children who lack relevant social skills. We must lastly note that for some purposes a high level of social skilfulness is essential. So, social skills training is required for students who undertake to help their peers through specialised counselling and mediation. (The social skills needs of these students will be examined further in Chapter 16.)

Helping in difficult circumstances

The kind of help that is needed when a child is being bullied by a more powerful person or group of persons is frequently not easy to give. In our school survey more than two-thirds of the students agreed that students themselves should seek to stop others from bullying; yet less than half of these students indicated that they, themselves, usually or always tried to intervene

Cooperation

From 'Cooperation' in *Creating a Peaceable School*,
R.J. Bodine, D.K. Crawford, and F. Schrumpf (1994), p 11.

when they saw it happening. Why do students so seldom help in this way? There are doubtless many reasons. But if we are serious about getting students to help stop others from bullying, we have to view the matter in its complexity and appreciate the difficulties that confront the would-be helper.

The following diagram is intended to capture some of the issues and dilemmas that confront the would-be helper when it seems that someone is being harmed by another person or persons.

Model 9.1:   To help or not to help

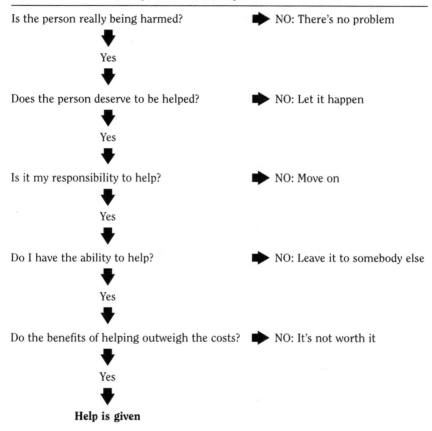

Is the person really being harmed?   NO: There's no problem

    Yes

Does the person deserve to be helped?   NO: Let it happen

    Yes

Is it my responsibility to help?   NO: Move on

    Yes

Do I have the ability to help?   NO: Leave it to somebody else

    Yes

Do the benefits of helping outweigh the costs?   NO: It's not worth it

    Yes

Help is given

The model above attempts to elucidate the many considerations that arise when people consider intervening in a situation in which bullying is taking place. They generally occur in rapid succession, so that you sometimes are not aware of why you have acted or not acted. By examining the steps in the decision-making sequence, it is possible to see how education or training could result in more realistic and helpful decisions being made about how to help. Let us now consider each step in turn and see what implications there can be for a teacher or counsellor using the model with students.

Is the person being harmed?

In some situations it is quite clear that an individual *is* being hurt and wants the aggressor to stop, and the aggressor is enjoying the situation. The hurt being suffered may be physical or psychological, often both. This is normally apparent in the expressions and reactions of both bully (or bullies) and victim. But the interpretation of what is happening may be difficult for several reasons:

(i)   The victim may deny that he or she wants any help. The victim may in fact collude with the bully in defining the situation as one in which 'we are only playing'. The victim may be embarrassed or ashamed at being in a situation in which he or she cannot cope, and wish to deny that the hurt is happening.

(ii) By contrast, the reaction of the victim may be (to the observer) out of all proportion to the apparent cause. The observer may feel that he or she would not be at all hurt or feel threatened by what is being done or said. The difficulty here is putting yourself into the shoes of the victim—with all the vulnerabilities that the observer may not have.

(iii) The 'victim' may in fact be manipulative, simulating a hurt that is not genuinely felt in order to get the 'bully' into trouble.

(iv) There may be others around watching who are doing nothing about it. This provides a strong cue that nobody is really being hurt. Unfortunately, they all may be deriving their judgements from the reactions of others.

Does the person deserve to be helped?

At first we may think it horrifying that the question is being asked. Surely we should help those in need and not consider whether a person deserves to be helped. (It is as well to remember, however, that in the New Testament parable, the Good Samaritan was really exceptional. And we are no different today.) We very often reserve our helping behaviour only for those whom we deem to be 'worthy' of our help.

A number of considerations may pass through the observer's mind:

(i)   What provocations (if any) has the victim given to be treated like that? The answer may come from a knowledge of what has actually gone on prior to the incident between the people in conflict. Or it may be based upon an appraisal of the character of the victim, who is perhaps known to have been provoking others.

(ii) The character of the bully may also provide a clue to whether the treatment is deserved. Does he or she normally seek to hurt others without justification?

(iii) If the victim belongs to an identifiable social group—being Aboriginal, Vietnamese, Australian, Disabled, Gay or Straight, etc.—you may form a judgement according to the worthiness of the group. Here prejudice may play an important part.

(iv) In the absence of the above cues, you may fall back on what you think about victims in general. For many people there is an assumption that victims generally deserve what they get. This is because it is sometimes threatening to feel that you do not live in a Just World, in which terrible things can happen to innocent people—like yourself! To maintain this view (which is somehow comforting) it is helpful to conclude that the victim you see before you really deserves what he (or she) gets.

Is it my responsibility to help?

This will depend partly on the level of moral development of the observer. Here are some ways of responding:

She has never helped me. Why should I help her?

My friends won't like me any more if I help a person like him.

This is a job for the authorities. A teacher should be here.

It is not part of my role as a student to get involved.

People should look out for themselves. It's dog eat dog in this school.

It is unfair for people to be treated like that, no matter who they are.

It would be a better school if each of us did something to stop it.

It may also depend on the range of people to whom you feel an obligation:

I will help him because he is my brother.

I owe Mary one for helping me.

I will do what I can because she is a fellow human being.

It would be useful to consider each of these responses in the light of Kohlberg's theory of moral development (see p. 154).

Do I have the ability?

The first consideration is what is needed to stop it. Appraisals of your ability may then follow. Therefore, if stopping it means using physical force, the strength and size of the observer will be a key factor. In some cases, however verbal skills may be at least as important: that is, being able to talk to the bullies persuasively. A further consideration is whether you can get help for the victim by involving other people.

Do the benefits outweigh the costs

This assumes a utilitarian kind of philosophy, and this does not always apply. Some students may act purely on impulse, from a sense of what they fiercely think is right. But many will weigh up the pros and cons.

Costs:

Being hurt by the bullies yourself

Being regarded as a 'dobber' (if you have told the teachers)

Having made powerful enemies

Time spent in getting involved

Being seen as a friend of a wimp

Benefits:

Gaining admiration from some others

Gratitude from the victim (but remember the help may be resented)

Having lived up to your values

Having helped (hopefully) towards a safer, happier school

In dealing directly with the problem of intervening to help students who are being bullied, the teacher must be prepared to examine all these considerations and more as they arise in a free and open discussion about what we can do to help. But it is important that teachers prepare themselves for the difficult questions that will certainly arise when there is an honest discussion of whether to intervene or not.

Where
it happens

In this chapter we focus upon the environment in which bullying occurs. We address the question of what can be done by the school and other agencies to make the environment a safer place for children who might otherwise be the target of peer-victimisation.

The term 'environment' is a very general term and our first task is to specify those aspects which are of particular relevance to schools. One simple distinction can be made between (a) the school premises; and (b) places through which the student must pass on the way to school and on the way home.

Of course the school is directly responsible for the safety of children on the school premises during school hours; the responsibility is less clear at other times and places.

The school's primary concern is with the former, but most, if not all schools, would recognise that they should, and often can, help in reducing bullying that goes on among children going between home and school.

Where bullying occurs

If we ask students where bullying occurs, they report that it happens in a variety of places: in the classroom; in the playground during the breaks; on the way to school, and on the way home.

The relative frequency of bullying in each of these environments is reflected in the results provided by students in our surveys when they have been asked how often (if ever) they had seen bullying between students going on in various places.

Figure 10.1   Percentages of students reporting that they had noticed bullying going on in four places

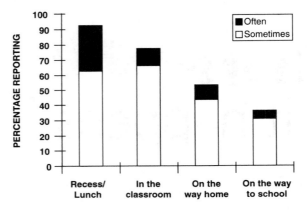

Adapted from Rigby and Slee (1995)

As you might expect, when children are at school students are more likely to report bullying as going on *outside* the classroom at recess or lunch time. It is also clear from these results that a good deal of bullying occurs to and from school, in particular on the way home from school. Let us now consider each in turn.

The classroom

We should not be surprised that, despite the fact that students spend more time at school inside the classroom than outside, the incidence of reported bullying is less in the classroom, for here students are under a much greater degree of surveillance and can also be expected to be occupied in set tasks in which they can be absorbed. If there is any surprise, it is likely to be about the large numbers of students who report that they notice bullying going on in their classrooms 'often'.

We should at this point remind ourselves that bullying can be relatively subtle, and the students reporting classroom bullying could have in mind hurtful teasing and innuendo rather than physical abuse. But even so, reported bullying may seem high, and we must ask ourselves why this could be.

A good deal of bullying goes on in classrooms when the teacher is out of the room. This may be because the teacher has arrived late or because the teacher has been called away. Anyway, children who are prone to be victimised by their peers are 'sitting ducks'. There is also a captive audience for the bullies to impress and with whom to share their amusement. But bullying can sometimes continue when the teacher is present, especially (of course) if the lesson is felt to be boring and not engaging the students' interest.

Classroom bullying can be so unobtrusive that the teacher is not aware of it. Gestures of derision directed by individuals or groups can easily occur unnoticed. There are times when some children refrain from asking a question of the teacher or giving an answer because they will be subtly ridiculed by others for having done so. Occasionally bullying may be skilfully orchestrated, as in a recent case reported to me of boys in a class all simultaneously raising their feet off the ground when a girl came in, suggesting she was unclean.

Corridors

Released from classes in which there is little scope for physical activity, crowded corridors along which students move to their next destination provide abundant opportunities for students to accidentally-on-purpose barge into, insult or generally upset the ones they may wish to bully. The achievement of orderly movement along corridors is a problem for many schools, but can be alleviated by ensuring as far as possible that the corridors are free of obstacles, such as lockers, bags, etc. In some schools it may also be desirable to stagger the times at which different classes use the corridors.

Outside the school building

In Australian schools students spend approximately one-sixth of their time either at recess or at lunch-time. In contrast to the rest of the day, supervision and surveillance are singularly lacking. It is during this time that bullying occurs most frequently. In our surveys more than 90 per cent of students say that they have witnessed incidents of bullying at recess or lunch-time 'sometimes' or 'often'. Also compared with harassment that occurs in the classroom, it is more likely to be physical, vicious and unremitting.

From this we are apt to draw the conclusion that bullying is an activity that occurs naturally among students when they are left unsupervised—we are left to speculate whether Golding's castaway boys in *Lord of the Flies* were not drawn from real life playgrounds. We must remind ourselves that while bullying is certainly not uncommon in the playgrounds, it is confined to a minority of students. The majority find the break periods times of enjoyment, as the following results of a recent Australian survey conducted by Phillip Slee show.

Among children (N=375) between the ages of 8 and 13 years attending an Adelaide Primary School, 44 per cent of the students enjoyed their playground 'a lot'. A further 35 per cent reported that they usually enjoyed their experience there. This suggests that the remainder, a group of approximately 20 per cent, gained little enjoyment from their recess or lunch breaks. In a further measure of enjoyment of the school playground, children were presented with an array of faces showing smiling or unsmiling expressions and asked which face best described them when they were in the playground. A large majority chose a smiling face. Some 14 per cent saw themselves as unsmiling.

Few studies have so far compared children's fear of bullying in different parts of the school. An exception is a recent study by Venu Sarma, a colleague from the University of South Australia.

Boys and girls between the ages of 9 and 12 years (N=128) attending two Primary Schools in Adelaide completed questionnaires in which they described how safe they felt from bullying (a) in the classroom and (b) in the playground. There were no gender differences in reported safety in either place. Some 21 per cent said they did not usually feel safe from bullying in the schoolyard compared with 12 per cent in the classroom.

It is a minority of students, but a substantial minority, that concerns us here: the children who are fearful, who are bullied, harassed, abused some-times by individuals, sometimes by groups or gangs, in many cases most days of their lives and for long periods in the places where they are expected to go out to play.

Supervision as a means of reducing bullying

It is often suggested that bullying in a school can be reduced by increasing the amount and quality of supervision at recess and lunch-time. Dan Olweus, has argued that staff surveillance is the most effective single means of reducing bullying in schools (Olweus, 1993).

This approach is certainly not popular with teachers. Often objections are raised. It is argued sometimes that it is much better to prevent students from ever wanting to hurt others than to go around on 'police duty', snooping, watching out for instances of bullying. Clearly it is. But in the meantime, until that happy day, if we want to reduce bullying there is probably no more effective short-term measure than the appearance of staff or senior students in the playground watching out for bullying. A second argument is that if bullying is suppressed in one place and at one time by teacher presence, it will occur elsewhere. The evidence for this proposition has never been provided; in fact, the Norwegian research suggests that there is no such displacement. Finally, it is sometimes suggested that the necessary surveillance makes unreasonable demands upon staff time and that there are other important duties, not to mention the need for staff recuperation, that have precedence. If this view is advanced, we must again evaluate the importance of the problem of bullying in the school. We might also consider ways in which students themselves can be involved in the process of surveillance. With the development of peer mediation in the school (see Chapter 16) staff supervision may indeed become unnecessary.

Effective supervision

What constitutes effective supervision? Although the research evidence is clear that the density of teachers present during break periods at school is correlated significantly with low levels of reported bullying, not all supervision is equally effective in reducing bullying behaviour. Indeed, some forms of supervision may be counterproductive.

Where teachers are present but take *no* action when bullying occurs, they may be seen as condoning bullying. The message is that the bullying is just fun or alternatively is accepted by the teacher as part of school life or even that certain people deserve to be victims. It is doubtful whether many teachers do feel this way, though I have met a few who do. It is more likely that the teachers who take no action are either unaware of what is happening or, if they are, simply don't know what to do.

A second way in which supervision can be counterproductive is when the teacher is extremely managerial, intervening everywhere. Such a person may come across to students as unbearably officious and absurd. The effect may be to encourage bullying, including the teasing of the supervisor.

What is appropriate action?

Probably of all problems confronting teachers, what to do about peer harassment is the most perplexing. Not surprisingly, many students do not see staff members as being committed to taking action against bullying. Our surveys in Australia show that only about one-third of students think that their teachers are always interested in stopping it. A similar proportion say that teachers are not really interested or only *sometimes* interested in stopping bullying. These results reflect the uncertainties staff members feel about their role in countering bullying.

The first issue is *what behaviours to stop* and *how to identify them*. Now, if we are concerned with bullying per se (as we are here), we must return to definitions. The essence of bullying, it will be recalled, is abuse of power, that is, an imbalance between two parties such that one is the victim of negative and hurtful behaviour. There may be other forms of peer interaction that we may also want to stop, especially fighting or quarrelling between students of about the same strength or power. This is not bullying. Nevertheless fighting may help to create an ethos in which bullying may flourish, as students perceive that out of conflicts a victor often emerges, providing a model that the bully may wish to imitate. Also, because of its disruptive effects, physical fighting is understandably not tolerated by teachers in schools and for that reason, if no other, teachers rightly feel it must be stopped.

Action must therefore be taken against both fighting *and* bullying in schools. It is nevertheless worth preserving the distinction. Our concern is

primarily with the latter, but in passing it should be observed that the supervisor's role is often made difficult by an inability to distinguish between real fighting and play fighting. Many would argue that physical struggles between students taking the form of 'rough and tumble' games and competitions in which they wrestle or push and shove each other, are healthy and desirable. But, for some, the show of aggression which is inseparable from such struggles is unacceptable or may be seen as a precursor to more violent and definitely undesirable conflict. Although the issue of precisely when to intervene cannot be resolved to everybody's satisfaction, it is well to bear in mind that a consensus on whether an incident is an example of friendly fighting or real fighting can generally be reached by watching the facial expressions of the combatants, their intonations when they speak—or yell— and the general atmosphere surrounding the struggle.

The resemblance of real conflict and play is something that the bully may well take advantage of in justifying his or her behaviour to an outsider, such as a supervisor. This has been well caught in the picture on the cover of the book of the play, *Only Playing, Miss!*, by Penny Casdagli (1990) reproduced above.

It is generally easier to see that an intervention is needed when there is an obvious imbalance of power and the bullying is physical. Where a group of students is physically abusing an individual there is usually no room for ambiguity; similarly when there is a large difference in size and strength between two children and the stronger continues to hurt the weaker who is unable to resist. In such cases efforts must be made to stop what is going on. Non-physical cases of bullying may be more difficult to identify. Sometimes, however, it is perfectly clear that a student is being verbally harassed by another and this must be stopped.

Ambiguity is sometimes present because the victim may try to create the impression that he or she is not being bullied at all. This may be because the victim prefers to suffer the indignity of being bullied to the greater indignity of someone—especially a teacher—intervening on his/her behalf. So there might appear to be a kind of collusion between bully and victim. A crude intervention by the teacher may stigmatise the student further and a vigorous and obtrusive intervention is often undesirable. You may wish to save the victim's face and so you may seemingly disregard the bullying and seek to talk with the person who is being harassed on some other pretext. This will bring the episode to an end, and give the teacher time to talk to the student and explore the situation further to discover whether help is needed—and wanted.

Cases of non-physical bullying sometimes emerge when students describe what has been happening to someone, sometimes themselves. This may happen during a session of supervision. It then becomes a matter of judgement as to whether the incident warrants further attention. It is difficult to set out clear guidelines here; but it is sound practice to take every report seriously. Some may turn out to be exaggerations, spoofs, manipulations, squabbles, part of the everyday scene of shifting alliances and fallings-out of people whose personal relations do not always run smoothly, like most of us. But you cannot take the chance of ignoring what you are being told.

Promoting pro-social behaviour in the playground

In this section we have been concerned with stopping undesirable behaviour from happening by putting it under surveillance. We should now ask whether teachers can play a more positive role in their period of supervision. Much depends on the relationships that have developed and can develop through interactions in the school yard or field. As we know, the teacher in the classroom is frequently caricatured; for many students the teacher is a rigidly defined stereotype rather than a person. The possibility is there for teachers to relate in a more human and personal manner. Depending on the teacher's interests and skills, the teacher might initiate or take part in games with students or participate in discussions with groups of students without the inhibitions and formality apparent in many classrooms. This kind of personal influence can be highly effective in promoting goodwill and generating interest in cooperative activities; both of which are quite incompatible with bullying.

Intervening

Intervening may take various forms. Often the presence of a teacher on the scene of a fighting or bullying incident *is* the intervention. The behaviour ceases. If it is necessary to take action to stop the bullying continuing there and then, it is suggested that it is often best to do so unobtrusively, especially if you suspect that it is really in the interest of the victim that it is done that way. How you proceed from there will depend on the seriousness of the situation. You may counsel or give practical advice to the victim—if this is wanted. A reprimand or admonition to the bully (privately as a rule) is sometimes all that is needed—but it is as well to make a careful note of what has happened in case there is any further bullying. Sometimes it will be necessary to meet with the perpetrator(s) of the aggression and the victim separately and/or together. The process of counselling and/or disciplining those involved may follow different courses, and these are to be examined in the next chapter.

   Occasionally a very serious and difficult situation arises when the conflict is hard to manage. This can occur when groups of teenagers are engaged in harassing an individual. They may not be inclined to take any notice of the objections of a teacher on duty. Indeed, a teacher who tries to intervene may become the target of abuse. Earlier (see page 165) we examined the grounds for decisions that people may make when they are considering whether to intervene or not. They were applied to students, but they may also apply to teachers as well. When a teacher is unsure whether to intervene for any reason it makes sense to talk about it with other staff. Occasionally it may be sensible to invite the assistance of colleagues if a personal intervention seems dangerous or likely to be counter-productive. If such assistance is not available, identify students involved in the incident for action to be taken later.

It is important that individual supervisors should not, as far as possible, operate in isolation. Where necessary, they should share their impressions and pass on information to other staff members about what has been happening between students. In this way problems associated with particular students or groups of students can be discussed and a coordinated plan evolved to deal with the difficulties. Trouble spots in the school where bullying occurs most often might be identified. For example, in the study conducted by Venu Sarma in Adelaide, one area that was identified as where bullying took place a great deal was the Bicycle Shed. Teachers were generally unaware of this. Thoughtful design and planning might have avoided this problem—a window in the shed positioned so that staff could readily see what was going on in the building would have been very helpful. Policies may also be developed so that areas in the school may be designated for use for particular activities or for particular age or gender groups, should that be seen as desirable.

Improving the school environment

To some extent this may be seen as closely related to the question of surveillance. A school where surveillance is easy because the area is open and accessible, is one in which bullying will be relatively low, provided of course that there is adequate supervision. So, from an anti-bullying point of view, the reduction or elimination of areas which are hidden from sight is a priority. Toilets are places where bullying is not infrequent in some schools, but the maintenance of privacy may have a higher priority and there are limits to what can reasonably be done.

A familiar argument is that bullying is a response to boredom on the part of some children who are particularly intolerant to low levels of stimulation. It would follow that bullying can be reduced by creating a more stimulating and interesting environment for children outside the classrooms as well as within. It has been observed that playgrounds have changed little, or not at all, over the last fifty years despite the vast technological changes that have occurred in society; sometimes these have led to improvements in class-rooms but rarely outside. Vast expanses of asphalt and playing areas bereft of greenery, or fields dedicated to football and cricket and little else are still commonplace. From closely organised activity in the classroom and the stimulation of up-to-date, state-of-the-art laboratories, computers, libraries and workshops, to the tedium of the dismal 'playground' in which there appears to be little to do and little to engage either the mind or the senses, is a downward step for some children who simply do not know what to do when they go outside. By teasing and bullying others they can get some relief from the monotony. Not surprisingly, it has been proposed that bullying can be countered by enriching the outside environment.

Nevertheless, there are problems with this approach. The most obvious is financial. For the richer private schools in Australia this is no worry; indeed, many of the schools are wonderfully resourced and have excellent grounds and facilities for a variety of games and other outdoor activities. But for a large number of state schools and poorer private schools it is difficult to produce the transformations that architects and planners would eagerly propose to make an interesting environment. In some schools changes in the environment can be made at a modest cost by involving children (and sometimes parents) in the necessary work and incorporating their ideas and artistry in the plans. Where funds become miraculously available, it is not always wise to make a sudden and radical change in the facilities to be available to the students. This can sometimes lead to an increase in conflict between children in the use of the facilities. Changes must be carefully managed.

A further view is that bullying can be a response to overcrowding. We know that the close and sustained proximity of others can be extremely unpleasant and frustrating. It can maximise both the provocation and the opportunity for a person to "take it out" on another. While general over-crowding is rarely the problem, it is not uncommon for children at school to be in a packed crowd for some parts of the day: for instance, outside the Canteen or Tuck Shop in a queue (or rabble); and in narrow corridors as children move from one class to another. If action cannot be taken, for practical reasons, to modify the environment, arrangements can often be made to stagger the use of areas, and thereby avoid this source of stress and consequent aggressive behaviour, which may lead to bullying.

To and from school: whose responsibility?

We know that a great deal of bullying goes on between students on the way to school and on the way home. It is possible to wash our hands of it, and argue that what goes on out of school hours is not the school's problem, that it is a matter for parents and the police. Certainly the responsibility of the school *is* diminished together with its capacity for taking effective action. Nevertheless the school can play a significant and important role in helping to reduce bullying outside the school, more especially when students are coming to school or going home. It is obviously in the school's interest to do so. Whatever has contributed to distress and disharmony among students outside the school must affect their behaviour and quality of life at school.

What can be done?

For a school that wants to influence the behaviour of its students *outside* school, the first step is to find out what is happening. Often information about student misbehaviour in which bullying is implicated comes to a school from members of the community, especially parents; sometimes from people who provide transport, sometimes concerned citizens. In addition, schools may hear directly from students who have been victimised by others. But remember that sometimes the victims are afraid or ashamed to speak out. A school may therefore feel justified in obtaining information using a general survey or by discussing the matter with students. By such means it becomes possible for a school to identify 'trouble spots'. These might include places on routes taken by students walking or cycling to and from school; at bus or tram stops or train stations; on transport arranged for students, commonly the 'school bus'; and on public transport, especially on train services which may be poorly supervised.

Where peer mediation programs have been effectively promoted in a school, it is often possible for students who are able to intervene at the 'trouble spots' to do so. For example, peer mediators travelling on the school bus may act so as to resolve interpersonal conflict (see Chapter 16). Where this proves to be too difficult, those involved in the problem can be identified and approached individually at a later stage.

But sometimes bullying occurs in places where there are few, if any, observers, and no one motivated or able to mediate. This may apply to students who are on foot or sometimes on bicycles. In the latter case the bullying is less likely to be physical (unless the cyclists are stopped) but they may well be treated to sustained and repeated abuse which can be equally hurtful. Students who are victimised in such situations need help. This can sometimes be provided by the school in the form of advice, as follows:

1   Students should be encouraged to report incidents of bullying to the staff or student mediators, or, if particularly serious, the police.

2   Although students have a right not to be harassed to and from school (and steps need to be taken to achieve that), it is often wise for them to consider ways in which the journeys to and from school can be made safer, for example, by avoiding certain routes or places, or travelling with others whom they can trust.

3   Advice can also be given on how to react when you are threatened by a more powerful person or group. Depending on the nature of the menace and the whereabouts of others, it may be sensible to:
    (i)   join a group of others you can trust;
    (ii) call out to someone for help;
    (iii) escape from the situation by going into a shop or Safety House.

Safety Houses

The role of Safety Houses requires a special mention. The Houses were established to provide assistance to children who are endangered by others, including children who bully them. The Safety House Programme began in Australia in 1979. It organised the provision of a network of safe places for children who are threatened, especially on the way to and from school. According to Safety House Australia, 20 per cent of incidents leading to the use of their facilities involve children being bullied by peers (SHA Newsletter, July, 1995). Currently there are over 90 000 Safety Houses throughout Australia.

A Safety House is a place where you go if you feel unsafe, frightened or unsure

The Safety Houses are chosen according to strict criteria. First, applicants must undergo a police check. The selected homes will normally be on a route taken by students to and from school and have an adult present during those times. The Houses must have a clear path to the door and possess a telephone. They can be identified by signs on letter boxes of the premises. Children going into these places will be listened to and taken care of by responsible adults who may contact parents and, if necessary, the police.

The school should provide information to students about this resource. The local police can be invited to the school to tell students about the purpose and location of the Safety Houses.

Kids Help Line

This organisation has already been mentioned as a provider of up-to-date and relevant statistics about bullying among young people. Many young people phone Kids Help Line over a wide range of personal problems and interpersonal difficulties. Sometimes a student may wish to talk to an adult about a bullying problem and may prefer to go outside the school for help.

This may be because the student is afraid that others at the school will find out; it may also be because it is thought that incidents outside the school are not the concern of the school authorities. We have seen that this is in fact a 'zone of uncertainty'. Kids Help Line has decided advantages. It is staffed by highly trained counsellors who are experienced in dealing with the problems of children; it enables children phoning in to keep their much needed anonymity, until *they* decide to bring it into the open; and finally it is extremely accessible and free! (Toll free call on 1800 55 1800)

Finding out
about bullying

Clearly you cannot begin to deal with specific bully/victim problems until you have relevant and reliable information about what has happened. In this chapter we will examine the various sources of information that become available to teachers and how this information may be used.

Learning about what has happened

Information about bullying incidents involving school students may come from a variety of sources and may vary in reliability. These include the following:

1   Students claiming to have been victimised by their peers.

2 Students reporting bullying incidents involving others.

3 Parents speaking on behalf of students.

4 Observations by teachers.

5 Reports from other members of the community.

Who handles the reports?

On this question the school must have a firm policy. One option is for *all* reports of bullying to go to the principal or deputy principal. This ensures that the reports are being taken very seriously and responsible action will follow. Alternatively, teachers and counsellors, who are often the first to hear of the bullying, may be given some discretion in separating the seemingly less serious cases from those that must be taken to 'the top'. When this option is taken, guidelines will be necessary to assist teachers and counsellors in making such a decision. Of course, seemingly trivial cases may be initially misjudged and later reclassified. Teachers should be allowed to change their minds as events unfold. The School Policy on Bullying must make it clear what procedure the school is to adopt.

Students claiming to have been victimised by their peers

When students say they are being bullied by others they commonly do not do so without a good deal of thought, and usually with reluctance. Often they don't want others to know about it, either because they feel it is humiliating to seek help or because they think it will not be to their advantage to tell. The reluctance to tell is evident in the results of research in this area.

Table 11.1 **Percentages of students who told someone after being bullied**

	Boys	**Girls**
Person told:		
Mother	30.7	44.1
Father	23.8	26.2
Teacher	15.5	19.1
Friend or friends	46.0	57.3

From: Rigby and Slee (1995)

It should also be added that for many children having told someone did not lead to an improvement in their situation. In fact, in about 50 per cent of cases there was no reported improvement. In about 7 per cent of cases things were seen as getting worse. Children, therefore, can have limited confidence that telling will help. We can therefore be pretty sure that when they do tell someone they are normally in considerable need of help.

The counsellor as confidant

The PRQ has also provided information about how often school counsellors are told by a student about being bullied. The answer has been quite seldom. Teachers appear to be told at least three times more often than counsellors. I found this puzzling and at first I supposed that it was because schools where the question was asked either did not have a recognised counsellor or, as is sometimes the case, shared a visiting counsellor with other schools. But further enquiries indicated that students mostly did prefer to talk to a teacher rather than a counsellor, even in schools where there was a full-time counsellor. Because counsellors are increasingly becoming skilled at dealing with bully/victim problems this was disturbing news. There may of course be many reasons for this. Teachers may be more 'handy': students can catch up with them before or after lessons. They may be more familiar figures. There are also more of them to choose from. But often the reason appears to be that the counsellor is seen by students as someone who attends to kids with a 'psychological problem' and admitting to having one may seem worse than saying one is being bullied. The message must therefore be that 'being bullied can happen to anyone' and that counsellors can indeed help with this 'normal' difficulty.

Responding to victims

When a student comes to see a teacher or counsellor about being bullied, it is very likely that he or she is telling the truth. Not always though. There will be the occasional student who is trying to get someone into trouble, and may even be trying to get in a pre-emptive strike—before the real victim tells his tale. But the teacher should always begin by listening sympathetically. In time, it may emerge that the victim has provoked the incident or is in some way responsible for the continuance of the bullying. More than likely, however, the victim is in need of as much support as can be provided. The first task is to listen carefully, non-critically.

You should listen to find out what the student wants to happen about the bullying. It may be that he or she simply wants to share the problem, nothing more. There may be a marked reluctance to have it taken further— and the student's wishes must be respected. Together the teacher and student might explore better ways of coping with the situation, for example, by becoming more assertive, getting friends to help, avoiding certain places.

Where the student has made it clear that he or she only wants to talk and doesn't want the teacher to tell others, normally the teacher will have an obligation to keep the matter confidential. In fact, the consequences of breaking confidence can be devastating not only for the child who may suffer more abuse because of what has been said, but also for the teacher. I learned recently of a welfare teacher who broke a promise to a student not to tell anyone about a bullying incident. To the profound dismay of the student the problem escalated. Parents were called in and sides were taken. The upshot was that other students hearing about the teacher's 'betrayal' of confidence boycotted her. She was forced to resign and moved to another school. This is, of course, an extreme case, but it shows what can happen.

There are times when the victim of the bullying may want the teacher to take action and to speak with the bullies. The teacher may agree that this is the proper course of action. What follows next will depend upon the seriousness of the case and the policy the school has adopted. We will examine alternative ways of dealing with bully/victim cases later in Chapter 13.

Whatever action or non-action is taken it is important that the victim should feel that he or she has been listened to and has been taken seriously. The victim should feel free to go back to see the teacher to talk further at any stage; indeed, an explicit invitation should be given to the student. The student should also feel free to change his/her mind about what course of action to take, and expect the teacher to listen carefully to the reasons for the change.

Occasionally, however, the teacher may be in a dilemma. It may be that the student is being quite seriously bullied and a very dangerous situation is developing. For example, the victim may be so incensed that he or she is likely to react very violently. Some victims we know have resolved to kill their tormentor. Some victims have actually taken their own lives. In such serious situations, the teacher should always explore the issue with the principal who may call in other colleagues to consider what action may need to be taken, despite the student's evident reluctance to have any steps taken on his/her behalf.

Students reporting incidents involving others

The greater the degree of awareness within a school of the seriousness of bully/victim problems, the more students are likely to initiate action to stop it. But there will continue to be many who are reluctant to talk. The mis-guided code of honour—you don't dob in others—will act as a brake on what is said. It should therefore be borne in mind that the informer is often taking a risk, and the decision to inform is often the uneasy outcome of a tussle between concern for a victim and taking the more prudent and safer course of inaction. Nevertheless we should not eliminate the possibility that the informing student is the exception: a student who wants to get somebody into trouble.

The value of a report from a non-victim or observer lies in it being generally a more objective version of what has happened. It provides an important means by which a victim's story might be corroborated. The informant is also a potential helper in bringing about a good resolution of the case, and may be treated as such. But remember that the informant's identity might also need to be protected.

Parents of students speaking on their behalf

This is a common source of information about bullying. Unfortunately by the time a parent has informed the school about it several things will already have happened:

(i)   The child will generally have suffered a good deal of bullying before the parent has got to know about it, most children are reluctant to tell their parents about it and go to them as a last resort.

(ii) Parents, too, are often reluctant to tell other people, including teachers. So that by the time parents communicate with a teacher about the child being bullied (or, more rarely, the child bullying others) the problem has further intensified.

(iii) The parent not uncommonly feels very strongly about the problem and may well feel inclined to blame the school.

It is natural enough for the teacher to be defensive and feel that the school is being unfairly accused of not providing adequate protection for the son or daughter. There may be some difficulty in listening carefully and sympathetically to what is being said. But the primary consideration at this stage is to gather information about what has actually happened and at the same time develop a cooperative relationship with the parent. The question of how this can be done is of very great importance and we shall examine the matter further in Chapter 14.

Observations by teachers

We can divide staff observations into: (i) those that were made after a case of suspected bullying has led the teacher to watch out for the bully or bullies; and (ii) observations that were made without such previous knowledge or suspicion. The latter carry more weight, since they occurred before any bias could have operated.

Teachers would naturally like to think of themselves as unbiased observers. But remember that their judgements of students are often formed in the context of a classroom situation in which the respect which they are shown, or not shown, by each student may be crucial in reaching a decision about his or her culpability. It is hard for the teacher not to draw upon earlier instances of cooperative or defiant behaviour as indicators of the student's innocence or guilt, even when the student is in conflict with others.

Reports from other members of the community

Occasionally reports of bullying come from other members of the community. Bullying, as we know, often occurs to and from school. It is sometimes observed among students travelling together on public transport and may constitute a problem for the driver or other passengers. Reports by school bus drivers of rowdiness and bullying not uncommonly come to the attention of teachers. Occasionally, an instance of bullying may be reported by someone who observes it happening in the street. Reports may also come from Safety Houses (see Chapter 10) and the police. Finally, reports may be forthcoming from medical practitioners who have seen and talked with children and identified health problems associated with being a victim of school bullying.

Weighing the evidence

Whenever there is some evidence, however slight, that a student has been bullied at school, it must be taken seriously. Naturally, the more sources there are providing converging evidence, the more confident you can be that bullying has taken place. However, this does not mean that if one source (e.g. that of a friend of a child who is being bullied) is not confirmed by another (e.g. a teacher doing supervision), you should ignore it. As we have said, bullying can be very subtle and the victim can be unusually sensitive. It is easy to dismiss an incident of bullying on the grounds that the child is 'over-sensitive'. You must be particularly careful about this. We are all hurt by different things—and if a person knows what hurts us and continually seeks to aggravate the injury, that is indeed bullying, no matter how foolish the reaction of the victim may seem to be to the outsider.

The truth, the whole truth and nothing but the truth?

Sooner or later, as the evidence accumulates and is sifted, there is a temptation to really get down to the bottom of it—to discover the truth, the whole truth and nothing but the truth. This can set into motion an increasingly complex process of examinations, cross-examinations, heavy documentation, etc. The temptation is strong and for some teachers irresistible. It is fun, exciting even, to play the parts of detective, judge and executioner. It enlivens the day and (we can tell ourselves) in the undeniably good cause of bringing the bully to judgement. But before you embark on such a course, it is well to remember that precisely how, when, where and why bullying begins is practically unfathomable. To fully unravel the story of its development is an extraordinarily demanding process. We should ask ourselves whether we are going to spend precious time in tracing the origins of peer conflict and precisely and judiciously attributing blame, or alternatively using the time to resolve the problem and bring about a lasting reconciliation between two or more students. What we need to know basically is whether a person has been victimised and who may be responsible.

The paper-work

This should be kept to a minimum.

It has been suggested that detailed records should be produced of every bullying incident, giving dates, times, places, witnesses, outcomes, statements by the supposed victim, declarations by the supposed bullies, teacher observations, whether parents notified, degree of parental involvement, other external contacts relating to the incident(s), for example, the police, Social Welfare, Safety Houses etc. etc. In setting up and maintaining such a system we are inevitably preparing ourselves for a legalistic battle in which justice is to be done according to the Courts of the Land, or at least, the Rules of the School. Is this what we want?

There are considerable dangers in this approach as applied to *every* instance of reported bullying. It is likely to become overwhelming in its complexity. In many cases it is unnecessary. Modelled on a quasi-legal system of justice, this approach results in many students possessing a 'record' as a bully or victim, and even if 'acquitted', the stigma can remain. He or she, it could be said, was, according to the school records, a bully or at least a suspected bully.

The problem of labelling is particularly acute when we examine one proposal that schools set up a 'register of bullying', indicating who bullied whom, when, where and how. It can be constructed so that cross-referencing of bullies and victims is easily achieved. It can be put on to computer. We can read from the screen or print-out that on the twenty-fifth of March, 1995, Manuel was bullied by Basil Fawlty, who had himself been verbally harassed on the twenty-fourth of March, 1995 by Sybil Fawlty. Sometimes it is argued that records of this kind should be destroyed after a period of time has elapsed so that students can begin again with a clean slate.

Still, there are exceptional cases for which detailed records must be kept. Unfortunately, it is not always possible to know in advance whether a case will turn out to be 'exceptional'. There is clearly a danger of omission. Nevertheless, it is wiser to take the risk of missing out on details that might subsequently prove useful, than to go mad in the direction of maintaining a labyrinth of detail on hundreds of cases of suspected bullying with the near certainty that injustice, often serious injustice, would be done to some students whose 'crimes' were recorded in the book. So, I would propose that records should be minimal in nearly all cases. They should normally simply enable you to identify persons about whom there seems to be a bully/victim problem and even such sparse records should be destroyed within a year. Judgements should be made on the available evidence regarding the seriousness of the bullying and where there is general agreement that the bullying is serious, more detailed records will need to be kept.

But what's serious?

We would take into account the factors detailed in the box shown opposite on page 193.

1 The degree of distress of the victim(s).
2 The concern of the parents, which will normally be a reflection of their child's distress and inability to cope.
3 The duration over which the bullying has occurred.
4 The amenability of the bully when confronted to recognise the hurt that has been caused.
5 The readiness of bullies to work towards a reconciliation.

Now what?

The general course of action that a school may take once the nature and seriousness of the bullying has been determined can vary quite widely. We must next ask what courses are open to the school and which one will it take.

12

What to do
with the bully

We keep hoping that it will not come to this, that methods of prevention have done the trick—but cases of bullying continue. There is no simple answer to the problem and in this chapter we will begin to consider the daunting question: what can we do with the bully?

It will become evident as we explore this question that there are options. In fact, there appear to be three basic approaches to the problem of bullying. Each of them has its supporters and critics. In some schools they go all the way with one or other of these approaches. In other schools there is a mixture of approaches as there is a mixture of philosophies of education. We all have our preferences, and before the end of this chapter mine will be clear enough.

But before these three approaches are presented, as we consider what we might do in a school about 'the bully', we should ask ourselves the most basic question of all: why do we want to do anything. What is the point of an intervention directed towards the bully?

What do you want to intervene for?

The first answer that people normally give is this: to protect children who are being victimised. This is almost invariably the first consideration. and increasingly it is being seen in Australia (as in some other countries) as a legal requirement. And people normally want the protection to be speedy and efficient.

A second answer is that they want the bully to change, so that (i) other students are not terrorised by the bully; and (ii) that the bully learns to lead a more constructive and satisfactory life for his/her own sake.

A third answer is that they want to deter or dissuade *other* students from following the course taken by the bully, because they want a safe, peaceable school.

In evaluating the interventions, it is useful to refer to these points.

Three broad approaches to treating the bully

We can distinguish three quite broad approaches to the way to deal with bullies.
1   The Moralistic Approach
2   The Legalistic Approach
3   The Humanistic Approach

Moralistic

In its purest form this approach assumes that by forcibly stating and reiterating the values and moral position of the school as they apply to bullying, bullies will desist. The moralistic approach requires that the student conforms to the stated or understood values of the school.

An example of how this can be applied comes from a primary school in South Australia, as explained to me.

A student has been found to have bullied someone. The student is asked to see the counsellor who describes the values underlying the School Policy as it pertains to bullying. The importance of showing respect and tolerance for others is emphasised. The student is then required to write an essay explaining that what he/she has done is contrary to the school's explicit values and requirements. It is explained that the essay is then to be given to the Deputy Principal who will decide whether it is acceptable. The student is also instructed to write an apology to the person who was bullied. Finally, the student's parents are invited to come to the school and the situation and the moral position explained to them.

The aim, of course, is to apply moral pressure. The effectiveness of this approach will depend upon the moral authority of the school and its acceptance by the student.

On the credit side, the approach can be said to be appealing to the student's sense of moral rightness and at the same time promoting the values of the school. However, it should be noted that in the application described above there is no real engagement with the bully; no attempt to understand the bully's values or motives and to find some common ground for discourse. Unfortunately with this approach the bully may (and often does) cynically acquiesce and bully again in ways which are harder to detect—and these are many.

Legalistic

This assumes a set of rules with which the bully is expected to be familiar. These are commonly described as 'sanctions'. There may be little or no moralising—the aim is to apply the law even-handedly. The penalties may range from mild to severe: from school chores, withdrawal of privileges, time-out, to detention, suspension, exclusion or expulsion—whatever is prescribed by the school and consistent with the Behaviour Management Policy. As part of the procedure parents may be invited to attend, and future consequences outlined. In the event of extreme physical bullying and injury, formal charges may be laid against the delinquent.

Sometimes the penalties prescribed at the school are described as 'consequences' as if they arise naturally and logically from the offence. 'You have done this—now the consequence is...' This, or some variant, is exceedingly common in dealing with bullying in schools.

To its credit:

(i) Administration in many cases is relatively quick. No counselling is required.

(ii) It sends a clear message to students as to what is acceptable behaviour between students and what is not.

(iii) By varying the severity of the penalty according to the seriousness of the offence, some 'justice' can be achieved.

(iv) The rules governing the use of sanctions in the case of bullying can be devised with the active collaboration of students themselves. This can make it likely that the authority behind the sanctions will be more acceptable than if it were simply teacher-based. In some schools the process has been taken a step further by enabling students to engage in a process of 'trying' bullies and determining appropriate sanctions. These so-called 'bully courts' run by students are controversial and have not to my knowledge been employed outside England. (They are discussed further in Chapter 15.)

These so-called legalistic methods have been criticised on the following grounds:

(i) In the interest of justice there is considerable pressure to establish the precise facts of the case (and treat the bully accordingly) and *in some cases* this may prove to be very time-consuming, frustrating, and for minor acts of bullying hard to justify.

(ii) Although penalties may deter some potential bullies, they may fail to make much impact on the 'hard core' bullies who may become defiant and redouble their efforts to make it worse for the informer(s).

(iii) The effectiveness of the approach depends very much on the students' perceptions of the efficiency of the surveillance of their behaviour and the risk involved in bullying someone. As we have noticed, acts of bullying are often difficult to detect and witnesses may be unwilling to report what they see.

(iv) Rarely does it lead to any long-term solution of the kind that may come if there is a genuine reconciliation between the bully and victim.

Humanistic

This is a very wide category, not easy to define. In the sense to be used in this book, it is conceived in the following way. *It is an approach that is based on a sincere desire on the part of the teacher/counsellor to understand the person who has bullied someone, not as a member of a category, a delinquent for whom there is a standard treatment. It implies listening (and refraining from preaching and laying down the law) and establishing genuine two-way communication as a precursor to, and essential element in, bringing about change, not only in the bully's behaviour but also in the bully's thinking and feeling.*

Its strengths lie in:

(i)   Its readiness to encounter the bully as a person to whom respect is due, irrespective of what the bully has done.

(ii) The invitation it provides for the bully to cooperate with the counsellor in bringing about some mutually desired change.

(iii) The promise it holds for a long-term resolution of the problem, which derives from the bully wanting to change, rather than merely complying (at best) as long as, but only as long as, there seems to be efficient surveillance.

As against this, it may be argued that:

(i)   Bringing about such change is very difficult and uncertain—especially when the bully is an 'unwilling client' and the counsellor is a school authority.

(ii) Some bullies are extremely manipulative and low in empathy and will not be prepared to meet the counsellor/teacher half-way.

(iii) It sounds like a soft option that would not gain the approval of some teachers and many parents, especially those whose children have been bullied.

It is not suggested that any of the approaches will be plain sailing. You are warned. *There is no simple solution.*

An impasse?

Have we then reached an impasse? Let us sit back a moment and take a wider perspective.

Bullying has been going on a very long time. Going back nearly 2000 years, the New Testament provides a startling example of bullying that accompanied the trial of Jesus (Mark, 14,65):

'Some of them began to spit on Jesus, and they blindfolded him.

"Guess who hit you?" they said. And the guards took him and slapped him.'

In the nineteenth century a very earnest proponent of muscular Christianity, Thomas Hughes, wrote his famous book, *Tom Brown's Schooldays*, which everyone knows is about poor little Tom being bullied by the odious Flashman at Rugby School.

What is less well known is that the book gave rise to a strong upsurge of interest in bullying, much as we are experiencing in the 1990s, and Thomas Hughes felt obliged to provide a preface to a later edition of his book (1857) in which he considered suggestions about what could be done to stop it. Hughes includes a little story, a sort of parable:

'A black soldier, in a West Indian Regiment, tied up to receive a couple of dozen for drunkenness, cried out to his captain who was exhorting him to sobriety in future. "Cap'n, if you preachee, preachee; and if you floggee, floggee; but no preachee and floggee, too."'

How should the Captain reply ? According to Hughes, he might say:

'"No, Pompey, I must preach whenever I see a chance of being listened to, which I never did before; so now you must have it all together; and I hope you may remember some of it."'

This comment made by Hughes is very interesting. It is not a matter of either/or, he suggests; if we are to change behaviour we must emphatically do both.

Now, 150 years later, the problem of bullying stays very much where it was: it goes on, with little sign of abating, despite generations of preaching. We have given up flogging, or its milder substitute, the cane. We sometimes pretend that we have given up punishment altogether. We first called it 'negative reinforcement', until Behaviourism lost credibility; then we invented 'consequences', pretending that these were provided by logic and nature; then 'sanctions' with a very correct political ring: what we applied to

Saddam Hussein in the Gulf War and should have applied to Adolf Hitler in the 1930s.

We are at last beginning to see that a combination of moralising and punishing is not really adequate if we are to do more than try, with limited success, to keep the 'hordes of bullies' at bay. Now this is *not* to say that we should not proclaim our values: indeed we must. Nor that we should completely abandon sanctions. Not at all. But surely we should do more than that.

Granted that counselling bullies is not easy. Granted that there are so many people baying for the blood of the bullies. Granted that in the last analysis we must protect the victims, even (we would agree) if we fail to convert the bullies. But the good news is that there are new ways of working with bullies that are what I have called humanistic and these offer prospects of success. In the next chapter we turn to these.

Humanistic
approaches
to bullying

I have suggested that, where possible, it is better to attempt to resolve problems of peer victimisation using so-called humanistic methods, employing counselling and mediation skills, rather than to resort to simple moralistic and legalistic methods of effecting change. *This does NOT mean, however, that schools should not have a clear moral position on bullying.* What is implied is that 'just moralising' about bullying is unlikely to have a positive effect in reducing peer victimisation in most schools. Likewise, it is to be doubted whether schools can do without sanctions in dealing with bullying on *all* occasions. Idealism does not stretch that far. But as the only or predominant method for dealing with bullying, punishment will not do.

Humanistic approaches to bullying are characterised by a sincere desire to understand and appreciate the needs of those primarily involved in the bully/victim problem, namely, the bully (or bullies) and the victim (or victims).

Central to this approach is the belief that success in working on the problem depends largely on the quality of the relationship that can be developed with those involved. And a good relationship, it is assumed, can only develop through the giving of respect and engaging in genuine two-way communication.

Variations in approaches within the humanistic framework

Within this general approach, which I have termed humanistic, in contra-distinction to moralistic and legalistic approaches, there is scope among practitioners for substantial differences of both theoretical and practical kinds. There are, for instance, different conceptions of the 'needs' of bullies, as well as those of victims. Different conceptions help to determine how the problem is defined and what features are focused upon in the course of interactions between teachers and students, and precisely what procedures are followed.

Self-esteem

One popular view is that in working with bullies it is best to focus on their need for self-esteem. It is assumed that bullying is a consequence of feelings of unworthiness or low self-esteem. If the bully can come to recognise that he or she is a valuable person, then the need to bully others will disappear. What is needed—so the argument runs—is genuine acceptance by significant others; only then can the bully be himself or herself. The teacher may begin by helping to provide this acceptance personally. This is the classical Rogerian conception of how individuals can be helped in therapy, and may be seen as applying especially to bullies, whose family backgrounds are often character-ised by parental and family rejection. However, the proponents of this approach must come to terms with an inconvenient empirical finding repeatedly found in studies of the self-esteem of bullies. As a group, bullies are not low in self-esteem (see Olweus, 1989 ; Rigby and Slee, 1993a). Still, it does not follow from this that *all* bullies have adequate self-esteem. Some feel inadequate. For them what may be called 'self-esteem therapy' may work. The point is that for bullies-in-general it is not a panacea.

A related view is that although the self-esteem of bullies is not generally low, it may nevertheless be maintained by the bullying behaviour insofar as that behaviour is effective in producing feelings of dominance and pride. If bullying should cease, it may be argued, there would be a need for support from an alternative source of achievement. Accordingly, the teacher may explore ways in which substitute achievement is possible for a bully. A boy who gains admiration from others (and consequent esteem) from pushing other boys around may learn that he can be equally admired by demonstrating his power in a more socially acceptable way, for example on the sports field.

Family

In exploring the forces that help to determine a bully's behaviour at school, family influences may be seen as playing a major role. This has led some educators to view family background, and especially the 'dysfunctional family', as the root of the problem, and to concentrate on ways in which the situation can be changed or come to terms with. It could be, as the relationship with the bully develops, that teacher and student might gain a deeper shared understanding of how a child's family experiences could result in the student's outbursts of anger and even acts of calculated cruelty towards peers at school. Appreciating the causes of this behaviour might lead the student to control or redirect such hostility. In practice, however, the effectiveness of this approach requires not only a high degree of insight and maturity on the part of the bully, but most probably considerable expenditure of time and effort on the part of the teacher/counsellor. Once embarked upon this course of action, the helper may feel obliged to visit the student's home and seek to influence the family's behaviour and lifestyle. Whilst this may be approaching 'the root of the matter', the resistance that may be encountered from the family could be discouraging. It might be justified, if at all, in exceptional cases, and then with the assistance of an experienced family therapist.

Skills acquisition

Another approach is to concentrate on identifying the skills a student may need to be motivated to stop bullying. Often a deficit in social skills is seen as the basic problem. However, bullies, as a class, typically do not have poor social skills; in fact, they may have above-average skills in this area, especially if they are effective practitioners, as many are, of indirect bullying. Yet some do lack social skills. Bullying is sometimes practised because of a seeming inability of a bully to influence people in other ways. Social skills training, as was said earlier, may have a part to play, but only in selected cases.

Occupational interest

Yet another approach within the Humanistic framework, so defined, is to assume that bullying is largely due to the students not being engaged in any pursuit that claims and sustains their vital interest. In short, the bully is bored. The present and the future seem quite futile. In this case, counselling may be directed towards helping the bully to find a real and enduring interest or occupation within school or outside or both.

Concern and responsibility

What ails the bully, it is often said, is a lack of concern for other people and a non-acceptance of responsibility for actions that cause distress. This view underlies some recent approaches to working with offenders in the community and with bullies in schools. It is proposed that bullies should be encouraged to become more concerned about those whom they victimise and personally be more responsible for their actions. To this we may murmur, 'well, of course; isn't that what we have been trying to do all along?' And in a sense, this is true, but for the most part, using traditional means: that is, preaching and punishing. The question is how can this be done more effectively in the humanistic manner.

First, we should consider why 'concern' and 'responsibility' have been put together in this heading. It is because they are inseparable when we address the problem of bullying. Changes in both are needed before there can be any fundamental change in the bully. Take 'being responsible'. The bully may be quite prepared to accept personal responsibility for the suffering of a victim, may indeed boast about it, glory in it. This bully is being responsible, according to his or her own lights if not society's. Without empathic concern for the victim there is no reason to change. Concern is needed.

'Concern' may not be enough either. There may be feelings of concern for the victim—but the bully may feel that he or she can do little or nothing about it. The bully's self-perception may be of one who is driven by impulses that are quite irresistible (it could be that some forms of 'therapeutic help', however well intentioned, may contribute to this belief). Or alternatively, the bully may feel that he or she is so much under the influence of a gang that 'sticks together' that there is no scope for personal initiative. Or an individual bully may be under the domination or 'spell' of another person, and 'personal' action is impossible. A sense of independence and personal efficacy is needed before a person can behave in a way for which he or she can take responsibility for any action.

Inducing concern and responsibility

This line of thinking, which stresses the need for personal concern for another and an acceptance of personal responsibility for change, is evident in the work of the Australian psychologist Alan Jenkins (1990). He has been engaged for many years in South Australia in the treatment of violent offenders to whom he offers, in the words of the title to his book, 'an invitation to responsibility'. Central to his method is an appeal to offenders with whom he works to become aware of the suffering they have caused, typically to their wives and children. He asks them to appreciate how these people must feel when they are abused. As in all applications of the humanistic approach, a personally accepting relationship with the offender must be developed in which a sharp distinction is made between the offence itself which is unacceptable and the person of the offender who is.

New approaches to bullying in school have much in common with Jenkins' invitation to responsibility. Among those who have followed a similar line of thinking and practice in their work with bullies are Barbara Maines and George Robinson in England who have developed and promoted a so-called 'No Blame Approach' and Anatol Pikas in Sweden who has proposed his 'Method of Shared Concern'. Both these methods have been employed widely in Europe and more recently in some schools in Australia. These will now be explored more fully.

No Blame and Shared Concern

The No Blame Approach and the Method of Shared Concern have a good deal in common, although, as we will see later, they differ in some important respects. But first let us note five assumptions they have in common.

First	An essential element in countering bullying is to arouse in bullies a sense of empathic concern for those they have victimised. Bullies do have the capacity or potential for making an empathic response to the plight of the victim, and moreover this potential can be actualised through a personal encounter.
Second	Concern can only be achieved in a strictly 'non-blaming' context. This does not mean that bullying is to be 'excused' but rather that feelings of concern will not be elicited if the bullies feel that they are being blamed and that punishment is impending.
Third	Once concern has been aroused, responsible positive action can be elicited and this will assist in the resolution of the problem.
Fourth	Bullying is typically a group phenomenon and to solve the problem you must encounter and work with the responsible group.
Fifth	Although concern and responsible action can result from a planned encounter, it will still be necessary to monitor future developments and to continue to encourage positive behaviours.

The No Blame Approach

The best account of this method can be found in an instructional video produced by the authors (Maines & Robinson, 1992). Its major features which involve seven steps are given below.

Seven Steps of the No Blame Approach

1   Interview the victim

In the interview the first objective is to discover, in general terms, what happened and who was involved. It is not intended that there should be a detailed investigation of the incident or incidents or an attempt made at this, or any subsequent stage 'to get to the bottom of it'. The focus is to be on the feelings of the child who has been victimised. The interviewer seeks to get permission from the child to tell the bullies how he or she feels about it. It is emphasised that the bullies will not be punished and that there is no reason to be fearful of informing. To provide a graphic account the child is asked to describe his/her feelings, if possible, in the form of a piece of writing, a poem or a drawing.

2   Convene a group meeting

This is to include the bullies, but also any colluders or bystanders; about six to eight is ideal. The victim is not included.

3   Communicate to the group how the victim feels

At the meeting the interviewer seeks to describe how the victim feels about the bullying, drawing upon the materials that have been provided by the victim. This may involve reading a poem or a description of how the victim feels. There is to be no interrogation and no blaming. The aim is simply to share information and produce an empathic response.

4   Attribute responsibility to the group

The interviewer points out that it is their joint responsibility to help by improving the situation for the victim.

5   Elicit helpful suggestions

Specific suggestions may then be elicited as to how the victim can be made happier. No promises are required from the children regarding any proposals to help.

6 Hand over responsibility to act to the group

It is explained that it is now up to them. (Nevertheless, the teacher undertakes to meet with them again in about a week's time to review progress.)

7 Individual meetings with participants

Each member of the group and the victim are next interviewed on their own. In this way the effects of the intervention can be monitored and the extent of the progress can be assessed.

Appraisal of 'No Blame'

Opinion is sharply divided about this method. To some it is idealistic and naive; to others it is very appealing because it is based upon an approach to children that can conceivably elicit strong feelings of compassion, a real change of heart and a reconciliation between bullies and victims. Much, however, depends on the teacher or counsellor using the method. Under some circumstances you can easily imagine the group of bullies (even with other 'non-bullies' present) being cynical and dismissive, and perhaps even ridiculing the teacher. It is likely to work better with younger children. Hard evidence from unbiased evaluators of the method is notably lacking. Nevertheless, it is hard to doubt that some teachers can make this approach work with some students. The positive thing about it is that it places the responsibility for change squarely on the bullies and expects cooperation—which in some situations can work wonders.

Is all bullying group bullying?

We might also like to challenge the assumption, made also by the author of the Method of Shared Concern, that bullying is essentially and always a group phenomenon. Surveys suggest strongly that many children see themselves as being bullied quite often by 'one other person'; not always by a group. It is possible that victimised children who claim to be bullied by individuals are unaware that those individuals who bully them are involved in groups or motivated by their membership of groups. But we must remember that there are also many children who claim that they engage in bullying others without the support of others. Are they mistaken or deluded? It seems unlikely that all bullying involves groups. This does not mean that the methods of 'No Blame' or 'Shared Concern' cannot be adapted so as to be employed with non-group bullying. But we might raise the question, to which currently there is no answer through research, of whether individual and group bullying are so radically different as to require very different approaches.

The Method of Shared Concern

This method was devised by Anatol Pikas for working with problems of bullying when a group of children have been identified as having bullied an individual or individuals, or are believed to have done so. Originally it was called the Method of Common Concern, but since 1994 the term 'shared' has been used in place of 'common'.

Accounts of the method have been provided in papers written by Pikas (1989) , and also by Cowie, Sharp and Smith (1992) and Fuller and King (1995). An examination and critique of the method are also to be found in Smith and Sharp (1994) and Sharp and Smith (1994). However, the method is understood best through participation in workshops provided by Pikas himself. During his visit to South Australia and Western Australia in 1995 the method was explored in some depth in his workshops, and the present account is based, in part, on the experience of attending one of these. Anatol Pikas is currently engaged in writing a book on his method and this will eventually provide an authoritative source from which teachers can work. In the meantime the rationale and the main steps in the method and some variations are provided below.

Rationale

It is assumed that children who engage in bullying are largely under the influence of the group with which they identify. But they are typically not comfortable with what they are doing. Sometimes they might feel glad to break free from the group and lose a sense of anxiety or guilt commonly associated with the bullying behaviour. In short, each member is seen as having a conscience that is periodically troubled. Nevertheless, being a member of the group is usually experienced as a source of satisfaction and enjoyment. To a lesser or greater degree the bullying of the victim may seem justified. The victim may sometimes be viewed as provoking the treatment and actually deserving it. But the bully remains a conflicted person, enmeshed in, and constrained by, a group.

As long as the enmeshment lasts there is powerful pressure to conform to the group and to remain insensitive and unconcerned about the victim's plight. To the extent that the teacher can 'reach' the bully as an individual, the latent concern of the bully for the victim can be acknowledged. Each person in the group needs to be 're-individualised' before any progress can be made. This can be done by the teacher or counsellor through the formation of a relationship with each individual member of the group in the context of a sharing of concern about the victim. Because the bully already has ambivalent feelings towards the victim, feeling some concern, albeit partially repressed under the influence of the group, there is a good chance that in a one-to-one situation the bully will take a step towards acknowledging his or her concern for the victim, and taking responsible action to improve the situation.

The Shared Concern procedure

The process can begin after information has been gathered from independent observers about a bullying incident in which it is believed that a number of students are involved.

There are four stages:

Stage one: Interviews with bullies

Each member of the group of bullies who have been identified, or more precisely, suspected of being involved in the bullying of a fellow student, is interviewed alone. Normally each will be taken by the interviewer (commonly the counsellor, but sometimes another teacher) from a classroom to a comfortable room where there can be no interruptions. The class teacher will naturally need first to be informed of what is happening and of the importance of keeping the class occupied so that those returning do not discuss what has happened. No reference is to be made to bullying. It is customary to begin with the group leader (if known) and to see each student in turn, usually for not more than ten minutes.

Chairs are arranged so that the teacher and the student sit at the same level side by side, but with chairs somewhat inclined towards each other, clearly not in a confrontative or adversarial way. After the student is seated, the teacher should wait for eye contact and then raise the issue of the victim having recently had a bad time. A statement to that effect may be said firmly and clearly, for instance: 'John has been having a rather miserable time lately'. Alternatively, there may be a more direct statement used, such as, 'I hear you've been nasty to John'. This is not to be said in an accusatory or hostile way but as a statement of fact. There is a clear invitation for the student to talk about it.

How the student may respond may vary. The student may acknowledge that John has been hurt but deny any personal responsibility, and perhaps blame someone else. Sometimes the bully will remain silent, uncommunicative; in which case a suggestion may be made that he or she might not like to talk today and can go back to class. This may motivate the silent one to speak. In some cases the victim may be blamed (perhaps with some justice) and accused of provoking the negative treatment. Whatever is said by the bully, it is important not to get into any argument, to interrogate and to blame. The teacher's role at this stage is to share his or her perception of the situation and to emphasise the concern that is felt for the person who is being hurt.

Normally, there will be some reciprocated concern expressed by the bully and some acknowledgment of involvement in the situation, either directly or indirectly. As soon as this happens, the interviewer turns to the question of what can be done to help the victim. The interviewer may say: 'I was wondering what you could do to help John'. Suggestions may be forthcoming, such as leaving John alone or, more positively, including him in a group activity. Once a suggestion has been made that is at all constructive and realistic, it is received and commented upon enthusiastically. Sometimes it is left to the teacher to make a suggestion that the student will find acceptable. The meeting closes with an agreement that they will meet again at a designated time to review progress.

The manner of the interviewer is as important as the 'script' that is used. The teacher should be calm, empathic, never angry or indignant. The teacher needs to be ever attentive to what each bully is saying or even suggesting by non-verbal activity. Throughout the interview there must be continued acceptance and respect shown for the bully as a person. Although the method can be viewed as an attempt to persuade, the persuasion must not be 'heavy', but subtle.

What can be expected to result from such an interview? Again there will be variations. Occasionally a bully may refuse to show any concern or accept any responsibility, but experience shows that most of them will. Generally they are surprised and relieved at not being interrogated and blamed. They may feel pleased that they have been consulted rather than abused. They will not feel angry towards the teacher or towards the victim, especially if it is made clear that the victim has not initiated the enquiries. They are generally prepared to make constructive suggestions or to accept reasonable proposals. Importantly, they are not now motivated to confide in other members of the group regarding what they have promised to do to help the victim (this may seem like admitting a betrayal). When each group member, one after another, has expressed concern and indicated steps that he or she will take to help the victim, each has begun to act as a responsible individual.

Stage Two: Meeting with the victim

After speaking with each student who is suspected of bullying, the victim must then be interviewed. The interview can start with an open-ended question: 'How are things going?' The victim will quickly recognise the purpose of the meeting and is generally prepared to discuss the circumstances of the bullying. In listening to the victim, the teacher will need to decide whether the victim is a classical, passive, non-provocative victim, or alternatively has played some role in provoking the bullying. Subsequently, ways may be explored as to how matters can be improved; for example, by not provoking the bullies or by becoming more popular and supported by others. An agreed plan of action is devised and a future meeting arranged.

Again the manner of the interviewer is important. It must be highly supportive, especially initially. But the matter needs to be treated as a problem involving *some* responsibility on the part of the victim. Generally the victim feels grateful for having been able to talk to someone sympathetic and supportive, and may be prepared to accept some responsibility for developing better relations with others.

Stage Three: Preparation for a joint meeting with the victim and the group

First it is necessary to see individuals again, quite briefly, to check on progress and motivate them further. If all goes well, plans can be made for a successful meeting between the group of bullies and the victim; this will make it clear to everyone that the bullying has really ended and a final resolution or conciliation has been achieved. There may sometimes be repeated meetings with individual students and/or the entire group without the victim being present. At these meetings the teacher must note the progress that has been made and offer congratulations when agreements have been kept or bargains honoured.

At some point it will become evident (ideally at the suggestion of a group member) that the victim will be welcome at the group meeting. It is important that the group and the victim are adequately prepared for this event. It must be agreed that each member of the group will make a positive and sincere comment about the victim with him present. Next, the victim must be contacted and assured that he will be welcome and that indeed positive things will be said about him or her.

Stage Four: Group meeting

If the group members have been well prepared the teacher can sometimes act primarily as a facilitator, enabling students to indicate their goodwill and acceptance of the victim. For this to be done publicly by group members will greatly strengthen any individual commitments that have been made. But in cases in which victims have been seen as provocative, a different scenario can be expected. The group members will then require some assurance and guarantee of change in the behaviour of the victim. The teacher then takes on the role of mediator, seeking from both sides suggestions or proposals that are acceptable to the other. The meeting may then conclude with an agreement as to how the victim, as well as the bullies, will behave in future.

Appraisal of the Method of Shared Concern

Compared with the No Blame approach, with which this method has much in common, Shared Concern is more elaborate and highly developed. We will now examine and evaluate the differences in the two methods.

1 With Shared Concern the victim is only seen *after* each of the bullies has been interviewed. This effectively deprives the teacher of the opportunity to gather information from the victim before seeing the bullies. Information must therefore be gathered from other sources, from bystanders, teachers and by personal observation. However, one important advantage of not beginning with the victim is that the victim cannot be blamed by the bullies for informing. The victim is consequently less endangered.

2 With Shared Concern the bullies are seen individually in the first instance, not as a group as in the No Blame approach. This is consistent with the assumption Pikas makes that in the context of the group, each member is constrained from acting as an individual. In a one-to-one context they are more likely to act in an individually responsible way. It may be added that it is considerably easier for the teacher to meet and work with an individual than to confront a group that is motivated to maintain its solidarity. To some degree, the procedure suggested by the No Blame approach partially overcomes this difficulty by including some 'non-bullies' in the group, and this can lessen group solidarity.

3 A third difference is that the Method of Shared Concern does recognise differences between victims. The impression conveyed by the authors of the No Blame approach is that victims are invariably passive or innocent and are 'doing their best'. This is inconsistent with what is known about types of victim, some of whom are provocative, and others themselves engage in bullying. After the bullies have been seen individually, the victim is interviewed and the teacher is then able to form a judgement about the victim's behaviour and how this may be contributing to the problem.

4 With the Shared Concern Method, the process of resolving the problem is not complete until there is an acceptance and demonstration by the group of bullies that the problem has been resolved. This is realistic. Unless the group disintegrates, which seems unlikely, it will continue to influence individual members, and unless there is a group acknowledgment of an acceptance of the victim or a resolution of difficulties with the victim, the members may subsequently be under pressure to resume their former state—that is, as 'troubled bullies'.

5   A consideration for a school is the amount of time needed to employ the method. Given the focused and planned nature of the interviews, there is no reason why they should not, in most cases, be quite brief, extending not more than ten minutes or so. Each school must, however, carefully consider its resources, including the availability of staff, teachers or counsellors, who are motivated to practise the method. Not all teachers find the approach congenial. And naturally the staff must consider its priorities in addressing the problem of bullying in this way in their school.

6   Finally, there is the question of parental involvement. It is sometimes suggested that if children are to be interviewed about their involvement in a bully/victim problem parents should be informed. This is based in part on a possible misunderstanding of the Shared Concern procedure. Accusations are not made; blame is not levelled at anyone. The method seeks to elicit support for victims, not an admission of guilt. Children are not in the dock.

In summary, the Shared Concern Method draws upon principles and assumptions shared with the No Blame approach, principally in the crucial need to have the victim's plight appreciated by the bullies and responsible action to remedy it elicited in the absence of blame and coercion. But the Shared Concern Method goes further in recognising the need for one-to-one counselling; in providing greater protection for the victim; in taking into account individual reactions by both bullies and victims; and by involving bullies and victim in a joint and final meeting at which the problem can be seen to be resolved.

Both methods, it should be noted, assume that bullying behaviour is embedded in a group context, and certainly this is, clearly, often the case. But we must entertain the possibility that bullying is sometimes practised by isolated individuals. As we have seen, students often see it this way, and complementary methods are needed to deal with such cases. They can nevertheless incorporate the philosophy of No Blame in seeking to develop feelings of concern for the victim and inviting responsible action from the bully.

Training in working with bullies in a school

We have already seen (Chapter 11) that teachers often feel inadequate and intimidated at the prospect of dealing with bullies. This is understandable. Bullies are often tough, aggressive people; most teachers are not. Increased confidence in doing this work is sorely needed. How can this be provided? The short answer is practice—but practice in what? It has been suggested that there are strikingly different approaches to working with bullies. Teachers will not learn and practice a method unless they are convinced that (a) it has good prospects of working; and (b) the school in which they are employed will support its use.

Convincing potential users of the value of the Method of Shared Concern can be done in different ways. One is through the provision of research evidence as to its effectiveness, and there are already good indications that in most cases in which it has been applied the results have been favourable (Smith and Sharp, 1994). A second way of persuading teachers and counsellors of its potential usefulness is to involve them in a role play in which they engage as 'practitioners' and 'bullies', in a simulated application of the method—and then reflect upon its effectiveness.

In running workshops for teachers, I have frequently used role play as a means of introducing the Method of Shared Concern and generating discussion of the approach based upon the experiences of participants. This is done as a preliminary to a more detailed consideration of the method.

In the role play, instructions are provided for people who will play the part of 'bullies' and 'teachers'. Some get the part of an exaggeratedly traditional authoritarian teacher (Teacher A); others get a part not dissimilar to that exercised by teachers in the first stage of the Shared Concern Method. Instructions for role plays are given below.

BULLY

You are part of a group that goes around teasing and bullying kids at your school.

You like belonging to this group. It's lots of fun. There is boy named Tom who is now the target. He gets ridiculed, called names, tripped or even hit, and is often left out of things for no particular reason. Occasionally you feel a bit sorry for him. But making fun of Tom is really very amusing—and after all he is a wimp and sort of deserves what he gets. Some teachers have been watching what is happening to Tom and asking questions. So you are not surprised when you hear that a teacher wants to talk to you.

You will be asked to go to one of the teachers who will interview you for about five to ten minutes.

Try to behave as you think a boy or girl of twelve or thirteen would probably behave in the situation.

When you have finished, leave the scene and jot down your impressions and the feelings you had during the interview.

TEACHER A

Over the last few weeks you have noticed that Tom, one of the students you teach, is being continually teased and bullied by some students in his class.

Tom is a smallish, introverted boy who gets upset easily. This only encourages the bullies. You feel strongly that you want to stop the bullying

You send for one of the students whom you believe has been bullying Tom. This is your approach.

1 Stand up when the student comes in and face him/her, *standing throughout the interview*.
2 You have good evidence that the student has played a part in bullying Tom but you want to hear it confirmed by the student. *You want to find out exactly what happened.*
3 You feel very angry and you are going to tell the student what you think about people who bully others. *You are not going to accept any excuses.*
4 You make it very clear that such behaviour will *not* be tolerated.
5 You explain that the student will be punished. You warn the student about what will happen if Tom is bullied again. You emphasise that the student will henceforth be *watched*.

Take between five and ten minutes; then afterwards jot down some impressions on how the interview went.

TEACHER B

Over the last few weeks you have noticed that Tom, one of the students you teach, is being continually teased and bullied by some students in his class.

Tom is a smallish, introverted boy who gets upset easily. This only encourages the bullies. You feel you want to help Tom.

You send for one of the students whom you believe has been bullying Tom. This is your approach.

1   Ask the student to sit down, then take a seat alongside, partly facing the student. Wait until there is some eye contact, and begin by pointing out that Tom is having a bad time of it recently. You then ask the student what he or she knows about it.

2   Listen carefully without blaming the student in any way.

Continue to share your concern for Tom.

Sooner or later the student is likely to show some comprehension of the problem that Tom has. When this happens, move on and ask what can be done to help him and how the student could help.

3   If no offer is forthcoming, make a suggestion, such as being careful *not* to tease Tom (since he easily gets upset), or to include him in some activity. (What is suggested may arise naturally from what has already been said during the interview.)

4   As soon as any positive proposal has been made, support it—but make a time to see the student again to see how things are going.

5   Remember to remain calm, non-blaming throughout, focused upon sharing *your* concern for Tom and seeking some constructive action from the student.

The entire interview should take between five and ten minutes.

Afterwards jot down your impressions of the interview

Following the role play, participants share their feelings and reactions. Of special interest are the reactions of those who play the part of the bully. Almost without exception the 'bullies' who were interviewed by participants who adopted the authoritarian approach (Teacher A) report increased hostility not only to the teacher but to the mythical person who was allegedly victimised! They also generally feel more inclined than before to identify with the group of bullies and to continue the practice of bullying. By contrast, 'bullies' who were seen by the teacher whose approach was more understanding and non-blaming (Teacher B) are much more inclined to be cooperative. Although we cannot draw firm conclusions from a role play, the effect of the experience in role playing is frequently enough to convince teachers that the Method of Shared Concern is worth examining further.

When teachers are convinced of its potential value, it is best to role play scenes that commonly occur in the conducting of the Method of Shared

Concern. Pikas himself is a supreme master in setting up and orchestrating these scenes. He is also skilful in demonstrating how teachers can react to alternative ways of responding by the bully whilst continually maintaining an attitude of respect for the bully, concern for the victim and a commitment to producing a solution to the problem. This approach also provides the role players with opportunities to receive feedback from the leader and other participants about their performance.

Evaluating methods of intervention with bullies

Earlier we considered three criteria by which interventions could be evaluated (see Chapter 11). In brief these were:
(i)   to ensure the protection of the victim;
(ii) to change the behaviour of the bully—both for the sake of other future victims and for the sake of the bully's future; and
(iii) to deter or dissuade other students from engaging in bullying. How do the approaches discussed so far measure up?

The safety of the victim

We have seen that this is the major consideration. It is instructive to compare the various approaches according to their effectiveness in ensuring the continued safety of the child who has been victimised. As we have seen, in the Method of Shared Concern steps are taken to protect the victim by not requiring the victim to provide evidence that can be used against the bullies. To a lesser degree, the No Blame approach provides some security for the victim in guaranteeing that the bullies will not be blamed or punished over the incident that is reported by the victim.

When the victim is believed to have informed on the bullies and the bullies are subsequently punished, the danger to the victim may actually increase, as occurred in a case that was reported recently. This occurred when several boys attending a secondary school were suspended for having continually attacked another boy without provocation over a period of months. The attacks had included frequent kicking of the boy in the backs of his legs which, as a consequence, had become badly scarred. The bullies were identified and it was suggested that the matter was so serious so as to be handed over to the police. This option was rejected by the parents of the victim on the grounds that it would be too traumatic for their son to endure. The attacks continued, however, with friends of the suspended boys joining in. As a consequence the boy (aged sixteen) was provided with two bodyguards who escorted him everywhere while he was at school. This was for only part of each day because the protection costs were so expensive. The abuse, now verbal, continued and persisted when the boy left school several weeks later. The family were extremely disturbed by the situation and like many families in similar circumstances wanted to leave the area in which they lived.

We have, of course, no way of knowing whether the bullies could have been dealt with more effectively through the use of counselling and mediation. But there was certainly a chance that a breakthrough would have been possible. But no such approach was tried. The bullies were seen as the enemy; they were to be punished and taught a lesson. Unfortunately the treatment produced only defiance and a resolve on the part of the bullying group to continue the war.

What we often ignore is that bullying is maintained by allegiances to groups, however misguided their missions may be. We may also forget that there are means of continuing guerrilla warfare that are difficult, if not impossible, to stamp out. As far as possible, and as long as possible, it is desirable to explore means by which non-punitive measures can be employed to resolve the situation.

There is unfortunately little quantitative evidence of a direct kind on the relative endangerment of children after different methods have been applied to intervene with bullies. Nevertheless there is some relevant evidence from the Sheffield research that indicates that following applications of the Shared Concern Method, the group does not usually bully again. Two-thirds of the cases have been reported as having been cleared up. This is encouraging. When bullying does recur, it is more usual for a different victim to be chosen. The original victim almost always is helped by the method.

Changes in behaviour

We may ask whether different methods of intervention may have *enduring* effects on those who are so treated. In a shrewd analysis of the process of social influence, Kelman (1961) identified three ways in which attitudes and behaviour could be affected by alternative treatments. He described these as:

(i)   compliance;
(ii) identification; and
(iii) internalisation.

They can be applied instructively to expected consequences of treatments of bullies.

Compliance generally occurs when behaviour is under the control of forms of reinforcement, positive or negative. Punishment then is seen as being generally effective as long as, but only as long as, effective surveillance is seen to be happening. As we have seen, surveillance is extremely difficult to maintain as far as bullying is concerned, because there are so many subtle ways in which it can be practiced and detection avoided.

Identification, according to Kelman, occurs when behaviour is maintained through admiration of a person whose behaviour you wish to copy, that is, to be like him or like her or alternatively in a role relationship with that person, such as that of follower. To the extent that the teacher is an admired role model (and this is more likely to be so if the teacher can make genuine and helpful relations with the student) pro-social behaviour that is incompatible with bullying is likely to be maintained—and without surveillance. It follows that any change in a bully's behaviour effected in this way is likely to continue, as long as the model remains admired! Surveillance is unnecessary as long as this condition is maintained. But its continuation cannot be guaranteed. The student may choose one day to admire somebody who is quite different: somebody, perhaps, who is a bully.

Internalisation, referring here to the adoption of behaviour congruent with your own values, is again independent of surveillance and, most importantly, is also independent of the maintenance of admiration for someone. Value structures can also change but they are much more resistant to change than behaviour that is under the control of contingencies of reinforcement or the vagaries of fluctuating likes and dislikes that a person may have for someone.

In the light of Kelman's analyses, a No Blame method such as the Method of Shared Concern is more likely than other methods to result in the development of sustainable behaviour grounded in a process of internalisation rather than identification or compliance. This line of thinking is certainly consistent with commonsense. To the degree that behaviour is seen by a student as being self-chosen, not in some way coerced or wooed into being, it is likely to be enduring. To act otherwise from how you have chosen to behave must create a great deal of dissonance in the 'ex-bully'.

Effects on others

The effects of such a method on bullies' behaviour towards other students are not easy to assess. Many of the considerations raised above are relevant to the question of whether the use of particular methods of treating bullying will dissuade others from bullying or encourage others to try it. Unquestionably, the use of well advertised 'consequences' (with good methods of surveillance) for bullying *can* deter some children, but generally these are the milder kinds of bullies, that is children who are averse to taking risks. Those who are really tough are sometimes actually encouraged by the threat of punishment. They see it as a challenge.

We must also bear in mind that children are often influenced by the behaviour of dominant peers who used to bully others but have stopped of their own volition. If we can provide in a school more examples of these kinds of children our job is made much easier. Humanistic methods offer better prospects of producing them.

Mixing approaches and methods

Are different approaches compatible? It is often asked whether it is possible to combine components of moralistic, legalistic and humanistic approaches in a school policy in dealing with bullies.

When this question is raised it often results in a hot debate, in which conflicting and inflexible positions are taken: one committed to only 'humanistic methods' and opposed to any practice which involves discipline and punishment; the other arguing that reliance upon such an approach as the Method of Shared Concern is idealistic, unrealistic and impractical. This is likely to be a continuing debate for some time. My own view is that a humanistic approach such as that proposed by Pikas is certainly desirable as a first stage in all but the most serious cases of bullying and that, in a sense, the use of punishment is always second best. I agree with Moberley (1968) who puts the matter as follows:

> 'Though it is often right to punish, this is only because no better alternative is available at the moment to those in authority. For punishment always entails some loss as well as gain; it includes some element of pretension on the one side and of surrender to coercion on the other; it rests on presumptions that are never wholly true. Like

some physic, it includes an element of poison and is not chiefly good for food. *To be obliged to punish offenders, not only implies that we blame them; in some degree it implies our own moral incapacity...'* (page 381, my italics)

The future

What of the future of humanistic methods? I think it is positive. We have become much less convinced than previous generations of the value of preaching—especially to the seemingly unconvertible. Increasingly the use of punishment is being questioned as the primary response and principal means of dealing with delinquent and anti-social behaviour. We have always known, I think, in our hearts, that ignoring the problem will do no good. We are desperately looking for alternatives that are effective.

Are the new methods being tried? Yes, in many schools in Australia responsible and realistic teachers are trying out new ways to solve the old problem. For example, St. Peter's College in Adelaide, South Australia; Pembroke Secondary College in Victoria and Thornlie Secondary Senior High School in Western Australia are among many schools that have adopted the Method of Shared Concern as part of their counselling/behaviour management policy. Interested teachers should enquire of such schools how effective the new methods are. As we shall see, more and more schools are seriously considering, and some actually trying out, other humanistic methods—such as conflict resolution through peer mediation. As new methods are being developed and become known, we can expect that bullying will increasingly be addressed by methods based on an understanding and respect for individuals and by 'invitations to responsibility' that are hard to refuse.

Supporting
the victim

Most people would agree that children who are being victimised at school need support from others. Not all. As mentioned earlier, there are some people who believe that victimised children should learn to fend for themselves and should not be helped. But such people are in a small minority. If there is any disagreement, it is likely to be *what* kind of support and *how* it should be given.

What we know about supporting victimised children

Two years ago I teamed up with a lady from England, Ms Sonia Sharp, who had already done a great deal of successful work with peer victimised children in schools, to write an article for the *International Journal of Protective Behaviours* (Rigby and Sharp, 1993). We called it 'Cultivating the art of self-defence amongst victimised children'. What was said then is essentially what I believe now, although I think I have learned a few more things since, as you will see. But it seemed worthwhile to reproduce parts of that article in this book, which I now do with agreement of the Journal and the co-author.

> *'Although any child can become prey to bullying behaviour and indeed most children will have an experience of this unpleasant aspect of peer culture by the time they leave school, a small group of children do seem more vulnerable than others. These more vulnerable children often share some common features although there has been no study which establishes whether these characteristics are the cause or the consequence of being bullied. Research has established that they are often introverted, have few if any friends and are especially lacking in self-esteem. They offer little or no effective opposition to the bullying pupils. It is as if they do not know how or, for some reason, cannot bring themselves, to defend themselves. Some adults may lose patience with them, as evidently did the Australian poet, C.J. Dennis (1950) who gave this advice:*

> *Get a _____ move on*
> *Have some common sense*
> *Learn the _____ art of*
> *Self de- _____ -fence!*

> *What are the behaviours that are helpful for frequently bullied pupils to learn? Can they be readily identified? If so, how can they be learnt?*

> *Bullied children are often advised to stick up for themselves or ignore the bullies by learning martial arts skills. For some children this may indeed be an answer. For many more children, however, who are temperamentally gentle or physically weak, this is unlikely to be a reasonable option. When we come to think of the children who are rarely bullied—the vast majority of children—they are certainly not martial arts experts. They are often not strong or physically robust children. The qualities they possess usually include a sense of confidence; an ability to cooperate with others; friendliness and a good*

sense of humour. In the remainder of this paper we will try to identify some of the protective behaviours which can be taught to those more vulnerable children who do not seem naturally to have access to a buffering temperament or appropriate social skills.

As an alternative to an aggressive response to bullying behaviour, children might be encouraged to ignore their tormentors. However, a completely passive reaction can make the bullied child feel more helpless and may even encourage his or her peers to think of the individual child as powerless as well. We would suggest that there is a third set of strategies which pupils can employ when faced with bullying. These strategies build upon assertive behaviour, aiming to empower the individual pupil to respond to the situation in a direct and constructive manner.

Social skills training for pupils generally has a long tradition in schools and in the community. All of us concerned with children recognise that self-protection is an essential part of social development and urge our children to be careful and to keep safe. Tiny Arora (1989; 1991) in Britain described a small support group for badly bullied pupils in a secondary school in the UK. She offered these pupils a twelve hour training programme, spread over a half-term, which included opportunities to learn and practice some assertiveness techniques; rehearse appropriate responses to bullying situations and extend their repertoire of general relationship building skills. She found that not only did these children become more assertive in their interactions with both peers and adults, but also their self-esteem increased and levels of reported bullying fell as the course proceeded.

Building upon Arora's work, The DFE Sheffield Bullying Project, directed by Peter Smith, at the University of Sheffield, England, sought to evaluate the effectiveness of protective behaviour training for bullied pupils. Nineteen pupils from three schools were monitored throughout the duration of a training group and then intermittently up to two terms later. The training group consisted of between four and six sessions, each session lasting between thirty minutes and an hour. As in Arora's study, a significant increase in the self-esteem and self-

confidence of the pupils became apparent and this maintained over time. Furthermore, the pupils selected more constructive and assertive strategies in response to hypothetical bullying situations, and reported actually implementing these strategies in real life contexts. The pupils also reported a reduction in being bullied. A related study focusing on children, carried out by Irene Whitney, with special educational needs highlighted assertiveness training offered in a support group setting as particularly valuable to children with learning and behaviour difficulties.

Thus carefully conducted studies have shown that by learning to employ protective behaviours, bullied pupils can increase their resiliency and actually reduce the extent to which they are victimised by others. Three principles are basic to this process.

The first is that when they are in situations in which they are being harassed, children should respond in an assertive manner, rather than passively or with aggression. It may be necessary for some children to learn the crucial difference between being assertive and being aggressive or passive. Secondly, it is desirable that wherever possible children who are being bullied should be able to enlist the support of others. This presupposes a capacity to call upon people who will help, including bystanders. The success of this strategy will also depend on the extent to which other pupils are sympathetic to the idea of supporting other pupils. Schools can do much to build a supportive peer ethos by teaching effective bystander behaviour to all pupils. Finally, such children should be able to make a realistic appraisal of situations in which they are in danger of being badly hurt, and to escape as soon as possible.

For children to apply these principles, they must be able to utilise specific skills in pressure situations. They should be able to recognise unreasonable requests and make assertive, non-acquiescing responses. They should know when they are being manipulated or coerced—and resist. Where name-calling is the form of abuse, children need to be able to stay calm and relaxed, and respond neutrally. How to get bystanders to intervene when it becomes necessary is a further skill that can be of great value to them. Finally, it is important for them to know how to leave a hostile situation.

None of the above skills is readily acquired through the simple act of being told about them. Children may indeed be strongly motivated to employ these skills, but are unlikely to perform them when required unless they have been clearly instructed. In fact, the skills need to be demonstrated for them and then repeatedly practised by the children through role play in a supportive social environment. By continual rehearsal—and appropriate reinforcement by the instructor and other children—the necessary skills can become part of a child's everyday repertoire. The more opportunities there are to practise the skills, the more effective they can become in 'real life' situations.

To identify these vulnerable children and assist them to develop self-defence skills is an important goal for any school. In addition, it is essential that schools examine the broader context of their social and educational environment to establish methods for preventing bullying behaviour from occurring in the first place, and for responding effectively to those pupils who bully others. This 'whole school' anti-bullying approach can provide an appropriate framework for more intensive training in protective behaviours for some pupils.

In reflecting upon what is now being done in some schools to help children who are frequently victimised by others, we are conscious of certain obstacles or hindrances to this work which can arise through the way people sometimes think about the problem of bullying. There is, first of all, in some quarters, an undue emphasis upon the so-called 'personality' of the victimised child, as if it were fixed and incorrigible. This we know from research is simply not true; and maintaining that children cannot change is certainly discouraging. Secondly, there is some evidence to suggest that schools find it easier to identify persistently bullied boys than girls (as mentioned earlier, girls do get bullied and schools who are intending to establish this kind of training need to ensure that their methods of identification do not discriminate against either gender). Finally, there is considerably more to it than crude exhortation for the child who is repeatedly victimised to 'get a

_____ *move on, have some common sense'. The art of self-defence clearly does need to be cultivated—and for the more vulnerable children this needs to be done thoughtfully and sensitively. It cannot be done overnight. Fortunately, we are becoming increasingly aware of how this can be achieved, and the future is much brighter for many children in schools than it was only a few years ago.'*

What kind of support is needed?

There are two kinds of support that can be provided for victimised children, and they need to be distinguished.

The first might be called moral or psychological support. This is provided when we listen sympathetically to a child's problems. We have seen that this can have an important effect of acting, at least partially, as a buffer between the stress of victimisation and consequent health problems. Both parents and teachers have been exhorted in this book to lend a sympathetic ear and to provide this source of support.

The second kind of support is more active. It may include giving moral support but also seeking to help the victimised child to acquire new skills (or practise old ones that have fallen into disuse) that could prevent the child from being bullied. Most people think that this is a good idea. But there are some who are sceptical. There are those who believe that some children are so disadvantaged and incapable of being assertive that training will be a waste of time or perhaps even damaging to them. We have not seen evidence to support this view. Vulnerable children can learn better ways to protect themselves. There are also some who believe that it is simply wrong to ask victims to adjust their behaviour. They are, it is said, doing their best. The bullies need to change their behaviour. I have sympathy with this view, which has been promoted by the proponents of the No Blame approach in England (Maines & Robinson, 1992). In a world in which we could guarantee that bullies would all stop, I would certainly be for it. Until that happy day, however, I would suggest that we do help victims to protect themselves better.

Providing practical support for victimised children

Children who are frequently victimised by others can be helped in different contexts and each has advantages and disadvantages.

One-to-one situations

The advantage in working with a child in a one-to-one situation is that focused attention can be provided without distraction. Some psychologists have specialised in this work and can be helpful in diagnosing problems and identifying more clearly the difficulties that a child may have with aggressive peers. For example, it may not be immediately evident whether the problem is due to a lack of appropriate assertiveness skills in a child's behavioural repertoire or due to a pervading state of anxiety or poor self-esteem that prevents a child from using the skills he or she might actually possess. In Melbourne, the psychologist Evelyn Field has been particularly active in helping non-assertive children to help themselves more effectively by learning more positive ways of responding to teasing and harassment.

The disadvantage of providing one-to-one therapy or counselling is that it is:

(i)   often less economic in the use of time than working with children in groups; and
(ii) whatever is 'learned' in the session in a psychologist's room with the psychologist may not generalise to situations in schools where there are other children and circumstances that are difficult to anticipate.

To some extent, this disadvantage can be minimised by gathering 'feedback' from the child on how interactions at school have proceeded, and making adjustments in the training accordingly. Also, where diagnostic needs require more intensive attention and individual therapy is seen as desirable, a child may be helped in a situation where there can be a sustained focus on the one child.

Help in the classroom

It is sometimes argued that help can be provided most effectively in the situation where bullying occurs and in the company of the children who are the principal actors, that is, bullies, the bullies' supporters, neutral bystanders, victims and the victims' supporters. In this case whatever is learned can, in theory, have immediate 'real world' application. This approach has been promoted in some schools in the United States where children who are victimised are helped by a teacher or counsellor in a number of ways, including facing up to the bully in the class with other children present (Batsche & Knoff, 1994).

The victim may be instructed in how to respond to a bully's threats by using what has been termed 'brave talk'. This means bringing it out 'into the open' with other students in the class watching as the victim, with the necessary prompting and encouragement from the instructor, refuses to be cowed by the bully and asserts that he or she will not take it any more, or words to that effect. The problem is that the bully and the class may see the incident for the role play that it is, and the usual relationship between bully and victim could quickly reappear. But where the inequality in power is not so extreme and with sympathetic support from other children in a class the method can be effective—but not without risk!

Groups for helping victims

These can have substantial advantages. First they are relatively economic compared with providing training in a one-to-one situation. But more importantly, they provide a context in which bully/victim problems can be explored with children who are 'in the same boat' and motivated to help one another. Not only can they constitute a 'support group' for victimised children, but they can provide for each other the opportunity for them to develop appropriate skills, under the direction of an instructor or leader, through interacting with other members as part of a planned programme of training.

In terms of providing learning that can be generalised to 'real life', the situation is much more positive than that provided in one-to-one training, but less so than learning and practising assertiveness skills in the context of a classroom. My personal judgement is that for many children who are easily victimised it is best to start in a relatively protected or safe environment such as that provided in carefully selected small groups with a sensitive and skilled leader. Otherwise they will feel overwhelmed and their behaviour in using 'brave talk' in a classroom will seem inauthentic, phoney. The learning in a 'protected group situation', being sweeping and non-specific, will still be a problem, and children in such groups will need to be persuaded to try out new behaviours that were learned in a secure situation, and then report on what has happened when they next encounter the peers who bully them.

Running groups for helping victims

The first problem is how to get together children who need help without further reducing their self-esteem by advertising their inadequacy. A broader description than 'victim support group' is needed: one that emphasises social skills that enable people to interact more effectively with others. Children identified as 'victims' by teachers and other pupils should to be approached. However, truly voluntary attendance is important. Parents of pupils should be informed and consent provided before the group work can begin.

How should the groups be composed? Experience shows that it is preferable to include children who have similar needs in that they lack assertiveness and are easily bullied by their peers. Although it may be tempting to include 'bullies' (as a challenge, perhaps) it is usually unwise to do. They would tend to disturb the 'safe' environment that is necessary, at least in the early stages of the work, with these children. The groups should be quite small, about six members is ideal.

It is best (if possible) to have two adult leaders. This allows one to be more directive and the other to observe developments more closely. They can alternate roles and importantly check out their perceptions regarding progress and problems after each meeting. They should each be knowledgeable about bullying, have daily contact with children, and ideally have group work training and a basic understanding of elements of social skill and assertiveness. Depending upon age group a period of between forty-five and ninety minutes is desirable. With younger children shorter periods may be needed. At least six to eight meetings are usually required with such programs.

Goal and aims

The leaders should be clear about what they are aiming to do. The overall purpose is to reduce the incidence and severity of bullying experienced by the group members. How this is done will depend in part on the expressed needs of the group, but these *sub-goals* are considered important: These are to help children:

(i) To be aware of new and better ways of relating and reacting to other children.

(ii) To feel more in control of their own actions and reactions: in short, to be more assertive.

(iii) To be better at making and keeping friends.

(iv) To see themselves more positively, that is, to have higher self-esteem.

You can be sure that the realisation of any (and hopefully all) these goals will contribute to the reduction of bullying.

The process

The process will normally consist of some direct instruction, but also role plays and discussion between members of the group. Together the children will learn how other children feel about difficult and threatening interpersonal situations. They will quickly come to see that they are 'in the same boat'. Under the leaders' guidance, they will begin to work out with others what can be done in situations in which someone tries to bully them. Through role-playing different responses to deal with bullying can be tried out. The students can begin to try out new ways of behaving outside the group, and then report back on what happened. Above all, the meetings should be fun; the children and the teachers should have a good time together, learn to appreciate each other and make friends.

What might be done in the training sessions

How the group leader operates will vary from person to person, depending on specific skills and familiarity with techniques. One outstanding worker in this area is Ms Sonia Sharp from the University of Sheffield, who has developed a series of techniques and group exercises to develop greater assertiveness among children who are often victimised by others. These have been employed in some Australian schools through her direct influence following a visit she made here in 1994. Some of the methods she uses are described below.

1   To begin with she stresses the need for children to differentiate between what they can tell others about the group activities, for example, the techniques they practise and those they should not, for example, what a member has told others about himself or herself in confidence. In short, children are to understand what is confidential to the group.

2   Children are then reminded that each of them has in the past been bullied by others, and that this should help them to be considerate in how they behave towards each other in the group. However, when they are *acting* a part, it is explained, this doesn't apply. This distinction must be understood.

3   The first exercise is to get children to share and 'open up' with each other. Because victimised children are frequently, introverted, shy and unasser- tive, this must be done gently. A highly successful method with these children is to give each person two sheets of paper on which, with the assistance of a partner, outlines of their feet are drawn. Each then goes off to draw or write on the paper some 'good' things about themselves on the 'best foot', for example the things that they like, make them happy, or enjoy; and not-so-good things on the other foot, that is, things that make them fearful, unhappy or worried. It is pointed out that they will later share what they have produced with a neighbour, and they should therefore not include things they do *not* wish to have mentioned. The leader models this activity first. This is a very safe activity. The children can first collect their thoughts in private and decide to share some things, not others. What they will say is down on paper and serves as a prompt. It also provides the first clues to the children's interests and concerns. This helps the group to develop a sympathetic interest in each other.

4   To begin to develop assertiveness, Sonia recommends a 'bout of boasting'. Each child is to shake the hand of a partner, look them in the eye, and say: 'Hi, my name is ———————— and I'm good at ————————'. Any tendency to change the wording to 'quite good at' is corrected, as also is avoiding eye contact. This can be done around a circle, allowing each person to see how others are doing it.

5 To develop assertiveness further, an exercise of simply saying 'no' to a request is then used. Each child takes turns in making a request to which an answer of 'no' is given by the partner; again this is done around in a circle. The leader watches carefully and picks out any incongruence between the verbal, 'no' and non-verbal behaviour; for example, smiling or looking embarrassed, while saying 'no', and the exercise is repeated—and success is reinforced. It is pointed out that there are reasonable and also unreasonable requests of the kind that bullies often make. Care is taken to discuss *when* the technique can be appropriately used, and when it can't.

6 The exercise of saying 'no' is later extended to apply to situations in which a demand is repeated several times—and the same or very similar answer is given, for example, 'No, I don't want to', 'No, I don't'. This 'broken record' technique is rehearsed with different kinds of requests. In practising this, the children can appreciate that firm and persistent refusals (without explanations) may eventually result in the bully feeling discouraged.

7 Responding non-emotionally to name-calling is developed in this way. Nasty or insulting names are written down on slips of paper (either by leader or members) and placed in a bucket. Each member draws out at random two or three slips. These are read and used to insult the group leader who replies in a so-called 'fogging' manner, that is, she uses a nebulous non-emotional reply. These can include: 'you might think so', 'probably', 'it may look like that to you', 'maybe' or 'possibly so'. In this way the children see how they can respond in a non-emotional way and so not become upset. They then practise this in pairs.

8 At the beginning of each meeting, children are asked to tell others their news, both good and bad. In addition, they may share biscuits. This gives the meeting the status of a club and emphasises the nurturing function of the group.

9 Particular difficult situations for children who are bullied are examined and role-played, for example, being pressured and jeered at by a group; having a group blocking their exit; and being physically pushed around. In each case, helpful responses are suggested, for example, maintaining a confident manner, escaping a situation, calling for help, pushing through a group. For the latter, it can be sometimes useful to bring in self-defence experts, depending on who is available, bearing in mind that

children who are often victimised are usually temperamentally gentle. At the same time some physical skills can often be very helpful for their confidence.

10 The success of the group does not depend entirely on the skills that are learnt. According to Sonia, the sense that someone cares about them, recognises their difficulties, and is prepared to help them to help themselves can develop in such children greater confidence and self-respect.

11 Evaluation of the sessions can include measures of:

(a) self-esteem;

(b) assertiveness;

(c) capacity to get help from others; and

(d) greater self-control.

It is also important to check whether children are putting into practice what they have learned outside the group sessions.

Exercises in group problem-solving with victims

In the course of providing social skills training for students who are continually being victimised, it is useful from time to time to pose problems which relate directly to possible bully/victim issues. Here are some examples, which are adapted from work undertaken by Arora (1991).

1 Name calling

You have just come out of Maths and are on your way to a Physical Education class. While walking down the corridor, you see ahead of you two boys who are messing about and calling out names to many pupils who pass.

- Think of as many things as possible which you could do or say.
- Choose the best three to act out.

2 Demanding money

You are in the playground, standing by yourself, when two bigger boys come up to you and start to push you, saying you have to give them two dollars. They know you have the money on you.

- How would you deal with this situation?
- Write down as many ways as possible, choose the best *two* to act out and explain why these are the best ones.

3 Physical threat

Some of your classmates have threatened to get you and beat you up on the way home after school. They know where you live and the route you take.
- How would you deal with this?
- Show two different ways in which you might solve this problem.

Resistance training

It is sometimes urged that victimised children can best be helped by building up their confidence through becoming physically stronger and more able to defend themselves physically. How this can be done is discussed at length in Tim Laskey's book, *How to beat the bully: a successful self-help course* (1992). Laskey strongly recommends the use of 'systematic, well-supervised Progressive Resistance Training to build strength, physique and confidence'. Activities he recommends include bodybuilding, power lifting and Olympic lifting. He goes on to suggest that if a boy is 'interested in boxing, it could be just the catalyst he needs to trigger a resurgence of confidence, pride and self-esteem' (p. 19). The same can be said of the martial arts of judo, karate, kung fu, taekwondo and ju-jitsu. And there is no reason why the suggestion should be restricted to boys. However, the key phrase is 'if he (or she) is interested'. It may be uncongenial or impractical for a child who is being victimised to turn to such remedies, and certainly no pressure should be applied for a boy or a girl to do so. In short, these suggestions may be useful for some children but not others.

More realistic, I think, is the work of Bill Bates, a police officer in Adelaide who provides programs for children (and their parents), frequently visiting schools to help young people protect themselves against bullies. Bill is a martial arts expert who for two years made a close study of children's physical abilities, finding that they were generally not structurally or physically strong enough to beat off assaults from older peers. He maintains that young people are often influenced by films and videos to believe that they can effectively defend themselves against a bigger person by kicking and punching. By reacting physically (and ineffectively) children can escalate the danger. Their actions may also lead to them being accused by teachers, and sometimes the police, of being responsible for the conflict. Alternative strategies are needed. These are provided through his program, *Living*

Safely (Bates, 1992) and includes developing better judgement in apprehending danger and taking evasive action.

The creative use of science fiction

An alternative approach to dealing with the problem of name-calling has been devised by an Adelaide psychiatrist who works at the Cranio-facial Clinic at the Adelaide Women's and Children's Hospital. The children he treats have suffered facial disfigurement and become the butt of insensitive children who ridicule their appearance. Dr Gerrard teaches such children to imagine that their heads are surrounded by a 'force field' which has the effect of causing insulting names called out at them to boomerang back upon the caller. This can produce a feeling of impregnability and calm. The caller is not encouraged to continue since he or she is evidently having no effect. The potential victim remains detached, unaffected. Research has demonstrated that this method is effective in raising the self-esteem of such children, which can become very low (Gerrard, 1991).

Evaluating interventions to help victimised children

Evaluation of the methods of intervention and training is very important. You would look for improvements in social skills, especially assertiveness, making friends, and self-esteem. Most of all, however, you would be looking for evidence that the children experience less bullying. Self-report measures can be used, supplemented by observations by teachers and other students.

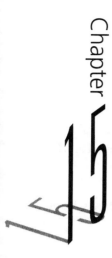

Parents, teachers and families

Parents and families can and do figure prominently both as part of the problem of bullying and as part of its solution. To a large extent, they must work with teachers in the interests of their child. This may not be easy. In this chapter we will examine some of the roles parents, teachers and families play, for better or worse—and some of the roles they might play for the better.

Parents learning about their children being bullied

Children are often averse to telling adults that they have been bullied by their peers; they are much more likely to tell their friends. But if they do tell an adult, it is likely to be a parent, especially their mothers. About one in three tell either mother or father, often both.

Sometimes parents suspect that it is happening but the child is not telling. Here is a set of warning signs, proposed by Dawkins and Hill (1995; Dawkins, 1995) based on their medical experience in England.

Table 15.1 **Warning signs that a child is being bullied at school**

Physical
Unexplained bruises, scratches or cuts
Torn or damaged clothes or belongings

Psychosomatic
Non-specific pains, headaches, abdominal pains

Behavioural
Fear of walking to or from school
Change of route to school
Asking to be driven to school
Unwilling to go to school
Deterioration in school work
Coming home starving (because lunch money was taken)
'Loss' of possessions/pocket money
Asking for or stealing money (to pay the bully)
Having few friends
Rarely invited to parties
Change in behaviour
    Becoming withdrawn
    Stammering
    Unexpected mood change
    Irritability and temper outbursts
    Appearing upset, unhappy, tearful, distressed
    Stopping eating
    Attempting suicide
Appearing anxious: may wet bed, bite nails, seem afraid, develop tic, sleep poorly, cry out in sleep
Refusing to say what is wrong
Giving improbable excuses or explanations for any of the above

Of course, with any of the 'signs' given in Table 15.1, it would be wrong to jump to conclusions that a child is being bullied. There are many alternative explanations. They are 'warning signs' not proof of anything. Where the signs suggest a health problem, it is generally wise to see a doctor who can explore the matter in greater depth. The doctor may initiate a line of questioning with the child that may lead to your suspicions that the child is being bullied at school being strengthened.

There may remain, however, the delicate question of how far you should go in urging the child to speak. Parents will inevitably have different views on this, and much will depend on the unique relationship between the parent and the child. You should certainly respect the child's reticence. It is no easy thing for a child to admit to being bullied. The child may fear that the action a parent might take would be extremely embarrassing and perhaps make matters worse. But there are cases when the child's health and well-being are being seriously threatened that a parent may seek information from other sources. Under some circumstances the child might be coaxed to speak about it. Children will generally do so if they feel secure that they will not be losing control of the situation, that is, if subsequent steps are to be planned with their unforced involvement.

There are some things a parent can do. One is to listen sympathetically, without the slightest hint of blame. This is sometimes all a child may want. It may help enormously to know that the parent knows and cares. The child may be given encouragement and sometimes directly helped to feel more confident or assertive in going to school knowing he or she has the parents' full support. But it may be that the situation requires further action, foremost of which is likely to be a talk with a teacher at the school.

Now let us pause and ask how the bullying is likely to seem to the parent if such an action is taken. What follows is a description of parental and school perspectives which, unfortunately, all too frequently are taken, with no good resulting for the child.

Parental perspective

The most common response is one of outrage. There is often a strong feeling that the school is in some sense responsible for allowing it to happen or in failing to prevent it. The child's view of the matter is likely to have been accepted without question. The parent wants strong action now. At the same time the parent may feel considerable guilt or shame in the fact that the child is unable or unwilling to protect himself or herself.

The parent may well have come to the school as a last resort, having talked at length with the child, who quite probably has been reluctant to have a parent go to the school. The parent is in the mood to interpret any scepticism or lack of support from the school as evidence of callousness or worse. The parent may have already considered that satisfaction would not really be forthcoming from the school and is prepared to 'take it higher'. Already in Australia there are cases of parents taking the school to court on grounds of neglecting to protect a child from being bullied. After all, it is said, the school is 'in loco parentis'. It is not uncommon for parents to come to a school angry about the situation that has developed and ready to blame the school.

Parents sometimes carry with them painful memories of how they themselves were treated at school by their peers. It is not at all uncommon for parents to have suffered the same kind of humiliation that is now the lot of their son or daughter. This may intensify their feelings of outrage. They may also feel guilty that they have not helped their child to overcome the difficulties they had themselves. They may even suspect that they have unwittingly contributed to the problem by failing to be a suitable model of proper assertiveness or by failing to provide their child with opportunities to mix with other children and learn through experience to cope better. Feeling vulnerable to criticism, the last thing in the world they want to hear is blame for their part in creating the problem.

Parents will also tend to interpret what has happened to their child in the light of their own cultural experiences, which may or may not be relevant. Recently an angry father complained bitterly to a principal of a secondary school that his son had been called a 'bastard'. Because the father was from England he saw this as a dreadful insult. He was cheerfully informed that in Australia being called an old bastard was almost a term of endearment, which is true. But he was told this in such a way that he was made to feel that he was a silly old Pom, out of touch with reality. Now the son really was being bullied. The effect of this altercation was to make the father even more resentful, and determined to go back to Britain where 'people treat each other properly'. It is not uncommon for cross-cultural misunderstanding to play an important part in preventing parents and teachers from cooperating effectively.

Teacher perspective

Now how may the teacher see it. The teacher may be (often is) unaware that the child in question is being bullied. As we have seen, children often are disinclined to tell the teacher, and bullying can go on for some time unwitnessed. Also, understandably, the teacher may feel distinctly annoyed at the implication that the school should know about it and have already taken action. The teacher may also be unconvinced that the story told by the parent on the basis of what the child has said is really accurate. There may be a feeling that the matter is being wildly exaggerated. It may be, too, that the teacher thinks that the child may have been provoking the attacks, or even feel impatient at the child's evident unwillingness to take effective action. The teacher may think that intervening in the case being presented isn't justified or, if it is, calls for skills that he or she does not have, even if (which they may doubt) they had the time.

In these circumstances the teacher may feel justified in blaming the parent, or at least pointing out that the parent could have inadvertently produced the situation about which the complaint is being made. Any blaming of the parent is almost certain to produce hostility. It is no use asking the parent to put things into perspective, as if an upset mother can simply disown her feelings and see the school's point of view at the request of the teacher. One mother I know who went to see a deputy principal about her son being continually bullied at school was told: 'Of course, Johnny is the centre of your life', as if with some shift in perspective the mother might see that Johnny was only one of many who could learn to react in a more positive and constructive manner. Of course Johnny is the centre of his mother's life.

Now teachers vary widely regarding the degree of sympathy they may feel for students who are victimised and also in the extent to which they see their obligations to help students who are victimised. One teacher recently informed a parent that what went on in the schoolyard (where a daughter was being repeatedly bullied) was none of his business. Another teacher I know feels continually obliged to look out for incidents of bullying outside the classroom. Teachers may have different philosophies regarding the responsibilities of victimised children to protect themselves.

Here is an extract from an actual letter to a parent clarifying reasons for conducting a school camp for Year 8 students.

'A school is a community and all of us involved need to consciously work towards building relationships and encompassing everyone in the community. Already it is possible to see those who are being pushed towards the 'outer'. NO student at _____ should be on the 'outer'.

The students who are 'in' need to find out how they can encompass those who may feel 'out'. *Those on the 'outer' need to get their act in gear so they stop putting themselves into positions that tend to cause them to be isolated. Hard as it is to accept, as a parent or a student, the students who find themselves non-accepted are often their own worst enemies.* Their isolation has nothing to do with a learning difficulty or a physical difference. They just seem to lack the necessary social skills to relate to their peers. With our faith in what Jesus can do in all our lives and your prayerful support we will work to encompass all into the _____ community.' *(italics added)*.

It is not hard to imagine the dismay of a parent receiving such a letter when she is desperately seeking help for a son who is being badly bullied at the school. At best, the letter is grossly insensitive; at worst it shows an extraordinary ignorance of how some students become isolated and bullied by their peers without any justification at all. True, it does contain a plea for those on the 'inner' to encompass the outsiders and that a lack of social skills contribute to the problems of children who are bullied. But rather than loftily surmising that 'they just seem to lack the necessary social skills...' why, we may wonder, is there no resolve to teach them such skills rather than pray for divine intervention.

Again we must say such statements are exceptional, but it is worth considering how often teachers (as well as students and other adults) have the urge to blame the victim. Where such an attitude is deeply entrenched in a teacher it is difficult to see how a parent can be helped with a child's problem.

Cooperation between parents and teacher

Given the different perspectives, it is not surprising that many meetings between parents and teachers on the issue of bullying are very unsatisfactory. They often increase the anger and frustration of parents, bewilder or antagonise the teacher, and do nothing for the child. Here is some advice to both parties:

To the parent

1 Before you to go to the school, make sure the alleged incidents involving bullying are carefully detailed. As far as possible, set down
   (a) what exactly happened;
   (b) who was involved;
   (c) where and when;
   (d) whether there was any provocation on the part of the victim; and
   (e) whether there were witnesses and if so who.
2 Ensure as far as possible that the child knows what action you are proposing to take, agrees with it, and be guided by his or her response.
3 Make an appointment with the principal or the principal's nominee; never barge in.
4 Don't attempt to sort out the bullies yourself. This is rarely effective and results in escalation.
5 *At the meeting, calmly present the concern as a problem that you are sharing with the school, and explain that you are hoping to work out some solution with their help.*
6 Do not accuse the school of negligence or demand that they fix it.
7 Be patient. The school will need some time to investigate and check on what has been said.
8 If you are not aware of it, ask about the school's policy on bullying. This will help you to find a basis for a joint plan.
9 Listen carefully and note what steps the school intends to take, and what part they would like you to play.
10 Arrange for a further meeting to assess what has occurred.

For the teacher

1 Recognise that the parent is generally under a good deal of stress.
2 Even if the parent expresses anger and directs it towards the school, remain understanding.
3 Make it clear that you do care and will do what you can.
4 Try to get the facts provided by the parent as clear as you can, but don't cross-examine or unduly emphasise inconsistencies in the parent's version of events.
5 Point out that you will need a little time (try to be specific) to investigate the matter yourself, but that you will certainly make contact again soon.

(There may, however, be some circumstances, when a child's personal safety is severely threatened when action needs to be taken *immediately*.)

6   Assure the parent of the existence of a school policy on bullying, and explain what it is—and the readiness of the school to take action against bullying.

7   Listen to the parent's ideas on what might be done and indicate that you are keen on developing a joint plan with the parent to overcome the problem.

8   Try to avoid getting into any argument and ABOVE ALL don't set out to blame the parent, even if you strongly suspect that the parent has contributed to the problem.

9   Make an appointment to see the parent again after you have enquired further at the school.

What the teacher may do

What the teacher does next will depend in part on the school's Policy on Bullying. But clearly it will include the gathering of some information about the incident, and seeing the children involved, and perhaps also other children and staff who can shed light on what has been happening.

Some parents may wish to be present at the meeting with the children to give moral support to their son or daughter. This must be sympathetically resisted. This is a matter for the school. Normally the parents will receive a 'version' of the interview from their child, and this may or may not be an objective account. If asked by parents, to comment on what happened, it is best for teachers to avoid going into unnecessary detail and, if at all possible, avoid disputing the student's version. It is best to emphasise positive aspects of what has transpired. The parent needs to be reassured that the school is working on the problem and that suggestions from the child's parents really are welcome.

A last resort for parents

Even though schools are increasingly taking the business of bullying very seriously, no one will be as concerned about a child's interests as the parents. It is sensible for parents to be patient. But occasionally parents may not get the cooperation that is their due. What then?

I suggest as a matter of course to parents that they keep a record of what has been said and decided upon at each meeting. If the outcome is negative, then they may decide to approach another teacher, or suggest to the principal that they would like to talk with someone else at the school. It remains very important that they stay calm and avoid abusing any of the teachers. They may try to find out whether other parents share their concern about bullying. If necessary, they can form a group to develop a strategy to make their concerns more vocal. Sometimes strong assistance may be forthcoming from the School Council. I know of one recent case where a parent was able to convince the chairman of the school council that his daughter's sickness and depression really were stemming from her being continually bullied by another eight-year-old girl at school. Pressure from this source radically altered the principal's perception of the matter.

It is well to remember that after years of ignoring the problem of bullying, there is now a new awareness of the issue in the community. Indeed, bullying is becoming a political issue, and political leaders are likely to be interested in helping to see that justice be done. In some cases the ombudsman has been approached. As a very last resort—legal action is a possibility. I believe that most schools in Australia are now sensitive to the issue and such courses of action will probably prove unnecessary.

The importance of policy

I have suggested guidelines and ways in which parents and teachers may cooperate for the good of particular children. But the cornerstone of such activity is the school policy. It is, in my view, essential that *the school formally and in writing acknowledges the right of parents to speak with school authorities if they believe their child is being bullied by peers*. There should be no suspicion on the part of parents that their presence is unwelcome. This does not mean that 'the customer is always right'. Parents as well as teachers can misunderstand a situation, especially one as complicated as children's peer relations. But parents do have a right to be heard. Many of them still have to fight for this right.

Helping children in dysfunctional families

We have seen that children from families which are dysfunctional are commonly disadvantaged in that they are more likely than others to become involved in bully/victim problems. Such children can sometimes be helped by skilled counsellors. But if their family background is one in which they have not developed a strong sense of belonging to a primary group and have in fact felt continually rejected in early childhood, the assistance that may be provided may have quite limited effectiveness. Not surprisingly, efforts have been turned to providing help for some children indirectly by working with parents of young children who have poor or inadequate parenting skills.

The practical difficulties of this strategy are great. First, there is the question of identifying the parents who need help. You may begin by assuming that these are parents from disadvantaged families, and although you can expect parenting skills to be generally less well developed in such families, there are, of course, many exceptions. Second, having identified families who need help, there is the practical problem of getting appropriate help to them. Many will reject any proffered assistance; many would regard it as an impertinence. The values and child rearing attitudes of social workers and other 'do-gooders' are unlikely to be attractive to families that are more inclined to use punitive methods of imposing or failing to impose discipline.

Selecting families to help, and actually gaining their active cooperation so that they can be helped, has often seemed an insurmountable difficulty. Recently, however, a proposal by Peter Randall, the Director of the Family Assessment and Support Unit at the University of Hull has shown a good deal of promise (see Randall and Donohue, 1993; Randall, 1995). It has been proposed that child care centres be freely provided for parents living in selected disadvantaged areas. These could take young children between three and five years old. Parents would, however, be required to make *some* commitment to participate in the work of the centre. Under the guidance of specially trained staff, the children would learn to develop more positive ways of interacting with both peers and adults and do so in a social environment in which good parenting skills were being modelled. The parents could learn first by watching; then, increasingly, by becoming involved in actually providing the guidance for the children, their own included.

Although success is by no means assured, parents involved in such a plan often do show a remarkable capacity to learn; are willing to try new ways;

and sometimes seek help and advice over the management of their older children in primary or secondary school. They are not pressured to change; they are offered something 'for free'; are treated with respect as having some expertise especially with their own children; and they are able to see for themselves that their own children are happier and better behaved if they are treated differently. Although this may seem to be a small step, it is in the positive direction of helping the community to be more responsible and caring. And it is directed towards one of the roots of the problem. A pilot project is currently being planned at the University of South Australia in Adelaide to explore the feasibility of this approach.

Families together resolving disputes

Is it possible that the families and family friends of bullies and victims who are involved in a problem can get together and resolve it? Some people have thought so. Strongly promoting this belief are Professor John Braithwaite (1989) from the Australian National University and Dr David Moore (1994) from the Charles Sturt University in the Riverina. That this belief is sustainable has become more plausible through the operation of Family Conferences, originating in New Zealand and subsequently tried with some success in New South Wales and South Australia.

Applying the procedure to a case of bullying, a situation is structured in which what has happened to a victim is described by him or her in the presence of the family and friends of the victim and also the bully and his or her family and friends. The victim is accorded the opportunity to be heard; the bully must listen. When the situation is expertly handled, the outcome can be extremely positive for all concerned. The victim has the satisfaction of knowing that what has happened has indeed been heard. The bully feels shame. But with the support of family and friends this can be 'reintegrative shame' rather than an enduring stigma. The bully acknowledges the wrong and experiences what can be a strong and sometimes unfamiliar emotion: shame. And the fact that shame has been publicly displayed and observed not only enables the bully to feel that a new start can be made, but also can strengthen the community that has participated in the transformation.

In Queensland, Margaret Thorsborne has successfully applied this general method in resolving bully/victim problems between school peers. She has organised so-called Community Accountability Conferences at which bullies and victims who have become involved in relatively serious cases of bullying meet each other in the company of their families and friends. She believes that less serious cases can often be resolved through the application of a No Blame Approach, such as the Method of Shared Concern. But sometimes this is not possible. When there is a strong element of denial of the harm that is being caused by a bully, and perhaps also by his/her support group, it may be necessary, she thinks, for them to experience together the reality of the victim's suffering and to come to terms with the shame it can produce in a public setting. A feature of the reconciliation that can result from such emotionally charged meetings is the simple act of having the two sides eating together afterwards, so they may 'break bread' in a symbolic expression of acceptance of a new and binding relationship.

This approach has been criticised on the grounds that a sense of shame for anyone is an undesirable emotion. It would certainly seem to run counter to those who plump for raising the self-esteem of everybody quick smart. But it is to be understood that 'shame' is a means rather than an end; a necessary precondition for a real and enduring change of heart. A further criticism is that families and friends of bullies are frequently not prepared to make the required distinction between the sin and the sinner: to disapprove of the offence but to accept the person who offended. In some cases this may be so. Therefore cases for which this method can be used may have to be selective. A third concern, not so much a criticism, is that the skills needed to run meetings effectively to produce the desired outcome are quite limited. However, we can say that if the change of heart of the bully and reconciliation between the bully and victim can be achieved this way, then the training in the required skills must be provided. There can be no doubt that this approach points us in the direction of a better, more caring society.

Students
as peer
helpers

We have already examined in Chapter 9 how the support of students can be enlisted by teachers to implement a school policy which students have themselves helped to formulate against bullying in the school. We have seen, too, that by learning how to cooperate with each other more effectively and to express their rejection of bullying within a school, students can help to counteract the influence of a macho culture or ethos which, to a smaller or larger extent, is found in every school. Now we turn to examine what specific roles students can fulfil as 'peer helpers' to prevent or directly counter bullying behaviour.

There are at least three reasons for believing that students can undertake peer helper roles that counter bullying. The first is that we already know that a substantial proportion of students in every school (more than half in most classes) are already sympathetic towards children who are frequently victimised by peers. Moreover, about one-third of students indicate that they want to talk about the problem of bullying with other students. From among these students some will certainly be interested in taking on a relevant and active helper role. Secondly, we have also seen that students are far more likely to turn to their peers for help and support when they have interpersonal problems than to adults and especially teachers or school counsellors. Students often do want to talk to other students about their school problems. And thirdly, there already exist models and examples of effective peer helping being undertaken by students in schools in many parts of the world, including Britain, the USA and Australia. Indeed, in Australia the movement to involve students in peer helping with a range of personal and social problems is continually gathering force. Schools are seeing that peer helpers can produce a change.

We can begin with an examination of different kinds of roles that have been suggested for students to help the others in some way. Some of these can be seen as making an *indirect* contribution to overcoming bullying, that is, they operate so as to provide a school climate in which the norm increasingly becomes one of helping rather than hindering. Other roles can have a more *direct* impact on the problem in that they seek to deal with conflict between students, including bullying.

Roles for peer helpers

Many teachers encourage students to help each other, and do so on a quite informal basis. A teacher may see that there is a child in the class who is particularly unhappy or distressed and that he or she could be befriended by another child who would be willing to help. This may work out well with a minimum of fuss. But there is much also to be said for introducing and maintaining a procedure whereby students are selected to fit specific helping roles and receive some guidance or training to carry them out effectively.

Helper roles can be classified first according to the purposes they are intended to serve, as is suggested in Table 16.1.

Table 16.1 **A classification of peer helping roles**

	HELPING ROLES FOR STUDENTS		
	Educational	Personal support	Intervening in peer-conflict
Role			
Indirect contribution to countering bullying			
Peer tutor	Yes	Yes	No
Peer orientation guide	Yes	Yes	No
Buddy	No	Yes	No
Peer outreach worker	No	Yes	No
More direct contribution to stopping bullying			
Peer support leader	Usually	Yes	Sometimes
Peer counsellor	No	Yes	Sometimes
Peer mediator	No	Yes	Yes

Table 16.1 provides suggestions as to how students may be helped by fellow students and describes the ends to which the roles may be directed. Of course, the roles may be defined in different ways so as to include or exclude particular functions. Each role is conceived as providing personal support. Some roles may take on a more formal kind of educational function, either in an academic or social sense, sometimes both. It may be that individuals in a school may take on more than one role. They are not seen as mutually exclusive. Next we will consider how each of them may operate, beginning first with roles that make an indirect contribution to the problem.

Indirectly contributing roles

Peer tutor

Some students find it very difficult to cope with academic demands. They may suffer a great deal of stress because of this. They may lose self-esteem and even become seriously depressed; some may become angry and reckless in their behaviour with others. In Australian schools failure to succeed academically is not usually a reason for being bullied (sometimes indeed bullying may be directed towards someone showing conspicuous academic success), but the emotional consequences of academic failure among those to whom it matters (still a large number) may result in students becoming involved in bully/victim problems. Depending in part on the personality of the student, the student's depression may invite aggression from others or alternatively may result in the student who is failing 'taking it out on others'.

The role of the peer tutor must focus on helping the learner with the academic task at hand. This naturally means that the potential helper must have the necessary academic skills and knowledge. Sometimes the helper may be better equipped to help if he or she has had to struggle to master what the learner needs to know. Part of the difficulty in peer tutoring is that the students tutored may be, at times, quite resistant to help, because they do not want to feel dependent on anyone. They have felt frustrated and hurt by their inability to cope with tasks that are perhaps 'child's play' for others. The peer tutor will need to know how to offer help without stigmatising the tutored one as a dunce or a fool. But with the best of intentions, the helper may find the proffered assistance rejected. It is not easy to help 'slippery fish' who will not accept what they evidently need. The peer tutor needs more than knowledge and goodwill. Understanding and emotional support in the form of sympathy and encouragement when the going is difficult are equally important, especially when perseverance is needed or new approaches must be tried.

Peer orientation guide

As we have seen, students coming to a new school are particularly vulnerable to bullying. This is especially true for many students starting secondary school, after having been relatively invulnerable and immune from bullying, as bigger children often are among mostly younger students in primary school. A new situation now confronts them. Not only are they now surrounded by bigger and stronger students, but quite unfamiliar demands are made upon them, including new school subjects, getting to know many new teachers and a strange new physical environment which is likely to be much larger and more complex than the one they left in primary. Commonly, support from staff is nothing like as accessible. There is no single class teacher who gets to know each child well through continual contact. In many secondary schools it is possible for a student to remain unknown in any real sense by any single staff member during the first month or so of the time spent in a new school. Such virtual anonymity combined with the stressfulness of having to make many social readjustments to a new school can result in some children becoming profoundly dispirited—and targets for peer abuse.

Peer orientation guidance can be provided at two levels: at the feeder schools for final year students, and at the secondary school when new students arrive. These may also include those transferring from other secondary schools. Some schools arrange for some students from the secondary schools to visit the feeder schools to talk about the new school to which the primary school students will shortly be going. To this extent, they have an educational role. They can provide reassurance (and scotch fantastic rumours about initiation rites and other horrors in store) and promise to meet the new students and help them when they arrive. This can have the effect of enabling the new students to feel more confident.

Despite such help, some students will inevitably feel 'lost' when they begin their new school, especially if they have few friends, which is often the case when a student is transferred from another secondary school. More sustained help may be needed by such students to make the adjustment. But the help must be unobtrusive, not imposed conspicuously on children who, nervous and hesitant though they might be, want to appear independent and avoid embarrassing attention.

The buddy

Some children become particularly distressed at school. The causes may be external, for instance due to a family break-up, perhaps, or the death of a family member. Or the child may become depressed and isolated because of rejection by others, perhaps the victim of social prejudice. Or the problem may arise from shyness or an incapacity to make friends easily. Whatever the cause, it may be clear to everyone that a child is finding it extremely difficult to cope. Such children are often bullied. Sometimes they may become extremely angry and even violent towards others. They often have no friends at school. Close personal and sustained emotional support is needed. What can be done?

The suggestion that someone become that person's friend immediately raises difficulties. To be real, friendships must be unforced. Friendship starts, as C.S. Lewis has argued, when two people see the same truth, and one turns to the other and says: 'What you, too? I thought I was the only one.' We must be aware of the artificiality of manufactured and imposed friendships.

Close personal support is nevertheless needed at times, and if a student feels that he or she can provide it for another, especially during a time of stress, then it is good to provide it. The 'buddy' must understand both the need a person in distress may have for closeness and support (which is characteristically provided by 'true friends') and what a person in the role of a 'buddy' can realistically do to help a fellow student who is distressed. It may be best, at least initially, for the buddy to be seen as a 'special friend' who can make opportunities or arrange occasions when the one who needs help can share his or her thoughts with another person. This might be at a game they agree to watch together. Whether the relationship develops as a true friendship will be uncertain. No obligation can be placed upon a buddy. It is an undertaking that often requires considerable maturity on the part of a person taking this role and good judgement on the part of a teacher negotiating the arrangement.

Peer outreach worker

While some students may be conspicuously in need of social support, especially in a small school or in more senior classes, in a large secondary school it is not unusual for a student to be seriously distressed without anyone knowing about it. The role of the Peer Outreach Worker is to look out for such students and either personally or by referral ensure that appropriate help is forthcoming. Again the cause of the trouble may entail factors outside or inside the school. Bullying may or may not be an important factor. If bullying is taking place it is likely to be of an indirect kind, such as exclusion from groups, and, as such, may have attracted little attention. Because girls are more often subjected to indirect and subtle forms of peer abuse, the work of peer outreach may more frequently involve girls.

More directly contributing roles
Peer supporters

The role of such students may be quite broad, sometimes taking in a strong social educational role for younger students as well as counselling and mediation functions. In Australia schools frequently are able to gain practical assistance from the Peer Support Foundation which operates in most of the states. Staff from schools can receive from them in-service training and materials so that they can subsequently train students to be peer supporters.

As the name suggests, peer supporters are there to support and help their fellow students to live happier, less stress-filled lives. They listen and make suggestions, and in so doing fulfil some of the functions of a counsellor, in an informal way. Depending on the policy of the school, they may also take on an educational role in the area of social and personal development. They may lead small discussion groups with younger students in class time or at camps or at workshops, focusing on such issues as harassment. In some schools there is a regular weekly commitment. An example of peer support in action in South Australia is at the Elizabeth City High School where Year 11 students are each year selected to be peer support leaders and provide a weekly social education programme for Year 8 students. It will be recalled that in the first year of high school the stress on students, especially those most vulnerable to peer harassment, is particularly great. Peer support leaders may also undertake active interventions in cases of conflict between students, and this can sometimes include bullying.

The value of the contribution of peer support can be seen not only in the direct and indirect help that it can provide to younger students with personal school-related problems, but also in the effects it can have on the personal and social development of the older students providing the service. They are able to grow in stature and maturity. We should also not ignore the beneficial consequences involvement in the programmme often has for teachers. As they begin to form more positive relations with students in the school, the sense of isolation and detachment from the student body that many teachers experience may gradually be overcome.

Peer counsellor

The peer counsellor is conceived as the person to whom students go if they want help with a personal or social problem. Alternatively (or additionally) the peer counsellor may be accessible by telephone and provide counselling by that medium. This latter method has much to commend it, as it allows a greater measure of anonymity to the person seeking advice and also greater control over the situation by the person seeking help. In either case specialised training is needed and the work may be seen as an adjunct to that being provided by the school counsellor with whom the peer counsellor must work closely. Peer counsellor is a more formally conceived role than that of peer supporter, and it is unlikely to have a general educational function.

Opinion is much divided on the question of how effective students can be in the counselling role. For example, in 1994 Robert Myrick, an American educational authority, warned against entrusting too much responsibility to large numbers of students working as counsellors. 'Very few students', he wrote 'can learn to counsel other students. Counselling is a special skill that takes extensive preparation and practice' (p. 243). By contrast, some other authorities, such as Anatol Pikas in Sweden, believe that all students can develop appropriate technical skills in order to help their peers, especially those who are in conflict with each other. He nevertheless has strong misgivings about the creation of a special body of students who may be seen as *the* ones who provide remedies for the problems of others. There is gathering evidence that some students can be effective in the counselling role with their peers; the proportion that can, and the counselling tasks that are appropriate for them, is for schools to explore.

Given the demands on full-time students at school (and these can be academic, social and sporting), a number of students may take turns in carrying out this role. The work of such counsellors needs to be very carefully defined, especially in relation to that of the school counsellor with whom peer counsellors would normally need to work closely.

I would suggest that the role of peer counsellor be defined exclusively as dealing with peer relations; other matters that arise would be referred to the school counsellor or teachers with whom the 'client' would like to speak. It would nevertheless be desirable for students as clients to have the option, at least in some cases, of seeing either a peer counsellor or a professional school counsellor. What is *not* desirable, however, is to view peer counselling as basically a means of simply taking the load off counsellors and teachers.

Whether the terms used to describe the work of the peer counsellor should be the same as those describing that of professional counsellors is an issue that the school may wish to discuss. To describe students who are helped by the peer counsellor as 'clients' will, to some, seem unwise. It has been argued that the use of the term 'client' might empower students in their role of counsellor, but it might also help to create a class of person who become dependent on external help and, in a sense, 'dis-empowered'. Much depends on the way peer counsellors present themselves to those they seek to help—as dispensers of miraculous cures or as 'one of them', seeking a solution to a problem *with* a peer. If training can be directed towards this latter style of helping others, the terms that are used to describe helper and helped will not matter.

Finally, should a peer counsellor also be involved in interventions in resolving conflict situations? In practice, conflict resolution is commonly seen as an extension to the role of the counsellor who is a staff member. In some cases, therefore a peer counsellor may also have the role of mediator in student disputes.

Peer mediator

This is the role that is seen by some as being most directly relevant to the bully/victim problem in a school. Mediation can be said to occur when two or more people in conflict are helped by a third party to negotiate a constructive solution to their problem.

There are conditions in which a successful mediation are more likely to occur. This does not mean that mediation is impossible in less propitious circumstances; only that it is harder. Here are the ideal conditions.

(i) The persons in conflict are of equal or roughly equal power. As we have seen, when bullying occurs there is an imbalance of power and this raises difficulties for the mediator whose acceptance by the people in dispute may depend upon taking an unbiased position.

(ii) There is a readiness on the part of both parties in a conflict situation to seek mediation. Where there is an imbalance of power, the bully may be reluctant to accept mediation because the current situation is to his or her advantage.

(iii) The mediation process is voluntary.

These considerations have led some to declare that resolving bully/victim conflicts is really outside the range of what mediators can be expected to achieve. If this is so, the effects of successful mediation on bullying must be limited to those that are *indirect*, that is, through the gradual creation of a school climate in which people in conflict are prepared to listen to one another and resolve their differences peaceably. This can be very helpful. In an atmosphere created by successful mediation individuals are more likely to build bridges that enable their conflict to be resolved. The process is caught is caught neatly in a cartoon provided by Johnson and Johnson (1991, p. 361).

From Teaching Students to be Peacemakers, Interaction Book Company, Minnesota.

How mediation can best proceed was outlined by Dale Bagshaw (1994) at a recent international conference in Adelaide on Children's Peer Relations. She identified nine points in the process.

---

1 *Establishing credibility and trust in both parties*
Mediators must present themselves confidently and show great care in not favouring either party. (It must be acknowledged however that some student mediators may be known to the disputants and not considered as neutral in the situation. A matching of disputants and mediators may be necessary.) Credibility and trust will need to be developed gradually.

2 *Explaining the mediation role and outlining the process*
This is necessary so that the disputants do not feel that they are in a highly ambiguous situation which they will have to struggle to shape and structure to their own interests. The mediator should not move on until the disputants indicate an acceptance of the suitability of the process to resolve their difficulties.

3 *Instilling confidence in the process*
This can only happen if neither party feels coerced and if there is a 'general' understanding that what is said between them will go no further. (But remember that complete confidentiality may not be possible, e.g. if dangerous threats are made.)

4 *Agreed rules*
Once a general understanding and acceptance of the process has been reached, practical details must be provided, such as ground rules about taking turns and not interrupting the other speaker. This may culminate in a formal agreement regarding the procedure and the governing rules; then mediation can begin.

5 *Getting to know how each sees the problem*
Each disputant must be helped to explain how he or she sees the issues underlying the dispute. At each step, the mediator must make a neutral summary of what has been said, and ensure that each has understood the other clearly. This skill is central and needs to be practised; failure to be seen as fair and neutral will invariably result in a disastrous loss of credibility and trust.

6   *Finding out what is really important to each of them*
    Some issues will appear more important to them than others; the task
    of the mediator will then be to prioritise them and see that each is
    dealt with in turn.

7   *Focusing on common ground*
    This means encouraging the disputants to discover their mutual
    interests. In this way each disputant may come to see how the desires
    of both parties may be satisfied. If each disputant continues to defend a
    position as the only way to gain satisfaction, little progress can be made.

8   *Finding acceptable solutions*
    This will require getting suggestions from the disputants (or making
    acceptable proposals) which can lead to a negotiated settlement, as an
    alternative to fighting or withdrawal. The mediator must get each of
    them to appraise the consequences of the various proposals quite
    realistically, or the settlement will be short-lived.

9   *Reaching an agreement*
    This should be written down using the language used by the disputants
    and the conditions clearly spelt out. Each disputant should be praised
    for the part played in reaching the agreement.

It should be clear in examining these nine points that the skills of
mediation are not easily acquired and in some situations the skills may be
difficult to exercise, for example when disputants have a long history of past
conflicts, are disinclined to listen to each other, are very distrustful, and have
poor problem-solving skills. Clearly some students will be able to practise
mediation in difficult circumstances more successfully than others. Such
people are typically confident in their dealings with others, considerate and
caring. With training and practice, however, elements of the mediation process
can be mastered by many students.

Mediation in practice in schools

Recently, the Department of School Education in New South Wales has
taken the lead in Australia in promoting and evaluating peer mediation in

schools. During 1994–95 the Department in collaboration with Community Justice Centres of New South Wales developed and trialed a school-based mediation programme for secondary schools. Schools nominated teachers to undertake an intensive two-week mediation training program provided by Community Justice Centres. The teachers then selected and trained students in mediation in relevant skills, using role play procedures, and monitored the interventions conducted by them.

It was found that the most common causes of dispute were gossip and rumour (what we have called indirect forms of bullying), followed by name calling (verbal abuse), threats of violence, fighting and loss of property (New South Wales Department of Education, 1995). In evaluating the project,the report is cautious stating that 'it is too early to draw general conclusions about the program's long-term outcomes, although results to date indicate that this model of peer mediation appears to be an effective dispute resolution process in public secondary schools in NSW' (p. 20). The report also quotes Cameron and Dupuis: 'It has been estimated that it takes students two years to accept peer mediation as a dispute resolution process and teachers five years' (p. 7). It is early days yet.

But we should note that some schools in Australia have reported successful outcomes and widespread acceptance by their staff members. Amongst these is the Giralang Primary School (see Bingham, Daly, Mitchell and Skinner, 1994). If you have any doubts about the competence of students, even in primary schools, to undertake mediation roles with their peers, the record of five years of operating the program should dispel them. The principles by which they work are these:

Mediators lead by example

Mediators are courteous, caring and cooperative, recognising that if they behave in this way they are more likely to see others do the same

Mediators are not police officers nor prefects

Mediators do not try to make people obey the rules

Mediators help solve conflicts between people

Mediators do not become personally involved in conflict; if a mediator experiences difficulty in trying to stay impartial, they pass the mediation to another mediator

Mediators do not take sides

There is general agreement that successful mediation of conflict situations in schools can contribute towards making a school a more peaceable place (see especially Bodine et al., 1994) and this will help reduce problems of bullying. What is *not* agreed, however, is whether bullying can be addressed *directly* by mediating approaches. We will defer this problem for the moment and return to it on page 269.

The selection of peer helpers

Before you can begin the process of peers helping peers in a school a selection process may be undertaken. What kinds of people are best for the helping roles? Personal qualities are important. Basic to these is the capacity to get along with and help other students. Generally such qualities are found in students who have positive attitudes towards themselves, others and their school. They are friendly, sensitive and caring. Beyond these characteristics, a peer helper generally needs to have good listening and verbal skills. Normally the peer helpers will be older students, partly because of the need for maturity in judgement, but also because the peer helper is more attractive if he or she is older (a Big Brother or a Big Sister). Students are more apt to admire and to imitate older students.

There may be a temptation to include as a peer helper a student whose behaviour has hitherto been somewhat anti-social; even a bully. And there is evidence that a new role can indeed change a seemingly entrenched behaviour pattern. Nevertheless it is a risk, and if it is to be taken, it should only happen after the program has been operating successfully for a while and it is clear that the team of helpers will be a good socialising influence. Finally, it is wise to start small with a limited number of peer helpers with whom the leader can very confidently work: an expansion can come later.

There are various ways in which appropriate persons may be selected for the helping roles.

1   Students who are seen as likely to be good at carrying out particular helping roles may be informally approached by staff and/or members of the Student Representative Council and invited to take on the role.

2   A description of each of the roles, together with a rationale for their creation, could be circulated among students and staff who would then be asked to nominate individuals they saw as most suitable.

3 The roles could be described and advertised; and students asked to apply prior to being interviewed by a panel representing both students and staff.

4 Once a team of peer helpers has been formed and functioned for a time effectively, they can be invited to participate in the selection procedure.

Whatever the selection procedure, there must be good collaboration between staff and students. The judgements of students are essential: they are more likely than teachers to know who would be acceptable to students seeking help, and a collaborative process ensures that the student body would be supportive.

The question will arise whether peer helpers could fulfil more than one role. In part, this may be influenced by the availability of helpers. But in principle there is no reason why the roles of peer orientation guide, buddy, peer outreach helper and peer counsellor should not, at times, be carried out by the same person. However, some specialisation (and then rotation of roles) is preferable, if resources permit. Peer tutoring might also sometimes be provided by a person who has another helping role. But here, where knowledge and understanding of relevant academic content with which a student needs help is central, it is likely that the work of tutoring will be separate, and strong primary links will need to be made between the helper and the staff member(s) who have responsibility for the student's academic progress.

But can't everybody be peer helpers?

At this point it might be suggested that the work of peer helpers, including peer mediators, is of the kind that *all* students should and can engage in. The creation of a special class of person who administers 'help' may seem to run counter to the democratic ideal. Involving everybody is certainly what we should aim for. However, in many circumstances the numbers of students who *want* to spend time in providing the kinds of help we have described is limited. The training that is needed for the helping roles is often so intensive that it can only be provided for small groups of trainees at a time. But, as I have said in Chapter 9, the broader goal of engaging all students in the process of countering bullying in a variety of ways must be pursued also.

Training of peer helpers

We can distinguish between two aspects of the training:
1 General human relations training intended to develop a more sensitive awareness of others and an ability to relate to them better in a helping relationship.
2 Training that is specific to the role in question.

Both require time and commitment. In some schools specific human relations training may be provided, for example as part of Social Studies. In some American schools, courses in Peer Counselling are actually provided for students in first and second year high schools, and it is not unlikely that some Australian schools will follow suit. Ideally, some basic exploration of human relationships and even training in social skills can be provided as part of 'normal' lessons, or as part of the training provided by peer support leaders in some schools. This can provide a basis upon which further training can be built.

Human relations training

Although a general understanding of interpersonal dynamics and problems associated with interactions between people is no doubt desirable, the training for peer helpers must focus upon what is practical and relevant to their roles. Basic to the training is developing the capacity to observe and listen to others. Practical exercises can be very helpful. For example, a student's ability to concentrate upon what another person is actually doing may be increased by mirroring another person's behaviour as he or she behaves in front of them. Empathic ability may be improved through an exercise in which students are asked to describe the mood they are in, or have experienced recently, to another student who will then attempt to repeat what he or she has been told, catching as closely as possible the intonation and feeling that has been expressed. A further skill to be practised, of more direct relevance to the counselling situation, is paraphrasing a communication about a problem, retelling it and checking its accuracy with the speaker.

Training for role performance

There must clearly be orienting meetings in which students as helpers are provided with guidance, guidelines and, in some areas, specific rules to follow. The roles for peer helpers have been differentiated, but they have much in common, and some rotation of roles is desirable. The helpers may therefore be seen together at least at the beginning stage.

Throughout the training it must be emphasised that the skills that need to be developed are first getting people to talk about their problems and worries; next, being an attentive and sympathetic listener rather than an expert adviser; and thirdly, having the capacity to generate ideas with the client and explore options rather than to advise or impose solutions.

Probably the best approach in training peer helpers is initially for the trainer be rather directive, beginning by providing a clear model and instructions on how a peer helper may introduce herself/himself to others and then elicit from them, in a sympathetic and supportive way, exactly what their problem is and the kind of help they are seeking. Role playing of a standard helper-helpee situation is a useful starting point. Attentive listening and reflecting back what has been said, can be first modelled then enacted by students in role play. Subsequently, you can move on to other situations in which different ways of responding may be employed, depending upon the demands of the situation.

In their instructional video, Cowie and Sharp (1994) identify four such situations of relevance to peer counsellors—with the angry client, the upset client, the silent client and the client who begs the counsellor to treat any revelations as strictly confidential. Each situation makes different demands on the counsellor. With the angry client you may be tempted to say 'cool it' rather than facilitate the expression of anger; with the upset client you may wish to provide advice prematurely; with the silent client it may be difficult to maintain the necessary contact—you may run out of things to say and grow impatient; with the client insisting on secrecy you may be led to acquiesce when the seriousness of the revelation may not justify a counsellor actually maintaining secrecy.

Although at the initial stage, trainers should be quite directive and demonstrate 'traps for young players', it is important not to leave trainees with the impression that there is one correct way to deal with every situation. (You should be mindful of the advice given by one counsellor-trainer, Jourard, who claimed (tongue-in-cheek) that when the trainee could conform to a given model of counselling provided by the trainer to perfection, he would give the trainee a certificate or gold star, but if, after a year or so, the trainee was still impersonating the trainer the award would be taken back.) Gradually flexibility and improvisation need to be encouraged.

During training a great deal of emphasis should be placed on feedback sessions when the peer helpers meet and describe their experiences as counsellors and the thorny questions and uncertainties that have arisen in counselling sessions, or happen to worry them in retrospect. Here the trainer must constantly encourage and support the peer helpers and show faith in them. But throughout, the trainer will need to suggest better ways of dealing with situations and explore options of which the helpers may not have been aware. Increasingly the trainer should be able to mobilise the group to help in providing helpful suggestions.

Inevitably, there will be a focus on what student helpers might handle personally and what should be referred on (and to whom), either because the issue arising might be more appropriately handled by someone else (for example, when traumatic events at home are reported or a suicide threatened) or is, for some reason, particularly difficult for a given counsellor to handle personally. You should also expect discussion to centre on areas where there might be problems of whether confidentiality can be assured or maintained. A distinction might be made between areas in which a counsellor can promise confidentiality, as when personal friendships or animosities are confided, and areas in which serious consequences may follow if what is learned from a student is not disclosed, for example, a threat to harm someone.

Who should do the training?

Should the training for peer helpers come from teachers or counsellors who may themselves have been specially trained (as in the service provided by the Peer Support Organisation) or is it better for the peer helpers to be trained by experts who visit the school? There are arguments either way. When teachers are themselves trained and then train others there is a greater degree of involvement of staff, and consequently the school may become more inclined to 'own' the problem towards which a solution is being directed. Staff may also benefit, as we have seen, through the relations they build up with the students who provide the support and with whom they have made a common cause. On the other hand, direct training of students by better qualified and more experienced external trainers can be advantageous. External trainers are in some ways able to influence children more because they are not the conventional 'authority figures' which teachers and counsellors often are. This second model—direct training of students to be peer counsellors—is favoured by Kids Help Line, which has provided training sessions for interested students identified by teachers responsible for career guidance or social welfare. Such students would normally already have a leaning towards engagement in counselling work, being in some cases interested in following a related career such as Social Work. Max Kau, with KHL in Victoria, is currently trialing such a model which highlights five basic skills needed in peer counsellors which he identifies as Listening, Attending, Responding, Caring and Helping (LARCH).

Mediation revisited: Direct applications to bully/victim problems

Earlier it was argued that mediation methods can be used effectively by suitably trained students in schools to assist in the solving of disputes in which there is an equality of power. There can be little doubt that under suitable conditions the practice of peer mediation in schools can result in a reduction of undesirable conflict between children. And this can produce a change in the school ethos which will arguably become less supportive of bullying. In short, peer mediation can have an *indirect* effect in reducing the incidence of bullying.

We must now ask whether it can also have a *direct* effect in resolving conflicts where bullying has occurred, that is where there is a definite imbalance of power.

Answers to this question are controversial. To some extent, the answer you can give depends on the definition or description of the mediation process that you adopt. Where mediation is defined narrowly so as to apply only to cases in which the mediator can be absolutely neutral regarding the outcome—as long as the disputants agree to it—the difficulties of mediating in circumstances where there are large asymmetries of power are very great indeed. Because bullying is essentially unjustifiable behaviour, an outcome that enables the bully to continue with the bullying behaviour is obviously unjust and unacceptable. Unless the power differential can be reduced, at least for the purposes of mediation, a successful resolution to the problem is unlikely.

However, the term 'mediation' is sometimes used in a broader sense. The mediator may be seen as basically one who facilitates the negotiating process between individuals in dispute. To facilitate the process the mediator may concentrate on developing in the disputants social skills that are likely to help in the resolution of their difficulties; for example, being able to listen more carefully or to act more assertively rather than aggressively. A certain amount of counselling may be involved. If all this is done well, such mediation may become a much more practical proposition. This approach is arguably more appropriate when the disputants are children, since the process clearly has an educational aspect which, if emphasised with adults, would appear more as an impertinence on the part of the mediator.

Whichever conception of mediation is adopted, the asymmetry in power between bully and victim will have an important bearing on *how* (and perhaps whether) the dispute can be resolved. It is important, nevertheless, not to make too great a contrast between the narrower and broader views of mediation. It is rare in practice for disputes to involve an *exact* equivalence of power; some imbalance is in fact common. It is the large extent of the difference in power that is characteristic of the bully/victim situation that concerns us; not the fact that some difference exists.

The key question is what can be done to reduce the impact of power asymmetries so that successful resolutions are possible.

The first step is to make a close examination of the power differences. A first clue to the power differential between disputants may be found in the relative eagerness of bullies and victims to be involved in conflict resolution through mediation. The bully may be reluctant: actually quite pleased with the situation as it is. The less powerful is the one who may gain more from mediation.

Sometimes the nature of the power differences are not immediately evident and may only become so after the disputants have been interviewed. We should remember the asymmetries may be physical and/or psychological. With older children physical strength often plays a less important part than verbal facility. We need also to take into account differences in access to resources and links with power figures or groups. And as Milburn and Klimnowski (1996) have argued, 'power differences reflect not merely the resources available to the stronger party but also the needs, weaknesses and vulnerability of the weaker party'. We may also add the capacity to bluff.

Once the nature of the asymmetries has been identified, you may consider ways in which you can help towards providing a more level playing-field. Disabling the bully is not an option, but improving the capacity of the victim to state his or her position with confidence is. Counselling and support from the mediator may actually empower the victim so that he or she *can* act effectively, at least in the mediating situation with the bully present. This approach is favoured for example in the operation of the Student Mediation Program at the Cranebrook High School in New South Wales. The empowerment can take the form of encouraging the victim to act assertively but not aggressively. The victim will understand that at least in the mediation situation he or she is 'safe' and can count upon the mediator to ensure fair play. Any reduction in the power imbalance will enable the mediator to fit into the more neutral role. However, it will be particularly important for the mediator to insist upon adherence to norms or rules that constrain the adversaries and prevent abusive contests which will almost certainly disadvantage the victim.

In the course of examining the relationship that exists between the bully and the victim it may be discovered that in some ways the 'victim' is actually behaving provocatively. We may then more readily recognise the value of an ancillary counselling role directed towards helping the victim to avoid antagonising the other person. In such circumstances, there is scope for a negotiated 'settlement' in which the parties can begin to see they can both advantageously alter their behaviour. At this point, more conventional mediational skills come into play.

Where it becomes evident that the victim is not behaving provocatively and accordingly the mediator cannot maintain 'a neutral stance' regarding outcome, there can nevertheless be, indeed *must* be, an equal respect or regard for each of them. It is tempting to abandon this principle in cases of large power imbalances. But if this is done, the credibility and influence of the mediator is almost certainly lost.

Just as preparation for the mediation session may be desirable for the victim, there is much to be said for prior discussions with the bully. Again I would commend the Method of Shared Concern devised by Pikas (see page 209), as a model to follow in such interactions. To the extent that the bully can be brought to share a concern with the mediator for the plight of the victim, the task of mediation will be made easier.

We should also acknowledge that the reality of a situation may be that the bully already has been threatened by the school authorities. There may in some cases have been talk of suspension or expulsion. Coercion is therefore already present, but not of the mediator's making. Clearly it will be a factor in how the bully behaves in the mediation session. And herein lies an important advantage for a peer mediator. He or she will not normally be seen as being in league with the authorities, as a teacher or even a school counsellor would. A resolution that is facilitated by the student mediator may therefore be more genuine and durable.

In conclusion, it should be stressed again that mediation in bully/victim cases requires: (a) a conception of mediation that is broad rather than narrow; (b) a careful appraisal of the nature of the imbalance; and (c) steps being taken as far as possible to reduce the imbalance.

To some extent, it may also involve the exercise of some counselling skills to enable the disputants to move towards a negotiated resolution. In many cases it certainly isn't going to be easy. That is why it is most important that students who undertake such work first become expert in working with cases where the disputants are not unequal in power or have at least fairly similar power.

Judgements on peer mediation

Is peer mediation, especially in cases of directly dealing with bully/victim problems, a good idea? The jury is still out. Is this the way schools will go eventually in dealing with bullying? This is certainly the trend. How far will it go? For a possible look into the future I would strongly recommend an account of a radical intervention that has recently been conducted in a large English Comprehensive School using peer counsellors/mediators to deal specifically with the bully/victim problem in the school. The work of the school, and particularly the mediational efforts of students, has been faithfully recorded using positional cameras to provide an astonishing videoed recording of the students in action with bullies and victims, singly and together.

In the video, *Bullying* (Balfour, 1994), the initiative is taken by the principal who begins her address to the school assembly as follows:

'In this school you have the right to feel welcome, safe and happy, to enjoy your lessons and to do well. This will not happen if you are being bullied or if you are spending your time bullying others. Three years ago a girl at this school tried to end it all with an overdose. A girl in another local school did take her life—the result of bullying!

The principal then makes a direct appeal for help from students:

'If you'd like to be a counsellor and be trained to help there'll be application forms in the foyer today at lunchtime.'

Subsequently students volunteer to be trained as student counsellors and to work towards mediating in cases of bullying. We are shown some of the training sessions involving both teacher-trainers. Then we see the student counsellors in action, sometimes with victims, sometimes with bullies, sometimes with both parties in a mediation session. You are struck by the remarkable maturity and responsiveness of the student counsellors. They are able to listen without blaming—and as a result they are listened to. When the student counsellor asks a student who has bullied another how she would feel if she had been treated in a similar way, the question evokes a mixture of sympathy for the victim and shame for having hurt the other person, rather than the all-too-common defensiveness and resistance. You become aware of the much greater moral authority that students possess in their relations with other students than teachers often muster.

School communities as well as individual teachers differ widely on what they think of this approach. I have shown the video to many groups of teachers. Some teachers are both deeply moved and encouraged to explore this approach in their schools. Some are appalled. The dangers may seem enormous, and the professional expertise of counsellors greatly threatened. Others have sought on the basis of their own experiences to give a balanced judgement.

From some quarters there is cautious optimism. Judgement, it is sometimes said, about whether a student can act as a mediator, should be made in the light of the perceived difficulty of particular cases and the demonstrated skill and effectiveness of the would-be peer mediator. This view is taken by the staff who run the Giralang Mediator Program in Canberra.

Their experience with peer mediators over the last five years is that the most senior students of a primary school can intervene effectively in some less serious cases of teasing and harassment, but they recommend referral to a teacher when the mediators believe that they will not be able to cope with the situation. Peer mediators, it seems, can be effective in some, but probably not all, cases of bullying.

At Cranebrook High in New South Wales they are again cautious. Student mediators are asked to be particularly careful when:

(i)   the power imbalance appears too great for conciliation;

(ii) the parties are not willing to negotiate;

(iii) the disputants do not trust the mediation process or the mediators;

(iv) there are established procedures or legal requirements such that one person's interests have precedence over another; and

(v)   the primary issue is non-negotiable, as in clear cases of physical abuse.

Yet it should be said that despite such qualifications the students who mediate at Cranebrook often do find a way to help to resolve bully/victim problems.

Legalistic approach involving students

Now for something totally different. I have argued that a legalistic approach to dealing with bullies is less acceptable than one in which there has been a genuine attempt to explore the human dimensions of a problem and produce a 'change of heart' which will be enduring and therefore not requiring expenditure of time and effort (often futile) for long periods of time in observing and monitoring what is happening. Yet it may be concluded that in some cases a rule-bound punitive approach is unavoidable, either because humanistic approaches are unacceptable or inappropriate at a particular stage of a school's development, or because some individuals who bully others simply do not respond positively to a humanistic approach. Can students be involved in a legalistic approach?

Bully Courts

Some school authorities believe this is possible. It is argued that students can be given some responsibility for conducting enquiries into actual cases of bullying and making judgements, as in a court of law, and ensuring that appropriate sanctions are employed.

This approach requires the election or appointment of people from the school community who will constitute a so-called Bully Court. Typically, the members are a mixture of students and staff. It becomes their responsibility to examine cases of bullying that are reported to it.

How the courts operate is a matter for the school to decide. One procedure suggested by Michelle Elliott (1991) in Britain and subsequently followed in some English schools is as follows. The court is to deal only with cases that occur at school. They should not be trivial ones, that is, easily resolved by teachers. They should not be very serious ones either, such as may require the police. Finally, the Court may deal with only those cases for which approval has been given by a complainant. As we have seen, many students do not want action to be taken against the bully or bullies.

The process can begin when, and only when, a student makes a formal complaint against another student. For this an official form is provided on which the details are written. The bully or bullies are invited to attend the next meeting of the Bully Court. The complainant is also to be present, together with any witnesses of the event(s). There is to be no audience (it is not theatre). Each person attending the proceedings is asked to give evidence and then is questioned by the panel of students and staff. The panel then discusses each case in private and make their judgement. Penalties or sanctions may be prescribed and steps are taken to see that they are administered, unless there is a successful appeal to the principal who may apply a veto. Finally, as in a system of law, a record is kept of all proceedings and verdicts and these become precedents for other cases.

Are Bully Courts a good idea?

Schools must judge for themselves. To their credit, Bully Courts are a logical extension of the principle of empowering students in the context of a school policy aimed at controlling bullying by the use of sanctions, consequences or punishment for an offence. It has been argued sometimes that in the adult community it is quite unacceptable for individuals to attack others physically or verbally without victims having the opportunity to bring legal action against their attacker. Why, it is sometimes asked, should children not have a similar right and a similar means of obtaining justice. This is a persuasive argument.

However, although Bully Courts appear to be popular with students (according to Smith and Sharp, 1994), they have not proved to be popular with teachers. There are several reasons for this. Perhaps the most obvious is that teachers sometimes feel that the introduction of such a system would tend to take control of children's behaviour out of their hands with unpredictable consequences. It is further felt that the courts could easily be used by one group of students to exact revenge from another, and that penalties may well be too draconian. It is argued, too, that many cases of bullying do not warrant a heavy legalistic treatment, and that a counselling or mediation approach is likely to be more effective. Parents are particularly concerned that their aberrant children do not get a 'criminal record'. If Bully Courts are to be tried, it is necessary first to have a strong anti-bullying policy in place that is widely supported by students, parents and teachers. If Bully Courts prove to be divisive, they are unlikely to be successfully implemented. Parents, in particular, would need to be persuaded that the approach is a satisfactory one. Once there is generally agreement to try the method, considerable guidance would still be needed by teachers in the operation of the Courts.

We should make it clear that if a legalistic approach is used there is indeed much merit in involving students in the process of formulating general rules and, in some circumstances, helping to determine sanctions. However, the approach we prefer is one that seeks to involve students in the application of non-punitive methods, that is in preventing and, as far as possible, resolving bully/victim problems in a positive and constructive manner.

On empowering students

It has been continually emphasised in this book that bullying is a problem primarily for students to deal with and that many students are, in fact, deeply concerned about seeking solutions to the problem. We have seen that there is a variety of ways in which they can be empowered to help. First, I stressed the desirability of providing students with a range of helping roles and corresponding training to perform them. Discharging these roles can have a modelling effect and influence the extent of pro-social behaviour that goes on in schools. Such work can therefore have a very important preventative function in ensuring that bully/victim problems do not arise. Peer helping roles were delineated and seen as being complementary to the work of the school's professional counsellor. More specifically we considered the potential role of peer mediation as a means of resolving peer disputes and conflicts. Depending on how mediation was defined and practised, students were seen as potentially capable of mediating or at least conciliating, not only where disputants were of equal or roughly equal power, but also in bully/victim problems where there are typically marked power asymmetries. This is clearly a controversial area for which further action-based research is needed. What is already being done overseas and in some schools in Australia is nevertheless highly promising.

Finally in this chapter we examined how students could become involved in methods of countering bullying that are essentially punitive. Through the use of so-called Bully Courts, students may be empowered to act in concert with teachers to deal with cases of bullying by legalistic means. Although in some circumstances this approach may be followed, there are clearly shortcomings and dangers in using this method. It was concluded that it is much better to empower students to solve problems through pro-social means than through the use of punishment, however benignly conceived.

Epilogue

It is continually assured, especially in our Tolstoyan tendencies, that when the lion lies down with the lamb, the lion becomes lamb-like. But that is brutal annexation and imperialism on the part of the lamb. That is the lamb absorbing the lion instead of the lion eating the lamb. Can the lion lie down with the lamb and still retain its royal ferocity?

G K Chesterton, *Orthodoxy*

If I have somehow conveyed the impression that it is wrong to be fierce I shall have been much misunderstood. Lions have the right to be lions, and they would not be lions if they were lambs. What we should be concerned about is not ferocity but the way in which ferocity is directed.

There is a popular notion that bullies are cowards. Although this sentiment is widely endorsed, it is based upon a misunderstanding. Bullying is a miserable and deplorable act which we rightly despise. But by any objective observation bullies are highly aggressive, tough-minded, even bloody-minded people; insensitive and stupid, if you will; but not cowards. Typically their aggressiveness is expressed in all directions. That is what is wrong with it.

It may be unfashionable, but there is much to be said for the medieval ideal of the brave knight of whom Sir Launcelot was the prototype. In Malory's *Morte D'Arthur*, first published in 1485, the dead Launcelot is addressed by the sorrowing Sir Ector with these words: 'Thou wert the meekest man that ever ate in hall with ladies; and thou wert the sternest knight to thy mortal foe that ever put spear to rest'.

As C S Lewis (1986) comments, the important thing about this ideal is the double demand it makes upon human nature.The knight, he observes, is a man of blood and iron, a man familiar with the sight of smashed faces and the ragged stumps of lopped-off limbs; he is also a demure, almost maiden-like guest in hall, a gentle, unobtrusive man. He is not a compromise between fierceness and meekness; he is fierce to the nth degree and meek to the nth degree. When Launcelot heard himself pronounced as the best knight in the world, 'he wept as he had been a child that had been beaten'.

It is this combination of strength, indeed fierceness of the leonine kind, combined with humility and gentleness that we need today as much as it has ever been needed. We are not going to extol the virtues of wimps.

But we are not going to despise them either. Where confidence has been lost, it is right to help restore it. Hence we have been concerned in this book with understanding how children come to be victimised by their peers, how they can be helped to prevent this from happening, and how they can pick themselves up when it has happened. Should we extend the same sympathy and support to bullies as well?

There is a story of a social worker who one day came across a man who had been savagely mugged on the pavement. Looking down on this human wreck, the social worker mused: 'I bet the person who did this had some problems'.

Yes, again, we are committed to the idea that children who bully others are also in need of our help. We need to understand their circumstances and the forces operating on them. But tout comprendre is not tout pardonner. We do not intend to go soft on them.

Bullying is either a thoughtless or an evil act. The major thrust of this book is to clearly identify it, and treat it for what it is: a form of behaviour that is often destructive of the person who persistently practises it, and dangerous and damaging to those against whom it is continually practised. And that is why it cannot be tolerated.

Finally, if what has been written is construed as addressing an issue about children at school—and that only—again I will have failed. I hope that I have somehow given useful and practical advice to teachers and parents which will help individual children. But the questions I have raised, touching on the abuse of power and the development of character are timeless.

References

Ambert, A.M. (1994). A qualitative study of peer abuse and its effects: theoretical and practical implications. *Journal of Marriage and the Family*, 56, 119–130.

Argyle, M. (1983). *The psychology of interpersonal relationships* (4th ed.). Harmondsworth: Penguin.

Argyle, M. (1991). *Cooperation: the basis of sociability*. London: Routledge.

Arora, T. (1989). Bullying—action and intervention. *Pastoral Care in Education*, 7, 44–47.

Arora, T. (1991). The use of victim support groups. In Smith, P.K., and Thompson, D., *Practical Approaches to Bullying*. London: David Fulton, 37–38.

Askew, S. (1989). Aggressive Behaviour in Boys: to what extent is it institutionalised? In Tattum, D.A. and Lane, D.A. (Eds). *Bullying in schools*. Hanley: Trentham Books.

Bagshaw, D. (1994). Peer Mediation Strategies in Schools. In Oxenberry, K., Rigby, K. and Slee, P.T. (Eds). *Children's Peer Relations: Conference Proceedings*. Adelaide Institute of Social Research, University of South Australia, 22–33.

Balfour, Jane (1994). *Bullying* (a video). Camberwell: Australian Council for Educational Research.

Bates, Bill (1992). *Living Safely: a guide for children to keep safe using self protection and awareness*. Adelaide: Bill Bates.

Batsche, G.M. and Knoff, H.M. (1994). Schools and their victims: understanding a pervasive problem in the schools. *School Psychology Review*, 23, 2, 165–74.

Betjeman, J. (1960). *Summoned by bells*. London: John Murray.

Bingham, K., Daly, P., Mitchell, T. and Skinner, S. (1994). *Giralang Mediation Program*: Giralang Primary School: Giralang, ACT 2617.

Bodine, R.J., Crawford, D.K. and Schrumpf, F. (1994). *Creating a Peaceable School*. Champaign, Illinois: Research Press.

Bowers, L., Smith, P.K. and Binney, V. (1994). Perceived family relationships of bullies, victims and bully/victims in middle childhood. *Journal of Social and Personal Relationships, 11*, 215–232.

Braithwaite, J. (1989). *Crime shame and reintegration*. Cambridge: Cambridge University Press.

Brown, T. (1719). *Works*. Vol. iv, p. 113.

Brown, W. and Richardson, S. (1994). Skill Streaming in Early Childhood. In Tainsh, M. and Izard, J. *Widening Horizons: New Challenges, Directions and Achievements*, Melbourne: Australian Council for Educational Research, 51–68.

Cairns, R.B. and Cairns, B.D. (1995). *Lifelines and risks: pathways of youth in our time*. New York: Harvester Wheatsheaf.

Cameron, J. and Dupuis, A. (1989). The introduction of school mediation in New Zealand. *Journal of Research and Development in Education*, 24, No. 3, Spring.

Casdagli, P., Gobey, F. and Griffin, C. (1990). *Only Playing, Miss!*. London: Trentham Books.

Chesterton, G.K. (1959). *Orthodoxy*. New York: Image Books.

Cornes, G. (1995). E.J. Whitten—Footy's Mr Immortal. *Advertiser*, 19 August.

Cowie, H. and Sharp, S. (1994). Tackling bullying through the curriculum. In Smith, P.K. and Sharp, S. (Eds). *School bullying and how to cope with it*. London: Routledge.

Cowie, H., Sharp, S., Sellars, A., Lewis, J. and the Bully Line counsellors at Chaucer School (1994). *Time to Listen: peer counsellors challenge school bullying* (a video): Calouste Gulbenkian Foundation.

Cowie, H., Smith, P.K., Boulton, M. and Laver, R. (1994). *Cooperation in the Multi-ethnic classroom*. London: David Fulton.

Cowie, H., Sharp, S. and Smith, P.K. (1992). Tackling bullying in schools: the method of common concern. *BPS Education Section Review*, 55–57.

Dawkins, J. and Hill, P. (1995). Bullying: another form of abuse? In David T.J. (Ed.). *Recent Advances in Paediatrics*, 13, 103–122, Edinburgh.

Dawkins, J. (1995). Bullying in schools: doctors' responsibilities. *British Medical Journal*, 310, 174–274.

Dennis, C.J. (1950). 'The Austra-laise'. In Chisholm, A.H. (Ed.). *The selected verse of C.J. Dennis*. Sydney: Angus and Robertson.

Dietz, B. (1994). Effects on subsequent heterosexual shyness and depression of peer victimization at school. Paper presented at the International Conference on Children's Peer Relations. Institute of Social Research: University of South Australia, Adelaide.

Elliott, M. (1991). Bully 'Courts'. In Elliott, M. (Ed.). *Bullying: a practical guide*. Eron, L.D. and Lefkowitz, M.M. (1971). *Learning and Aggression in Children*. Boston: Little Brown.

Eron, L.D., Huesmann, L.R., Lefkowitz, M.M. & Walder, L.O. (1972). Does television violence cause aggression? *American Psychologist*, 27, 253.

Farrington, D.P. (1993). Understanding and preventing bullying. In Tonny, M. and Morris, N. (Eds). *Crime and Justice*, 17, Chicago: University of Chicago Press.

Forsey, C. (1994). *Hands Off! The Anti-Violence Guide to Developing Positive Relationships*. Melbourne: West Education Centre Inc., DEET.

Fuller, A. and King, V. (1995). *Stop Bullying!* Melbourne: Mental Health Foundation of Victoria.

Gerrard, J. (1991). The teasing syndrome in facially deformed children. *ANZ Journal of Family Therapy*, 12 (3), 147–154.

Gilmartin, B.G. (1987). Peer group antecedents of severe love-shyness in males. *Journal of Personality*, 55, 467–489.

Goldberg, D. and Williams, P. (1988). *A User's Guide to the General Health Questionnaire*. Windsor: NFER-Nelson.

Golding, W. (1955). *Lord of the Flies*. New York: Coward-McCann.

Gordon, S. (1995). *A Rubik's Cube Approach to Eliminating Bullying*. Adelaide: Mission South Australia.

Gordon, G. (1990). *The Demolition Job*. Adelaide: Bizcare Entertainment.

Herbert, Carrie (1992). *Sexual Harassment in Schools: a guide for teachers*. London: David Fulton.

Hughes, T. (1968, first published, 1857). *Tom Brown's School Days*. New York: Airmont Publishing Company.

Hyndman, M. and Thorsborne, M. (1994). Taking Action on Bullying: Whole school multi-stage approaches to intervention and protection. In Oxenberry, K., Rigby, K. and Slee, P.T. (Eds). *Children's Peer Relations: Conference Proceedings*. Adelaide: Institute of Social Research, University of South Australia, 122-37.

Jenkins, A. (1990). *Invitation to Responsibility*. Adelaide: Dulwich Centre Publications.

Jenkin, J. (1996, in press). *Resolving Violence through Education*. Camberwell: Australian Council for Educational Research.

Johnson, B., Oswald, M. and Adey, K. (1993). Discipline in South Australian Primary Schools. *Educational Studies*, 19, 3, 289–305.

Johnson, D.W. and Johnson, R. (1991). *Teaching students to be peacemakers*. Edinburgh, MN: Interaction Book Co.

Johnson, P. (1994). *Sticks and Stones (the Play)*. Byron Bay: Brainstorm Productions.

Kaukiainen, A., Bjorkqvist K, Osterman, K. and Lagerspetz, K.M.J. (1995). Social intelligence and empathy as antecedents of different types of aggression. A paper for the *IV European Congress of Psychology*, Athens, Greece, July 7th, 1995.

Keogh, L. and Rigby, K. (1995). Teachers' attitudes to peer victimisation among school children. Unpublished paper.

Kelman, H.C. (1961). Processes of opinion change. *Public Opinion Quarterly*, 25, 57–78.

Kids Helpline. (1994). *Information Sheet No 7: Bullying*. Brisbane: Kids Helpline.

Kohlberg, L. (1984). *The psychology of moral development: Essays on moral development*. San Francisco: Harper and Row.

Laskey, T. (1992). *How to beat bullying: a succesful self-help course*. Hindhead: Health Habit Publications.

Lewis, C.S. (1986). The Necessity of Chivalry. In Hooper, W. (Ed.). *Present Concerns: Ethical Essays*. London: Collins, Fount Paperbacks.

Maines, Barbara and Robinson, George. (1992). *The No Blame Approach*. Bristol: Lame Duck Publishing.

Malory, T. (1485). *Le Morte D'Arthur* (cited in C.S. Lewis, op cit).

Maugham, W. Somerset. (1977, first published, 1919). *The Moon and Sixpence*. New York: Arno Press.

Milburn, T. and Klimnowski, R. (1996). Power asymmetries in disputes and the mediator's role in reducing their impact and achieving successful resolutions in mediation. *Abstract for the Second International Mediation Conference: Mediation and Cultural Diversity*. Adelaide: January 1996.

Moberley, W. (1968). *The ethics of punishment*. London: Faber.

Moore, D.B. (1994). Pride Shame and Empathy. In Oxenberry, K., Rigby, K. and Slee, P.T. (Eds). *Proceedings of the Children's Peer Relations Conference*. Institute of Social Research, University of South Australia, 212–235.

Murray, Les. (1994). The culture of hell. *The Independent Monthly*, February, p. 18.

Myrick, R.D. (1994). *Developmental guidance and counselling: a practical approach*. Minneapolis: Educational Media Corporation.

Neti-Neti Theatre Company. (1990). *Only Playing, Miss!* (the video). London: Neti-Neti.

Newson, J. and Newson, E. (1976). *Seven Years old in the home environment*. London: Allen & Unwin.

New South Wales Department of Education. (1995). *Peer Mediation: Dispute Resolution Pilot Project Report*. Wetherill Park, NSW: Dept. of School Education.

Noller, P. and Callan, V. (1991). *The Adolescent in the Family*. London and New York: Routledge.

Olweus, D. (1980). Familial and temperamental determinants of aggressive behaviour in adolescent boys: a causal analysis. *Developmental Psychology*, 16, 644–660.

Olweus, D. (1989). Bully/victim problems among school children: basic facts and effects of a school-based intervention program. In Rubin, K.H. and Pepler, D. (Eds). *The Development and Treatment of Childhood Aggression*. Hillsdale, NJ: Erlbaum.

Olweus, D. (1992). Victimisation by peers: antecedents and long term outcomes. In Rubin, K.H. and Asendorf, J.B. (Eds). *Social withdrawal, inhibition and shyness in children*. Hillsdale, NJ: Erlbaum.

Olweus, D. (1993). *Bullying at school: What we know and what we can do*. Oxford, UK: Blackwell.

Parker, Tony. (1990). *Life after Life*. London: HarperCollins.

Peterson, L. (1994). Stop and Think learning: Motivating Learning in social groups and individuals. In Tainsh, M. and Izard, J. (Eds). *Widening Horizons: New Challenges, Directions and Achievements*. Melbourne: Australian Council for Educational Research, 70–83.

Pikas, A. (1989). The Common Concern Method for the treatment of mobbing. In Munthe, E. and Roland, E. (Eds). *Bullying: an International Perspective*. London: David Fulton, 91–104.

Polk, Kenneth. (1995). Youth violence: myth and reality. In Chappell, D. and Egger, S. (Eds). *Australian Violence: Contemporary Perspectives II*. Canberra: Australian Institute of Criminology.

Randall, P.E. (1995). Beyond the school gates. *Special Children*, May, 19–21.

Randall, P.E. and Donohue, M.I. (1993). Tackling bullying as a community. *Child Education*, 70.

Rigby, K. (1993). School children's perceptions of their families and parents as a function of peer relations. *Journal of Genetic Psychology*, 154(4), 501–514.

Rigby, K. (1994a). School Bullies. *Independent Teacher*, 10(2), 8–9.

Rigby, K. (1994b). Psycho-social functioning in families of Australian adolescent schoolchildren involved in bully/victim problems. *Journal of Family Therapy*, 16 (2), 173–189.

Rigby, K. (1994c). Family Influence, Peer-Relations and Health Effects among School Children. In Oxenberry, K., Rigby, K. and Slee, P.T. (Eds). *Children's Peer Relations: Conference Proceedings*, Adelaide: The Institute of Social Research, University of South Australia, 294–304.

Rigby, K. (1995a). New thinking about bullying in schools. *Independent Education*. New South Wales Education Union: Sydney, July, 3–6.

Rigby, K. (1995b). Peer victimisation and gender among Australian school children. Paper presented at the *IVth European Congress of Psychology*, Athens, July, 1995.

Rigby, K. and Cox, I. (1994). Cooperation among school children. Unpublished paper.

Rigby, K. and Sharp, S. (1993). Cultivating the art of self-defence among victimized children. *International Journal of Protective Behaviours*, 1(2), 24–27.

Rigby, K. and Slee, P.T. (1991). Bullying among Australian school children: reported behaviour and attitudes to victims. *Journal of Social Psychology*, 131, 615–627.

Rigby, K. and Slee, P.T. (1992). *Bullying in Schools*. (the video). Institute of Social Research, University of South Australia. Distributed by the Australian Council for Educational Research, Camberwell.

Rigby, K. and Slee, P.T. (1993a). Dimensions of interpersonal relating among Australian school children and their implications for psychological well-being. *Journal of Social Psychology*, 133(1), 33–42.

Rigby, K. and Slee, P.T. (1993b). Children's attitudes towards victims. In Tattum, D.P. (Ed.). *Understanding and Managing Bullying*, 119–135. Melbourne: Heinemann Books.

Rigby K. and Slee, P.T. (1995). *Manual for the Peer Relations Questionnaire* (PRQ). Adelaide: University of South Australia.

Rigby, K., Whish, A. and Black, G. (1994). Implications of school children's peer relations for wife abuse in Australia. *Criminology Australia*, August, 1994, 8–12.

Rosenberg, M. (1986). *Conceiving the self*. Malabar FL: Kreiger.

Safety Houses Australia (1995). Concern over child bullying. *SHA Newsletter*, July, p. 1.

Sarma, V. (1995). Bullying and the physical environment in two primary schools in metropolitan Adelaide. University of South Australia. Unpublished paper.

Schumacher, E.F. (1977). *Guide for the perplexed*. New York: Harper and Row.

Sharp, S. and Smith, P.K. (Eds). (1994). *Tackling bullying in your school; a practical handbook for teachers*. London: Routledge

Sharp, S. and Cowie, H. (1994). Constructive conflict resolution, peer counselling and assertiveness training: empowering pupils to respond to bullying behaviour. In Smith, P.K. and Sharp, S. (Eds). *School bullying and how to cope with it*. London: Routledge.

Slee, P.T. (1993). *Child, Adolescent and Family Development*. Sydney: Harcourt Brace Jovanovich.

Slee, P.T. and Rigby, K. (1993). The relationship of Eysenck's personality factors and self-esteem to bully/victim behaviour in Australian schoolboys. *Personality and Individual Differences*, 14, 371–373.

Slee, P.T. and Rigby, K. (1994). Peer victimization at schools. *Australian Journal of Early Childhood,* 19,1, 3–10.

Smith, P.K. and Sharp, S. (Eds). (1994). *School Bullying: insights and perspectives*, London: Routledge.

Snow, N.E. (1992). Perceptions of social situations by popular and unpopular disruptive adolescents. Unpublished thesis for Master of Psychology (Educational). University of Newcastle: New South Wales.

Spender, S. (1985). *Collected poems: 1928-1985*. London: Faber and Faber.

Storr. A. (1988). *Solitude*. London: Flamingo.

Thurber, James. (1967). *Thurber Country*. London: Sphere Books.

Whitney, I. and Smith, P.K. (1993). A survey of the nature and extent of bully/victim problems in junior/middle and secondary schools. *Educational Research*, 35, 3–25.

Widom, C.S. (1995). The cycle of violence. In Chappell, D. and Egger, S. (Eds). *Australian Violence Contemporary Perspectives II*. Canberra: Australian Institute of Criminology.

Resources on bullying

These are the resources that I wish every school had access to. Taken together, they comprise a wealth of thoughtful analysis, factual observations, and ideas for change. No longer can it be said that nobody cares or nobody has any ideas.

Books

Arora, C.M. (1991). The use of victim support groups. In Smith, P.K. and Thompson, D. *Practical Approaches to bullying*. London: David Fulton, 37–47.

Bates, Bill. (1992). *Living Safely: a guide for children to keep safe using self-protection and awareness*. Adelaide: Bill Bates.

Besag, V.E. (1989). *Bullies and victims in schools*. Bristol, PA: Open University Press.

Besag, V.E. (1992). *We don't have bullies here*. Newcastle-upon-Tyne: Besag.

Byrne, B. (1993). *Coping with Bullying in Schools*. Dublin: Columba Press.

Casdagli, P., Gobey, F. and Griffin, C. (1990). *Only Playing, Miss!* London: Trentham Books.

Elliott, M. (1991). *Bullying: a practical guide to coping for schools*. Glasgow: Longman.

Forsey, C. (1994). Hands off! *The Anti-Violence Guide to Developing Positive Relationships*. Melbourne: West Education Centre Inc., DEET.

Fuller, A. and King, V. (1995). *Stop Bullying!* Heidelberg: Victorian Health Promotion Foundation.

Johnstone, M., Munn, P., and Edwards, L. (1992). *Action against bullying: a support pack for schools*. The Scottish Council for Research in Education.

Herbert, Carrie. (1992). *Sexual Harassment in Schools: a Guide for Teachers*, London: David Fulton.

Maines, B. and Robinson, G. (1992). *The No Blame Approach*. Bristol: Lame Duck Publishing.

McGrath, S. and Gordon, S. (1991). *Safe Start, Safe Future: An integrated curriculum approach to child protection in early childhood settings based on the protective behaviours program*. Adelaide: Children's Services Office.

Olweus, D. (1993). *Bullying at school*. Cambridge: Blackwell.

Oxenberry, K., Rigby, K., Slee, P.T. (1994). *Children's Peer Relations: Conference Proceedings*, Institute of Social Research, University of South Australia.

Pikas, A. (1989). The common concern method for the treatment of mobbing. In Roland, E. and Munthe, E. (Eds). *Bullying, an international perspective*. London: Fulton.

Rigby, K. (1993). Countering Bullying in Schools. *CAFHS FORUM, Vol 1, 2*, 19–21.

Rigby, K. (1994). School Bullies. *Independent Teacher*, April, 8–9.

Rigby, K. (1994). An Evaluation of Strategies and Methods for addressing problems of peer abuse in schools. In Tainsh, M. and Izard, J. (Eds). *Widening Horizons: New challenges, directions and achievements*. Melbourne: Australian Council for Educational Research.

Rigby, K. (1995). Empowering students to help others. *Education Alternatives*, June, 12.

Rigby, K. (1995). New thinking about bullying. *Independent Education*, July, 3–6.

Rigby, K. (1995). What our schools can do about bullying. *The Professional Reading Guide for Educational Administrators*, Vol 17(i), November.

Rigby, K. and Sharp, S. (1993). Cultivating the art of self-defence amongst victimised children. *The International Journal of Protective Behaviours*, 1 (2), 24–28.

Rigby, K. and Slee, P.T. (1993). Children's attitudes towards victims. In Tattum, D.P. (Ed.). *Understanding and managing bullying*. London: Heinemann Books.

Sharp, S. and Smith, P.K. (Eds). (1994). *Tackling Bullying in your school: a practical handbook for teachers*. London: Routledge.

Smith, P.K. (1994). School Bullying: Interventions can work. *CAFHS FORUM, Vol 2 (1)* March, 28–30.

Smith, P.K. (1994). What we can do to prevent bullying in school. *The Therapist,* Summer, 12–15.

Smith, P.K. and Sharp, S. (Eds). (1994). *School Bullying: insights and perspectives*, London: Routledge.

Skinner, A. (1992). *Bullying: An annotated bibliography of literature and resources*. London: Youth Work Press.

Tattum, D.P. and Herbert, G. (1990). *Bullying: A positive response*. Cardiff: CIHE Learning Resources Centre.

Tattum, D.P. (Ed.) (1993). *Understanding and managing bullying*. London: Heinemann Books.

Videos

Jane Balfour Films Video. (1994). *Bullying.* Melbourne, ACER. (This is a useful 55 minute video on how students can assist in mediating in cases of bullying).

Maines, B and Robinson, G. (1992). *The No Blame Approach*. Bristol: Lame Duck Publishing.

Neti-Neti Theatre Co. (1990). *Only Playing Miss!* A 60 minute video recording of a play on bullying in schools. Obtainable from the Neti-Neti Theatre Company, 44 Gladsmuir Road, London, N19 3JU. Phone 71 272 7302.

New Zealand Police. (1993). *Kia Kaha: A resource kit about bullying for students, teachers and parents*. Commercial Union Insurance.

Rigby, K. and Slee, P.T. (1991). *Bullying in Schools.* A 25 minute video and instructional manual, produced by the Institute of Social Research at the University of South Australia. Obtainable from the Australian Council for Educational Research, Camberwell, Melbourne.

Questionnaire

Rigby, K and Slee, P.T. (1993). *The Peer Relations Questionnaire (PRQ).* This is a widely used instrument for assessing bully/victim problems in schools. Adelaide: University of South Australia. Ph. (08) 302 6945.

Rigby, K. and Slee, P.T. (1995). *Manual for the Peer Relations Questionnaire;* Adelaide: University of South Australia.

Subject index

Author index